Looking at *Bacchae*

Also available from Bloomsbury

Looking at Medea, edited by David Stuttard

Looking at Lysistrata, edited by David Stuttard

The Gentle, Jealous God, Simon Perris

Euripides: Bacchae, Sophie Mills

Euripides Plays: 1, translated by J. Michael Walton and David Thompson

Six Greek Tragedies, edited by J. Michael Walton

Looking at *Bacchae*

Edited by David Stuttard

Bloomsbury Academic
An imprint of Bloomsbury Publishing Plc

B L O O M S B U R Y
LONDON · OXFORD · NEW YORK · NEW DELHI · SYDNEY

Bloomsbury Academic
An imprint of Bloomsbury Publishing Plc

50 Bedford Square	1385 Broadway
London	New York
WC1B 3DP	NY 10018
UK	USA

www.bloomsbury.com

BLOOMSBURY and the Diana logo are trademarks of Bloomsbury Publishing Plc

First published 2016

© David Stuttard and Contributors, 2016

David Stuttard has asserted his right under the Copyright, Designs and Patents Act, 1988, to be identified as Editor of this work.

British Library Cataloguing-in-Publication Data
A catalogue record for this book is available from the British Library.

ISBN:	HB:	978-1-47422-148-1
	PB:	978-1-47422-147-4
	ePDF:	978-1-47422-150-4
	ePub:	978-1-47422-149-8

Library of Congress Cataloging-in-Publication Data
A catalog record for this book is available from the Library of Congress.

Typeset by RefineCatch Limited, Bungay, Suffolk
Printed and bound in India

To Mark Katz and Tamsin Shasha

Contents

List of Contributors

David Stuttard is a freelance writer, classical historian, dramatist and founder of the theatre company, Actors of Dionysus

Edith Hall is Professor of Classics at King's College, London

Alan H. Sommerstein is Emeritus Professor of Greek at the University of Nottingham

Ioanna Karamanou is Assistant Professor of Greek Drama at the University of the Peloponnese

Rosie Wyles is Lecturer in Classical History and Literature at the University of Kent

Chris Carey is a Professor of Greek at University College London

Richard Seaford is Emeritus Professor of Ancient Greek at the University of Exeter

James Morwood is Emeritus Fellow of Wadham College, Oxford

David Kovacs is Hugh H. Obear Professor of Classics, University of Virginia

Alex Garvie is Honorary Professorial Research Fellow at the University of Glasgow

Hanna M. Roisman is Professor of Classics, Arnold Bernhard Professor in Arts and Humanities at Colby College, Maine

Sophie Mills is Professor of Classics at the University of North Carolina at Asheville

Betine van Zyl Smit is Associate Professor of Classics at the University of Nottingham

Preface

Bacchae is at once exciting, terrifying, and intensely dramatic. Performances can still provoke a devastating effect on modern audiences. A story of power, it explores what happens when Dionysus, an implacable god, meets Pentheus, a mortal king, who refuses to recognize his divinity and resists the introduction of his worship. Thus, although some of its themes are universal, with Greek religion playing such an important role in its plot, *Bacchae* is firmly rooted in the beliefs and values of the fifth century BC, when it was written and first performed.

This collection of new essays by twelve international authorities on not only Greek drama in general but on *Bacchae* in particular sets the play firmly within its historical context, teases out many of the issues which it raises, and examines some of the ways in which it has been received in more recent times. It covers areas such as *Bacchae*'s dramatic antecedents, the other two plays with which it perhaps formed a trilogy, its performance context and how the first production may have been staged; it looks at the play's themes, including religion and revenge; it examines the bacchic chorus; and it considers some productions of the play in modern times.

As has been the case in other volumes in this series, I have allowed authors great latitude to choose those aspects of *Bacchae* on which they wished to write, and most were relatively unaware of the content of each other's essays. The collection, therefore, provides a useful overview of some of the issues surrounding the play which concern scholars in the second decade of the twenty-first century. As before, there is the occasional small overlap between some essays, with which I have not interfered, as well as some healthy disagreement in emphasis and interpretation. While I suggested that authors use the forms 'BC' and 'AD', I respected the wishes of one, for whom it was important to use 'BCE' and 'CE'. Line numbering within the essays refers to the standard editions of the Greek text.

Many of the quotations from *Bacchae* are taken from my own translation, which is printed after the essays. It dates from 1999, was supported by the Arts Council of England, and was originally written for a production, which I directed for Actors of Dionysus, and which featured Tamsin Shasha as an extraordinarily androgynous and aerial Dionysus. Readers wishing to use the translation for productions of their own can contact me through my website, www.davidstuttard.com, where applications for performance should be made before the commencement of any rehearsals.

David Stuttard
Brighton, 2015

Acknowledgements

The meat of this volume are the essays by twelve outstanding contributors, to whom I offer my profoundest thanks for their patience, diligence and generosity. I have greatly enjoyed working with all of them, and have personally learned much from each of their essays. My thanks go, too, to the excellent team at Bloomsbury: Charlotte Loveridge, who first commissioned the book; Alice Wright, her successor, who championed it; Anna MacDiarmid, who has guided it to its completion; the fine copy-editor Ian Howe; Kathy John, who orchestrated the proofing process so efficiently; and Catherine Wood, who designed the cover. My thanks, too, to Rosie Wyles for reading through the introduction and commenting so helpfully upon it.

My translation dates to 1999, and was written for a UK tour, which I directed for Actors of Dionysus. I subsequently directed scenes using this translation for performance in the Graeco-Roman theatre at Ephesus, and an 'audio' version performed on the high seas with Swan Hellenic. I am grateful to all the actors involved in these productions for enhancing my understanding of the play.

Finally my thanks go to the 'home team': our cats Stanley and Oliver, Dionysiacs both (though thankfully not enthusiasts for *sparagmos*), who help to maintain balance; and most especially my wife Emily Jane, my foundation and my cornerstone, whose unflagging support is so central to everything I do.

Introduction – *Bacchae* in Context

David Stuttard

In politics a speaker who has passion without wisdom can be very dangerous.

Bacchae is one of Euripides' most disturbing plays. Its basic plot can easily be summarized. After years spent in the East, the god Dionysus returns to Greece and his homeland, Thebes, accompanied by female devotees (called bacchae, after another of the god's names, Bacchus). Here he finds that, while the prophet Teiresias willingly accepts his godhead, his grandfather Cadmus does so only out of expediency. Moreover, many of his aunts and female relatives refuse completely to accept his divinity, so he drives them 'like cattle from their houses, maddened on the mountainside, hallucinating and delirious'. Meanwhile King Pentheus threatens to persecute Dionysus and his followers, spurring on the god to take grim revenge. He causes Pentheus to be torn apart by his own mother Agave and his aunts in the hallucinatory belief that he is a wild animal; when Agave realizes what she has done, she is horrified, but the implacable Dionysus drives both her and Cadmus into exile, effectively destroying the royal house of Thebes.

Using this basic storyline – a storyline, which (as Alan Sommerstein and others show in this collection) drew heavily on earlier plays – Euripides wove a richly complex tragedy, pulsating with questions which are as alive today as they were in the late fifth century BC. They include issues of gender and identity, madness and rationality, vengeance and repression, foreignness and fanaticism so extreme that it leads young men (or, in this case, a young god) to gloat in icy triumph over an enemy's severed head.

However, what Euripides meant to convey in *Bacchae* and how modern readers or audiences understand the play are not necessarily the same things. In many respects *Bacchae* is a product of its age, both a response and challenge to beliefs that were widely held at the end of the fifth century BC. It is a play, too, which assumes an easy familiarity with certain myths, which may be unknown to most modern audiences. So, to set both *Bacchae* and this collection of essays in context, we shall briefly consider some of those issues: the god Dionysus and the myths surrounding him, as well as the circumstances in which Euripides wrote the play and in which it was first performed.

Dionysus and his associated myths

Uniquely for a surviving tragedy, the protagonist of *Bacchae* is a god: Dionysus. Appropriately, he is the god of drama (indeed, as is demonstrated in this collection, Dionysus can be seen to be 'directing' much of the action of our play). In Athens, it was at his festivals that drama was performed, and his priest was given a seat of honour in the auditorium.

But Dionysus had other spheres of influence, too, most notably alcohol – not only wine, consumed (watered down) by Greeks with every meal, but beer, which was drunk mainly by northerners and Egyptians. His was the exuberant life force which caused the grape to swell and the green ivy to burgeon even in the most inhospitable of places.

Essentially, however, Dionysus was the god of transformation. Like other gods, he could metamorphose into whatever creature he might wish (in *Bacchae* he is regularly imagined as a bull) – but he also had the power to alter his followers' perceptions of reality, whether through drink or through drama. Two generations after *Bacchae*, Aristotle famously (if briefly) described the transformative power of tragedy: 'through fear and pity it accomplishes a purgation [*catharsis*] of these emotions' (Aristotle, *Poetics*, 1449b). Dionysus' ability to alter perceptions is central to the plot of *Bacchae*. Like the characters on stage, the audience is invited to see the world increasingly through the eyes of both the god and his alluringly sympathetic followers before realizing to its horror that in doing so it has become complicit in condoning acts of terrifying brutality.

Dionysus was an exotic god. Even the circumstances of his birth (so central to this play) were unconventional. The supreme god Zeus was enamoured of Semele, the daughter of Thebes' founder, Cadmus. So, in the guise of a handsome young man he seduced her, regularly visiting her by night but never revealing his identity. Not unexpectedly, Zeus' wife, Hera, was jealous. Disguised as an old woman, she befriended the now pregnant Semele and sowed the seeds of doubt in her mind. Why would her young lover not tell her who he was? Surely he would if he were honourable! On his next visit, Semele begged Zeus to grant her one wish. Fervently the god agreed. But when he heard it – 'reveal to me who you really are' – Zeus hesitated. For his raw essence was the lightning flash, which Semele could not experience and survive. Nor, though, could Zeus renege, once he had promised. But even as the fire consumed her, Zeus stretched his hand inside Semele's womb, plucked out the embryo which she was carrying, and swiftly sewed it into his thigh. In time he was delivered of a son, Dionysus. Meanwhile in Thebes, the site of Semele's incineration became increasingly venerated. It forms part of the setting of *Bacchae*, and in historical times it was considered so sacred that in the second century AD the traveller Pausanias records that no one was allowed to enter 'Semele's house'.

Some versions of the myth went further. They suggested that Dionysus possessed the heart of an earlier child of Zeus called Zagreus, who had been entrusted to Titans to bring up in Crete. However, encouraged by Hera, the gypsum-painted Titans attacked Zagreus and, when he changed into a bull in order to escape, they tore him limb from limb and ate him – all except his heart, which Zeus implanted into Dionysus even as Semele was conceiving him, and his genitals, which were rescued and revered on the island of Samothrace, where they played a part in a Mystery cult (see below). The tearing apart of animals (*sparagmos* in Greek) became part of the cult of Dionysus, and was apparently actually performed by his adherents in Classical Greece.

Thanks to the unorthodox circumstances of his creation Dionysus was called 'Twice Born', *Dithyrambos*, and honoured with choral songs called dithyrambs at his Athenian festival. Evidence shows that Dionysus was already one of the panoply of gods worshipped in the Mycenaean Bronze Age but, despite his long Greek pedigree and indisputably Greek parentage, there was something decidedly foreign about him. Legend told how, after his final birth, he embarked on a journey east through Asia as far as India before returning to his homeland, riding a chariot drawn by panthers. Early Greeks imagined Dionysus bearded and swathed in leopard skins, clutching his *thyrsus*, a fennel stalk wrapped in ivy and topped with a pine cone, a wand possessing magical properties. By the fifth century BC, however, artists and playwrights such as Euripides began to envisage him as beardless and effeminate, an intensely charismatic youth, garlanded with grapes and vine leaves. In his wake trailed his *thiasos*, a riotous group of followers, who included rampant satyrs (half-men half-horse creatures) and ecstatic women, variously called bacchae, bacchants or maenads (after the Greek word meaning 'to be mad' or 'to rave').

Despite his charm, Dionysus could be unrelentingly savage. In Thrace, when King Lycurgus refused to recognize his godhead, Dionysus exacted vengeance by driving him insane and causing him to mistake his son for a vine, which he vigorously pruned by chopping off its extremities, in reality the boy's hands and feet. (There is an echo of this myth in *Bacchae*. Holding

Pentheus' severed head, Agave proudly proclaims, 'I've brought home / a gift / from the mountain / a vine shoot / a tendril / sliced / dripping / the spoils / of the hunt.') The gods were horrified, but not at Dionysus – at Lycurgus. They demanded his death and he was torn apart on the mountainside by man-eating horses. The parallels with Pentheus' fate in *Bacchae* are clear.

Dionysus also played an important role in Mystery cults, where initiates were promised the hope of life after death. At the important sanctuary at Eleusis near Athens, he was honoured as the god of the vine alongside Demeter and Persephone, goddesses of grain, in a sacrament involving bread and wine, the overall message of which (rebirth after death) may loosely have prefigured the Christian Eucharist. Once more the ritual involved transformation, this time from the terror of the uninitiated to a feeling of calm certainty. As we have already seen, the genitalia of Dionysus' alter ego Zagreus played a part in the similarly transforming Mysteries of Samothrace.

Euripides and the social and political background to *Bacchae*

Bacchae was probably written in 407 BC when it is generally accepted that Euripides had left Athens and was living as a guest of King Archelaus I of Macedon. Now in his seventies, Euripides had long been one of Athens' leading playwrights but in the city's drama festivals, where competing plays were judged by a panel of citizens, he had won only four times (unlike one of his rivals, Sophocles, who won twenty times). The reasons for this are debatable. Perhaps it was something to do with Euripides' downplaying of the visually spectacular – the comic playwright Aristophanes raised laughs by criticizing Euripides' penchant for dressing his characters in rags. Perhaps, too, it was because of his tendency to reduce the role and impact of the chorus, sometimes (as in his *Electra*) rendering them virtually redundant. At the same time, his tragedies were populated by edgy and often anti-heroic characters; and they were shot through with potentially unpopular or provocative sentiments, especially concerning the gods (although this is challenged by David Kovacs in this collection of essays).

Evidence suggests that Euripides belonged to a circle of intellectuals who actively questioned accepted views of religion. These friends included Socrates, to whom tradition relates he showed his scripts before they were performed, and Protagoras, who may have read aloud his agnostic tract, 'On the Gods', at Euripides' house. Neither philosopher was well loved by the common man. In the late 430s BC, Protagoras' writings are said to have been burned in Athens' Agora (marketplace) before he himself went into exile, and in 399 BC Socrates was condemned to death by a jury of five hundred of his fellow citizens. Athens was not always a city of intellectual tolerance.

Indeed, by the last decade of the fifth century BC, tolerance may have been in particularly short supply. Since 431 BC Athens had been embroiled in a series of long and costly conflicts (generally grouped under the heading 'the Peloponnesian War'), which had seen her often fighting on several fronts against a coalition of city-states led by Sparta. In 413 BC, a huge expedition against Sicily had been massacred. It should never have sailed in the first place, but the charismatic and dangerously egotistic general Alcibiades had easily convinced the democracy – only for the People to turn against him, when he was later accused of impiety. For two years Alcibiades lived in exile, first trading secrets with the Spartans, then giving advice on strategy to the Greeks' ancient enemies, the Persians. But in 411 BC Alcibiades was forgiven, reinstated as an Athenian general and given *carte blanche* to wage the war, which was now focused in the eastern Mediterranean. In 407 BC, he returned to Athens, where he was welcomed with open arms and awarded the unprecedented title of *Strategos Autocrator* (Commander-in-Chief), arguably giving him total power over (what remained in name at least) the democracy.

By now Euripides had probably left Athens – his final stage production there (the usual trilogy of tragedies followed by a comedic 'satyr play') was in early 408 BC. It included the infamous *Orestes*, a play which portrayed its central character as a psychopathic murderer and turned the generally accepted version of the story on its head. It is, writes the classicist and translator William Arrowsmith, 'a kind of negative tragedy of total turbulence, deriving its real power from the exposure of the aching disparity between the ideal and the real ... Euripides' prophetic image of the final destruction of Athens'. Arguably, this description could apply equally well to *Bacchae*.

The war had taken a heavy toll on Athens. Not only had many of its citizens been killed, but (according, for example, to Thucydides) both public and private morality had already been seriously undermined. For Euripides, whose plays suggest that he was deeply suspicious of the power of the mob and whose beliefs may not have endeared him to the People, an invitation to the court of Archelaus I must have offered a welcome opportunity to leave behind the maelstrom of Athens – especially as Alcibiades, who could manipulate the People to his own ends better than any other politician alive, was expected imminently to return to the city. Especially, too, since Euripides' last production (his *Trojan Trilogy*, culminating in *Trojan Women*), which Alcibiades had attended on the eve of the Sicilian Expedition, could possibly have been interpreted as a warning to the Athenian People against being seduced by Alcibiades' enthusiasm for rekindling the war.

For the most part Macedon had remained untouched by the Peloponnesian War. In fact (despite its advanced culture) many Greeks still sniffily refused to accept it as fully part of Greece – only two generations earlier its then king, Alexander I, had been forced to argue strongly for his Greek identity in order to be allowed to take part in the Olympic Games. Now Archelaus I, keen to be recognized as a patron of the Greek Arts, issued invitations to pre-eminent practitioners to join him at his court. They included the artist Zeuxis, inventor of *trompe l'oeil* and two prominent Athenian tragedians: Agathon (whose victory celebration after a dramatic contest in 416 BC provides the setting for Plato's *Symposium*) and Euripides. Euripides' intended role is not known, but it is possible that he was to provide plays for the Olympia, a festival in honour of Zeus and the Muses held in the shadow of Mount Olympus at the Macedonian sanctuary-town of Dion. So in 408/407 BC, Euripides set to work on three tragedies, *Iphigenia in Aulis*, *Alcmeon in Corinth* and *Bacchae*, a trilogy discussed here by Edith Hall and Ioanna Karamanou. Evidence for *Alcmeon in Corinth* is scanty, but both *Iphigenia in Aulis* and *Bacchae* are large-scale spectaculars, well suited to Archelaus' purpose.

In neither play is there a rag in sight, but this is not the only way in which they could be seen as running counter to the trend of Euripides' late tragedies. In *Bacchae* he not only significantly reinstates the chorus, elevating it to be one of the key components of the play, but one of his central themes appears to be the importance of worshipping the gods. He even makes a god the protagonist (something unique, as we have already seen, in any surviving tragedy). Moreover (as Richard Seaford argues in this collection), *Bacchae* can be shown to contain allusions to the Mysteries, which would have been clearly recognizable to all initiates. The twentieth-century scholar Gilbert Murray even followed the nineteenth-century philosopher Friedrich Nietzsche in suggesting that in his final years Euripides underwent a religious conversion, writing *Bacchae* as a warning to non-believers.

Great works of art are open to many interpretations. Some are discussed in these essays, and there is no need to repeat them here. However, I would tentatively add an observation of my own: it is not impossible that in writing *Bacchae* Euripides may have had at the back of his mind his own experience of Athenian democracy and the devastating effect which a charismatic figure such as Alcibiades (in life every bit as charismatic as Dionysus in this play) could have on it. Give in to such charisma at your peril, he appears to say, for married to it is a cold psychopathy, which cares only for itself.

Euripides died before he could see his new trilogy performed. According to his ancient biography, he was enjoying a siesta beneath a tree when, mistaken for a wild beast, he was torn apart by King Archaelaus' hunting dogs. It is a vivid image, but one which is surely too uncannily similar to the end of *Bacchae* to be true.

In 406 BC, Sophocles responded to news of his rival's death with dignity and humanity, dressing his chorus in robes of mourning for an appearance prior to that year's festival of Dionysus. As a further act of honour, Euripides' son (Euripides the Younger) was invited to stage his father's final trilogy – perhaps at the City Dionysia of 405 BC. The fickle audience, which had so often rejected Euripides while he was still alive, awarded it first prize. As Rosie Wyles points out in her essay here, if this date is correct, a few months earlier Aristophanes had shown his appreciation of the man he had once mercilessly lampooned. In *Frogs* he imagined a contest in the Underworld to see which of two dead poets should be reborn to save their city. One was Aeschylus, the other Euripides. Curiously the protagonist of *Frogs* is none other than Dionysus, also the protagonist of *Bacchae*. Was this more than a fortuitous coincidence? Might Aristophanes have seen the script of *Bacchae* in advance (or learned its premise) and placed Dionysus in the spotlight as his own deliberate and very touching tribute to the now-dead tragedian?

Later in 406 BC Athenian military policy began to unravel. Despite Alcibiades once more being *persona non grata* (he had fled to self-imposed exile after a defeat involving his second-in-command), the Athenian fleet won a victory over the Spartans near the Arginusae Islands just off the shores of Asia Minor. However, torn between pursuing the enemy and rescuing the shipwrecked, Athens' generals chose the former course of action. A storm blew up; the shipwrecked were drowned, their bodies lost at sea; and in Athens the mob bayed for the generals' blood. Unconstitutionally (despite – so it was later claimed – the opposition of Socrates) the generals were tried together and the six who did not escape were executed. Emotion had triumphed over expediency, but to Athens' cost, for at a stroke the city had rid itself of some of its best military leaders. As Teiresias warns in *Bacchae*: 'In politics a speaker who has passion without wisdom can be very dangerous.'

In 404 BC Athens, reduced to starvation (when its grain supply from the Black Sea had been cut off), surrendered to Sparta and her allies. The city's population was saved from massacre and enslavement only when one of the victors reminded his colleagues of Athens' past greatness by singing a line from Euripides. Sixty-nine years later, Thebes, the city of Pentheus, on which Dionysus wreaks revenge in *Bacchae*, was not so lucky. Alexander the Great, not only a Macedonian and an initiate in the Mysteries of Samothrace but a charismatic leader soon to be recognized at Siwah as the son of Zeus, was angered because Thebes refused to recognize him as its king. He besieged the city, defeated it and burned it to the ground.

Greek tragic conventions

Despite its (probably) being intended for performance in Macedonia, *Bacchae* remains in essence an Athenian tragedy and follows the conventions of that genre. Thus the script is divided between a chorus of fifteen (who performed in the flat, circular *orkhestra* and both entered and exited through side passages or *eisodoi*) and individual actors (who could also perform on and make entrances and exits via a low-platformed building called the *skene*). All of these performers were male. To enable them to represent a number of characters, masked actors doubled roles – in *Bacchae* even the 'protagonist' (literally 'first actor') doubled, playing both Dionysus and Teiresias, while the 'deuteragonist' ('second actor') played Pentheus and his mother Agave. When this actor delivered the lament over Pentheus' head, he was actually holding in his hands the 'Pentheus' mask, which he had worn earlier while playing that character.

In contrast with the repressed Pentheus, Dionysus' mask and costume were undoubtedly flamboyant, mirroring descriptions in the text which speak of him as curly-haired and lavishly dressed. However, for most of the play Dionysus is disguised as a mortal, so it is not impossible that for his final apotheosis he was re-masked and re-costumed in even greater magnificence, a physical underscoring of his divine power.

The chorus, on the other hand, remained the same 'characters' throughout the play. In fact, however, the fifteen members probably possessed no individual characteristics. Rather they wore identical masks and similar (if not identical) costumes, the nature of which is discussed by Rosie Wyles. In tragedies, the chorus invariably entered after a prologue delivered by one or more solo actors. This entrance was called the *parodos*. Usually they then remained on stage, punctuating the drama with choral songs, often called *stasima* (singular = *stasimon*) but also sometimes called odes.

Realism was not of prime importance to an ancient audience. Theatre acoustics meant that actors were forced to speak 'up and out', addressing the audience more than each other, and, because they wore masks which concealed facial expression, they needed to convey emotion through both vocal delivery and physical gesture, possibly involving their entire body. In moments of high tension the actors, who usually spoke their lines, sang, though what the music sounded like is largely unknown. In addition, the choral 'odes', which play such an important part in *Bacchae*, were not only sung but danced, with the choreography, music and rhythm of their lyrics reflecting the emotion of the scene.

Athenian tragedy had other conventions, too, which are well represented in *Bacchae*. Usually (but probably not always) death and physical violence were not represented on stage. Rather, audiences learned of such things through messengers. *Bacchae* contains not one but two 'messenger speeches', both virtuosic descriptions of the power of the bacchae, the second of which, a chilling report of Pentheus' murder, is followed brilliantly but unsettlingly by an ecstatic choral dance. This in turn heralds the entry of Agave with Pentheus' head. In Greek tragedy it is not unusual for an actor or object representing a corpse to be brought on stage. Those who have died inside are usually revealed lying on a trolley (the *ekkuklema*) rolled out from the stage building. In *Bacchae*, however, (as in other plays, such as Sophocles' *Antigone* and Euripides' own *Hippolytus*, where deaths have occurred in the countryside) Pentheus' remains are brought through one of the two *eisodoi*. Uniquely for any extant tragedy, however, these remains are not intact: while Agave carries the head, Cadmus and perhaps other attendants bear other anatomical parts.

Euripides' tragedies often ended in the appearance of a god, frequently represented as flying or hovering above the *orkhestra*, when an actor wearing a harness was hoisted up from behind the *skene* and suspended from a crane or *mekhane* (hence the Latin term *deus ex machina*). It is likely that this technique was employed at the end of *Bacchae*, too.

Bacchae also calls for a number of special effects, not least the partial destruction of Pentheus' palace in an earthquake. Whether or not this was actually shown on stage is discussed by Rosie Wyles. Much, however, was left to the imagination. Sophocles is famously said to have introduced 'painted scenery', or rather a 'painted *skene*', but quite what this means is hotly debated. Perhaps painted panels were introduced into a slotted frame. If so, it is tantalizing – if ultimately fruitless – to speculate that Zeuxis was somehow meant to be involved in the production intended for Archelaus I, in the same way that Picasso contributed to productions by Diaghilev. In fact, not even Zeuxis could compete with the real landscape of Dion, for – if it were performed at the theatre there – many of the Macedonian audience could see not just the stage but the nearby peaks of Mount Olympus.

In Athens the 'backcloth' to *Bacchae* was the actual sanctuary of Dionysus, just yards behind the *skene*, but the play easily survived transfers to other less likely venues. Edith Hall describes a performance (perhaps of just one scene) in 53 BC at the wedding of Pacorus, son of the Parthian king, Orodes II, to the daughter of the Armenian king, Artavasdes II (himself an accomplished writer of tragedies). When an actor playing Agave brought on the head of Pentheus it was not a prop but the actual severed head of the Parthians' bitter enemy, the Roman general Crassus, who had been killed shortly before at the Battle of Carrhae.

However, perhaps *Bacchae*'s strangest (re)incarnation was in the mediaeval Byzantine drama, *Christus Patiens* (The Suffering Christ), for which the (anonymous) author mined large sections of Euripides' play, reworking them to suit the new Christian context. This text is particularly valuable, as it allows scholars to reconstruct at least part of an important passage towards the end of *Bacchae*, which is missing in the play's manuscripts.

Today, more than ever, *Bacchae* continues to enjoy popularity – for reasons which the contributors to this volume (and not least Betine van Zyl Smit in her essay on the play's reception) so clearly demonstrate.

1

Perspectives on the Impact of *Bacchae* at its Original Performance

Edith Hall

Although Dionysus was already worshipped by the Greeks in Mycenaean times, his cult was believed to be an import from barbarian lands, and *Bacchae* enacts an ancient myth narrating its problematic arrival at the mainland Greek city of Thebes. The story is one of several mythical illustrations of an archaic Greek imperative: those who doubt the power of the gods must be disabused of their disbelief. The royal house of Thebes must be punished because it questions the divine paternity of Dionysus, its most illustrious offspring. Yet *Bacchae* is more than an exemplum of divine prerogative expressed through the consecutive motifs of resistance, punishment and acceptance. Not only is Dionysus the protagonist: his drama is a study of his own elusive personality and of his devastating power.

Bacchae expresses Dionysus' function as god of altered consciousness and illusion. In an unforgettable encounter, Dionysus, disguised as a mortal, puts the finishing touches to the Bacchanal disguise of Pentheus, his mortal cousin and adversary, before leading him to the mountains to be dismembered by the women of the city he is supposed to rule. Pentheus is in a Dionysiac trance; he can no longer distinguish between reality and illusion; he has assumed the identity of someone other than himself. The spectator is invited to contemplate the experience of any performance which entails the impersonation of one being by another. Drama demands that performer and spectator collude in a suspension of the empirically 'real' world. Pentheus dresses in a maenad's attire, just as each chorus member had done before actuality was forsaken and the drama began; in the original production this also required assuming the identity of the opposite sex, for all the performers would have been male. *Bacchae*, therefore, is a meditation on the very experience of theatre – a mimetic enactment of the journey into and out of illusion, the journey over which Dionysus presides in the mysterious fictive worlds he conjures up in his theatre.

The Greek mind was trained to think in polarities; to categorize, distinguish and oppose. If the personality of Dionysus can be reduced to one principle, it is his demonstration that conventional logic is inadequate for apprehending the universe as a whole. Dionysus confounds reason, defies categorization, dissolves polarities and inverts hierarchies. A youthful god and yet an immortal, respected by the elderly Cadmus and Teiresias, he cannot be defined as young. He is male and yet in his perceived effeminacy and special relationship with women cannot be defined as conventionally masculine. Conceived in Thebes yet worshipped abroad, he is neither wholly Greek nor barbarian. He conflates the tragic and comic views of life, as the patron deity of both genres. His worship can bring both transcendental serenity and repulsive violence: the slaughter of Pentheus, followed by his mother's invitation to the bacchants to share in the feast, entails three crimes considered abominable by the ancient Greeks: human sacrifice, infanticide and cannibalism.[1] Dionysus may be worshipped illicitly on the wild hillsides of Thebes, but he is also the recipient in Euripides' Athens of a respectable cult at the heart of the city-state. So he cannot be defined as the representative of nature in opposition to civilization. In using delusion to reveal the truth he confounds conventional distinctions between fiction and fact, madness and sanity, falsehood and reality. In *Bacchae* Dionysus causes the imprisoned to be liberated, the 'rational' to become demented, humans to behave like animals, men to dress as women, women to act like men, and an earthquake physically to force the untamed natural world into the 'safe', controlled, interior world of the household and the city.

Until the climax, when the deluded Agave appears, Thebes is represented exclusively by males; the beliefs of the dangerous culture which the disguised Dionysus threatens to introduce have been articulated by women. But with Agave's gradual return to 'normal' consciousness, even this binary, gendered opposition is exploded. This Theban woman once doubted the existence of the god, but comes to know as she emerges from her Dionysiac mania that in the severed head of her son she bears the physical proof that Dionysus is a living reality in Thebes. The revealed truth is that the denied god, the outsider, the alien, has belonged inside all along.

The transhistorical appeal of *Bacchae* is partly due to its insusceptibility to any unitary interpretation. Its portrayal of the unrestrained emotionalism which can lead human crowds into inhuman conduct spoke loudly to scholars at the time of the rise of fascism;[2] its portrayal of the conflict within Pentheus' psyche has also fascinated psychoanalytical critics.[3] But ultimately it frustrates all attempts to impose a monolithic 'meaning'. It neither endorses nor repudiates the cult whose arrival in Thebes it narrates. It never did prescribe for its audience a cognitive programme by which to understand an inexplicable universe. It simply enacts one occasion on which the denial, repression and exclusion of difference – psychological, ethnic and religious – led to utter catastrophe.

Bacchae remained familiar throughout antiquity, a constant in the performance repertoire and in the visual arts and a favourite of the emperor Nero (Dio Cassius 51.20). It provided a familiar theme in pantomime, the wildly popular form of musical theatre which took tragic mythological narratives to every corner of the ancient Roman Empire.[4] In pantomime, pleasure was generated by the transformation of the dancer into different roles within the individual story: if he were dancing a pantomime version of the story told in Euripides' *Bacchae*, he would successively assume the mask and persona of Dionysus, Teiresias, Cadmus, a messenger and the delirious Agave (*Greek Anthology* 16.289). The musical sections of *Bacchae* were also performed at drinking parties. When Plutarch reports the death of Crassus (*Vit. Crass.* 33.2–4), the head of the slaughtered Roman general was brought into the presence of the Parthian king Orodes when a tragic actor, Jason of Tralles, was performing 'the part of Euripides' *Bacchae* which is about Agave'. Jason handed his 'Pentheus' costume to one of the chorus, and seized Crassus' head. Assuming the role of the frenzied Agave, and using Crassus' head as 'a grisly prop',[5] he sang from her lyrical interchange with the chorus, 'We bear from the mountain a newly cut tendril to the palace, a blessed spoil from the hunt' (1169–71). This delighted everyone. But when the dialogue was sung where the chorus asks, 'Who killed him?', and Agave responds, 'mine was this privilege' (1179), the actual murderer sprang up and grabbed Crassus' head, feeling that these words were more appropriate for him to utter than for Jason.[6] By the second century BC the role of the god Dionysus in *Bacchae* could even be realized as a solo aria by the star cithara-singer Satyrus of Samos.[7]

In contrast, the modern admiration for *Bacchae* is a relatively recent development. Despite the widely read and illustrated retelling of Pentheus' death at the end of Ovid's *Metamorphoses* Book 3, no Renaissance performances, Early Modern adaptations or eighteenth-century neoclassical plays took Pentheus as their theme. No performances of *Bacchae* featured during the first two decades of the revival of staged ancient Greek tragedy which began in around 1880.[8] The reasons for the neglect – or avoidance – of the play were ethical and religious. Although some Byzantine scholars heard Christian reverberations in the story of ritual dismemberment and divine epiphany, *Bacchae* did not sit well with the Christian sensibility of the Renaissance and Early Modern era. One devout eighteenth-century critic could hardly contain his revulsion, warning his readers that 'the refined delicacy of modern manners will justly revolt against this inhuman spectacle of dramatick barbarity'.[9] But an upsurge of interest in Dionysus and the connections between ancient Greek ritual and myth developed at the end of the nineteenth century, with the wide dissemination of Nietzsche's *The Birth of Tragedy out of the Spirit of Music* (1872) and Frazer's *The Golden Bough* (1890).[10] The interest in ritualism drew scholars magnetically to this extraordinary play, and it is now considered one of Euripides' supreme masterpieces. But in this essay I return to the very beginnings of the play's performance history at the end of the fifth century BC. I explore how reading *Bacchae* as the culmination of the group of plays with which it was first performed can illuminate the meanings – aesthetic, ethical and theological – which it engendered in its original performance.

   Bacchae was first performed as part of a tragic tetralogy, that is, a group of three tragedies followed by a satyr play. The two Euripidean tragedies which preceded it in the group were the surviving *Iphigenia in Aulis* and the lost *Alcmaeon in Corinth*; we sadly cannot identify the name of the satyr play. Like both *Iphigenia in Aulis* and *Bacchae*, plays about Alcmaeon were well known in the ancient repertoire. Aristotle paid them an indirect compliment in his *Poetics* by naming Alcmaeon alongside the more familiar Orestes and Oedipus when specifying ideal tragic heroes (Ch. 13). After Euripides' death, tragedies about Alcmaeon were written both by the fourth-century Astydamas and by the Roman Republican playwright Ennius. Alcmaeon was a prominent figure on the ancient tragic stage with numerous complicated adventures before the action portrayed in *Alcmaeon in Corinth*, including those portrayed in Euripides' earlier play about him, *Alcmaeon in Psophis*. He was Argive, son of Amphiaraus, a prophet and king. Alcmaeon led the second generation who besieged Thebes, the 'Epigoni'; like Orestes, he killed his mother (Eriphyle) in order to avenge his father, was maddened by the Erinyes, then purified. But in *Alcmaeon in Corinth*, Alcmaeon is in middle age. He arrives in Corinth to find the two children he had fathered long ago, during his matricidal insanity.

   The outline of the plot of *Alcmaeon in Corinth* must be reflected in a Greek mythological handbook, written in the first or second centuries AD under the Roman Empire, Apollodorus' *Library* (3.7.7). Earlier in his career, after the second siege of Thebes, Alcmaeon had a sexual relationship with Teiresias' daughter Manto. They had two children, a boy named Amphilochus and a daughter named Tisiphone. Alcmaeon had left Amphilochus and Tisiphone in Corinth for his friend Creon, the king, to raise. But Creon's wife had sold Tisiphone, a great beauty, into slavery, fearing that Creon might become enamoured of her. In Euripides' play, Alcmaeon came to Corinth, and was reunited with both his children, but only after a near-miss incestuous encounter with Tisiphone. He had not seen her for years, and purchased her as a slave before they recognized one another. His son Amphilochus subsequently founded Amphilochian Argos. There is a slight suggestion in the fragmentary remains that the tone of the play may have been intermittently amusing, as was so often the case in Euripides' 'happy ending' plays; this was certainly the tone adopted by Colin Teevan in his bravura new play on the theme, incorporating the remains of both of Euripides' plays about Alcmaeon as well as some of his unplaced fragments, in English translations which I provided for him. It was first produced under the title *Cock o' the North* at the Live Theatre, Newcastle upon Tyne, directed by Martin Wylde, in 2004.[11]

There is no obvious circumstantial link between the action dramatized in the three tragedies, except possibly in the figure of Teiresias, Alcmaeon's Theban father-in-law, who appears in *Bacchae* and may have done so in *Alcmaeon in Corinth*. Although we only have fragmentary knowledge of *Alcmaeon in Corinth*, we do know enough to understand the variety of settings which the spectator of the whole tetralogy enjoyed. They were taken, in their collective imagination, sequentially to a military tent near the wave-churned beach at Aulis, a sumptuous residence on or near the Corinthian acropolis overlooking the sparkling waters of the Corinthian Gulf, and to the ancient palace of the Theban monarchy in the dusty plains of Boeotia under the towering Cithaeron mountain range. The group of tragedies constituting Euripides' last full-scale production at the Athenian Great Dionysia thus took their spectators on a tour of three contrasting sites in central Greece that were also central to the Greeks' inherited mythology.

The plays also took the spectator on a voyage through mythical time, but in reverse chronological order. The Trojan War took place in the lifetime of Polynices' son Thersander (see Pindar, *Olympian Ode* 2.33–45), who in some early versions of the Troy story, by the time of the Greek expedition, had succeeded to the throne of Thebes and so led the Boeotian contingent.[12] The Greek expedition to Troy which prompts the action of *Iphigenia in Aulis* was understood as happening a considerable time *after* Thersander had besieged Thebes with the 'Epigoni', the sons of the 'Seven against Thebes'. The action of the second play in the group, the Corinthian adventure of Alcmaeon, the leader of the Epigoni, would have been understood by theatre audiences as preceding the Trojan War and therefore the incident at Aulis. But the third play, *Bacchae*, took the viewer far further back into mythical time, to a tragic incident involving the first three generations of Thebans – the founder Cadmus, his daughter Agave and his grandsons Dionysus and Pentheus. Pentheus was king of Thebes at least three generations prior to Jocasta, Creon and Laius, and at least five generations before the Trojan War. The audience of this group of plays witnessed an early stage in the Greeks' account of the evolution of their city-state civilization. The back-story is the birth of Dionysus, and so the audience relive nothing less than the very dawn of the religion they practised and the rites of the wine-god whose festival they were celebrating in the form of drama competitions in fifth-century democratic Athens. Very few tragedies, however, are set in mythical time so early that the cult of Dionysus has not yet been accepted in every major Greek city-state. Besides the Aeschylean *Prometheus Bound*, the action of which takes places many generations before the birth even of Heracles, no other extant Greek tragedy takes its viewer so far back in time.

All the myths dramatized in tragedy of course presuppose a world long before tragic theatre has been invented. In tragedy, songs are sung by bards and known from works of visual art: there are no plays within plays to be seen in Euripides' Aulis, Corinth, or Thebes.[13] There is some sophisticated 'metatheatre' – reflection on the nature of tragic mimesis – in *Bacchae*, but it is implicit rather than involving explicit references to the experience specifically of theatre.[14] There may have been strong inter-performative resonances, however, since all three plays had famous precursors and the meanings created by certain scenes may have been augmented or inflected by echoes of earlier plays. *Iphigenia in Aulis* demonstrably draws on Aeschylus' *Oresteia* and the various depictions of Clytemnestra in subsequent tragedies, including the *Electra*s of both Euripides and Sophocles; Aeschylus had also written an *Iphigenia*. The characterization of Achilles must also be informed by Aeschylus' famous Trojan War trilogy, the *Achilleis*.[15] In the case of *Alcmaeon in Corinth*, stories about Alcmaeon, derived from the lost epic *Alcmaeonis*, had long been a mainstay in the tragedians' repertoire. We have already noted that Euripides had himself produced a play about Alcmaeon's earlier experiences, his *Alcmaeon in Psophis*, one of the group (also including *Telephus*, *Cretan Women* and *Alcestis*) with which he won second prize in 438 BC. Sophocles had also been interested in Alcmaeon: the title of his lost plays include not only an *Epigoni* but an *Eriphyle* and an *Alcmaeon* which seems to have treated the theme of Alcmaeon's madness.[16] Two other fifth-century playwrights, Agathon and Achaeus, also wrote plays about Alcmaeon. *Bacchae* also had important precursors, notably Aeschylus' famous trilogy about the rejection of Dionysus by Lycurgus, king of Thrace, his *Lycurgeia*.

The centrality of Dionysus to *Bacchae* makes it appropriate that we owe what little we know of the circumstances in which this unforgettable play was originally produced to a remark by the god Dionysus in the only other surviving ancient drama of which he is protagonist, Aristophanes' *Frogs*. In line 67 of that comedy, the god Dionysus says that he is overwhelmed by a desire for the tragedian Euripides; Dionysus' interlocutor Heracles completes the line by adding that Euripides is dead. It was a single comment inscribed beside this line by an ancient scholar on a copy of the text which has preserved our priceless information that, after the death of Euripides, his son, under the same name, produced at the City Dionysia the following plays: *Iphigenia in Aulis, Alcmaeon in Corinth* and *Bacchae*.

This information allows us to date the premiere of *Bacchae* with some likelihood to 405 BC,[17] the same year in which Dionysus starred in the premiere of *Frogs*, a year when the Athenian democracy stood on the very brink of catastrophe. The *Frogs* scholiast implies that Euripides' son produced the group containing *Bacchae* relatively soon after his father's death, which makes a date later than 405 improbable. We know from the *Life of Euripides* that Sophocles appeared in black robes of mourning at the 'Proagōn' (on which event see further below) to the performances of tragedies in 406, when his rival Euripides had died. Sophocles, himself elderly, reduced the people to tears, with the heads of his troupe bare of the customary festive garlands. At a pinch, the plays could therefore have been produced in 406, if Euripides had already planned to produce these three plays and his son had been able to step into his shoes and the death caused no disruption at all. But the 405 date does seem most likely. For the purposes of this essay, however, it does not matter whether it was 406 or 405, since the historical and political context, about which much has been written, is less my concern here than the way in which the particular place taken by the performance of *Bacchae* in that particular group might have affected its nature as a performed experience, and its aesthetic, ethical and metaphysical impact.

The existence of the group of plays, as cited by the scholiast on *Frogs*, raises important questions about the way that tragic poets composed their plays, and planned their production in the drama competition. The scarcity of our evidence on key aspects of the festival administration has led scholars to make large assumptions and then treat their speculations as if they were articles of faith. The one certainty about these three plays is that they were produced posthumously and by Euripides' son. But we do not know whether he was acting on instructions from his father, or even according to a plan for a group which had been discussed within the family. It is perfectly possible that amongst Euripides' papers were unperformed plays, and that his son decided to propose these three (plus a satyr play of which we do not know the name) to the archon (magistrate) for posthumous performance.

Thinking about this process must make us focus on two uncomfortable facts. (1) Although we know when these three plays were first performed, we have no idea when they were first written. There is no reason why Euripides could not work on a particular play on and off for years, or write one mid-career which, for whatever reason, was not produced in his lifetime. (2) Although there is no reason to doubt that the three plays were performed in the order cited by the Aristophanes scholiast, we have no evidence that Euripides himself either wrote them with a joint production in that order in mind, or decided at some point, when looking for a set of three tragedies to put together in a single programme, that they would work satisfactorily in this particular arrangement. Such a decision might have been taken by his son, or it might have been virtually unavoidable if these three were the only, or the best tragedies left behind by his father at his death. But again, for our purposes it does not necessarily matter whether the group was originally conceived (or even at a later point developed) as a unified theatrical experience; what we *can* think about is how the decision to run these three plays together sequentially affected the meanings that they did in fact create in performance.

But the experience of performance began well before the drama competitions proper. The spectator at the Dionysia on that spring day not long before Athens lost the Peloponnesian War will have gone to the theatre excited at the prospect of seeing some hitherto unperformed works of the recently deceased tragedian. Euripides' popularity is emphatically stated in *Frogs*, definitely produced before these plays at the Lenaea of 405. It was the theme of several other comedies of the era: a character in one lost comedy announced that he would be prepared to hang himself for the sake of seeing this (dead) tragedian, and in another named *Euripides-Lover* a character discussed people who hate all lyrics but those by Euripides.[18]

How much did the spectators know about the productions before the great day arrived? The plays were submitted for the archon's consideration by a date between a year and a few months or so before the next festival. Each tragedian had to propose a tetralogy to be performed on a single day of the festival. For the 458 BC festival, for example, Aeschylus submitted his tetralogy the *Oresteia*, consisting of *Agamemnon, Libation-Bearers, Eumenides* and a satyr drama called *Proteus*. We know nothing of how much actual text he was required to submit, and little about the means by which the archon – probably in consultation with other officials – decided which three tragedians were to compete. It is likely that a poet whose production in a previous competition had proved disastrous could be excluded, and we hear of complaints when Sophocles, as a favourite poet, was not selected.[19] The three selected tragedians were at this time allocated their principal actors, their chorus, and also their *chorēgos*. This was a wealthy man who sponsored the production by funding the maintenance, costuming and training of the chorus of citizens made available to each competing tragedian.

After months of rehearsal, the drama competitions at the City Dionysia were inaugurated at the Proagōn, which means the formality 'preliminary to the competition' or 'before the competition'. After about 440 BC this was held in a roofed building called the 'Song Hall' (Odeon) next to the theatre. All the dramatists who were about to compete ascended a rostrum, along with their actors and chorusmen (wearing neither masks nor costumes), and 'announced' or 'talked about' their compositions.[20] It would be fascinating to know more about the Proagōn, especially the degree to which the details of the plot and special effects were made public, and how far the actual masked performances at the festival assumed knowledge of the personnel that had been gained when they appeared without their masks. How surprised were the audience by the twists and turns of the plots in *Iphigenia in Aulis*, *Alcmaeon in Corinth* and *Bacchae* when they were actually performed in full?

We know rather more about the ceremonies which took place on the festival day following the Proagōn, and their nature may have affected considerably the frame of reference within which the spectators understood the plays. From the perspective of *Bacchae*, the plot must have seemed related to, or even in some sense a continuation of, the religious rituals earlier in the festival, to which the physical effigy of Dionysus was central. The rites began with the procession called the 'Introduction' (Eisagōgē), which annually reproduced the introduction of Dionysus to his theatre in the city sanctuary. According to myth, this commemorated his original journey from Eleutherae (on the border with Boeotia, the region around Thebes) into Attica.[21] Instead of recreating the entire journey, the icon of Dionysus – a wooden pole with a mask at one end – was adorned with a costume and ivy. It was carried from his city sanctuary to an olive-grove outside the city called the Academy, on the road that headed out towards Eleutherae. A day or two later, after hymns and sacrifices, Dionysus was brought by torchlight in a great procession back to the theatre in his sanctuary from which he had been taken.[22]

Once Dionysus had been installed, the festival opened officially the next morning with the Pompē, or 'procession'. All the city was now in a state of high excitement: the Assembly could not be held, nor legal proceedings initiated, and it seems that even prisoners could be released temporarily on bail (which may have added extra meanings to Dionysus' escape from captivity after the earthquake in *Bacchae*).[23] The procession, which probably led from the city walls, would stop at each of several shrines on its way to the sanctuary of Dionysus in order to sing and dance for different gods, just as the chorus of *Bacchae* sings its ritual hymns in mythical Thebes. But the procession, at the same time, symbolically defined the relationships between the social groups that made up Athenian society. It was led by a virginal young woman from an aristocratic family (perhaps memories of her were prompted during the tragic performances by Euripides' Iphigenia and by Alcmaeon's daughter). She carried the ceremonial golden basket for the choicest pieces of meat from the sacrifice which will have 'set the stage' for the sacrifice theme in both *Iphigenia in Aulis* and *Bacchae*. The *chorēgoi* who had funded the productions wore expensive costumes, sometimes made of gold.

Provision had to be made for the public feast, and the many thousands of people attending the festival would have needed a great deal to eat: the bull specially chosen to be the principal sacrificial animal, as 'worthy of the god', which must have been recalled by the bull imagery in *Bacchae*, was accompanied by younger citizens in military training (*ephebes*). There were, in addition, hundreds of lesser sacrifices; the sanctuary of Dionysus must have resembled a massive sunlit abattoir attached to a barbecue. It resounded with the bellowing and bleating of frightened animals, was awash with their blood, and smelled powerfully of carcasses and roasting meat. The sight of the dismembered carcasses will have provided its own reverberations to the audience who heard about the maenads' activities in *Bacchae*.

The theatre itself was prepared for the culmination of the festival, the performance of the plays, by ceremonial activities. These began with a purification rite that may have involved yet another sacrifice, this time of very young piglets. The military atmosphere of *Iphigenia in Aulis* will have recalled the civic rituals which took place at this point. The ten *stratēgoi* ('generals'), the most senior elected officers of state, poured out libations of wine to the gods. A public herald made a series of announcements, naming recent benefactors of the city. When the theatre was full, there was a display of rows of golden money bars ('talents'), the revenue Athens had accrued that year from the states allied with her, who in practice were her imperial subjects and thus required to pay tribute. The imperial flavour was heightened by the public presentation of a suit of armour to all those sons of Athenian war dead who had achieved military age, before they were invited to take prominent seats near the front of the theatre.[24]

The production's three actors and their chorus were allocated months before the festival. The chorusmen were required to impersonate excitable women local to Aulis in *Iphigenia in Aulis* and female and male ritual followers of Dionysus in *Bacchae* and the closing satyr drama respectively. We do not know their identity in *Alcmaeon in Corinth*. It is also possible for us to reconstruct, at least in the case of *Iphigenia in Aulis* and *Bacchae*, exactly how the individual roles would have been assigned. In *Iphigenia in Aulis*, one actor played Agamemnon and Achilles, one Menelaus and Clytemnestra, and one the Old Man, Iphigenia and the Messenger. In *Bacchae*, one actor played Dionysus and Teiresias (god and prophet), another Pentheus and Agave (young man and his mother) and the third Cadmus and the two messengers. Since we know that some actors specialized in certain types of role – strong male heroes or young women, for example – we can speculate about which parts were taken by the same actor across all three plays. It is highly likely that the Agamemnon/Achilles actor played Dionysus/Teiresias; it is the most plausible guess that he also played Alcmaeon – a famous warrior in midlife – in the second play.

The continuity between the roles taken by the individual actors, who will not have been able to disguise their voices altogether, must have affected the impact of the performances. The actor who played both Agamemnon and Alcmaeon had intense scenes with two young daughters, although Agamemnon's daughter passes from happiness to misery, and Alcmaeon's, apparently, from misery to happiness. The actor who played both Dionysus and Teiresias in *Bacchae* will have had the opportunity to play a true priest and a god disguised as a priest; the Pentheus/Agave actor may have used his voice to reinforce the poignant familial relationship between these two characters. The changing between male and female identities of the second and third actors in *Iphigenia in Aulis* will have set up the issue of gendered transvestism explored so poignantly in the scene where Pentheus dresses up as a maenad in *Bacchae* in order to infiltrate the revels. It is likely that the same actor who specialized in impersonating old men and delivering messenger speeches played the elderly, morally refined slave in *Iphigenia in Aulis* and the kindly, ageing Cadmus in *Bacchae*. The whole group of tragic plays thus began and ended with scenes involving old men played by this actor, who was responsible for creating much of the pathos and ethical effect.

The issue of cognitive confusion certainly ran through the tragedies. Iphigenia and her mother need to be disabused of the delusion that they are in Aulis for a wedding: Clytemnestra's embarrassing first encounter in *Iphigenia in Aulis* with Achilles, who she thinks is about to become her son-in-law, gains its power from her misapprehension. There must have been a painful scene either enacted or narrated in *Alcmaeon in Corinth*, where the father and daughter did not realize that they were blood relations. And in *Bacchae*, of course, failure to apprehend reality accurately, epitomized in Pentheus' failure to recognize Dionysus physically, a concrete reiteration of the denial of Dionysus' godhead by Semele's sisters which had stimulated the action of the tragedy in the first place, is a major structuring motif: it culminates in Agave's deranged appearance with the head of her son, which she falsely believes, instead, to be the head of a lion.

The fundamental question asked by epistemology – how do we know what we know? – seems to have underpinned the plays' metaphysical signification. Like all effective tragedies (and we can assume all three were effective because they were victorious in the competition), they took their audience on a metaphysical journey through different ways of thinking about the reasons why humans suffer. *Alcmaeon in Corinth*, on the basis of our evidence, seems to have been a play where *eros* was important; perhaps the real-world importance of the cult of Aphrodite at Corinth figured large in a play about a beautiful maiden and the men – whether Creon and/or her unwitting father – who may have been attracted towards her. But this is speculation: the crucial role in changing the situation of the principal characters was apparently chance or coincidence. This was the force the Greeks called *tuchē*, which became more important to Euripides over the course of his life's work, is especially visible in *Ion* and was to become crucial to the plots of New Comedy. But the plays performed before and after *Alcmaeon in Corinth* were much darker: human error and premeditated divine malice are the driving force of the plots. In both, the movement of the plot is downhill towards doom. Yet the first and third plays stand at opposite ends of the spectrum of Euripidean metaphysics. The will of the gods is at its most obscure and unknowable in *Iphigenia in Aulis*; it is at its most starkly revealed in *Bacchae*. Human life is wrecked in both cases, but the possibility of evading the catastrophe seems to me to be far greater in *Iphigenia in Aulis*. From what little we know of the central play, catastrophe seems actually to have been avoided altogether.

Euripides did not write the whole text of *Iphigenia in Aulis* as it stands. There is a question mark over the authenticity of Agamemnon's 'delayed' prologue, positioned after the opening dialogue; there are several spurious passages scattered throughout the play, probably interpolated by actors after the fifth century. But by far the most significant interpolation begins with the appearance of the second messenger, or at least at that part of his speech which reports the disappearance of Iphigenia, whisked away by Artemis, and the substitution of a deer. This comforting alternative ending to the tragedy – perhaps inserted during the fourth-century crystallization of the tragic performance canon by an ancient theatrical company familiar with the hugely popular *Iphigenia in Tauris*[25] – radically affects both its theological meaning and its emotional impact. Modern directors often prefer, quite legitimately, to conclude performances with Iphigenia's unrelievedly tragic walk to her death at line 1531, the version I believe was originally performed in 405 BC.

In 1957 the insightful scholar Karl Reinhardt published an influential article 'Die Sinneskreise bei Euripides' or 'The Crisis of Meaning in Euripides'. This article was responding to the Existential tradition in literature, which Reinhardt traced explicitly through Kafka and Sartre, and which reveals the profound influence of Samuel Beckett's dramatic universe, the universe of the 'Theatre of the Absurd'.[26] For Reinhardt, *Iphigenia in Aulis* teeters on the brink of 'the sheerest absurdity'. Reinhardt's Euripides is less a poet of direct protest than a nihilist, an existentialist practitioner of the theatre of the absurd, dedicated to revealing the hollowness of the intellectual and linguistic strategies by which humans struggle to comprehend their situation. Some of the most powerful moments in *Iphigenia in Aulis* come when the characters on stage, unable to extricate themselves from absurd situations, resort to transparently hollow justifications, 'spinning' an argument, or attempting to make sense of their circumstances by conspicuously employing (in ancient terminology) the science of rhetoric.[27]

The role of spin/rhetoric within *Iphigenia in Aulis* is underscored by the manner in which almost everyone changes his or her mind, under rhetorical pressure, about the issue of the sacrifice. Euripides was fascinated by the factors which condition moral choices, and some of his tragedies explored the dangers attendant upon precipitate decision-making. In 406, the Athenians had precipitately executed no fewer than six of their generals, after an unconstitutional trial, as punishment for the great loss of life at the Battle of Arginusae; by 405 many must have regretted the whole tragic sequence of events and this will have affected their response to *Iphigenia in Aulis*, regardless of when it was first written.

Iphigenia in Aulis uses its myth to explore peremptory life-and-death decisions by showing how, during a military crisis, several members of the same family took and rescinded decisions about the life of an innocent girl. Agamemnon has summoned her to be sacrificed, changes his mind, but is incapable of sticking to the better moral course out of fear for his own army. Menelaus changes his mind, emotionally rejecting his earlier 'logical' justifications of the atrocity when he sees his brother's distress. Even Achilles allows himself to be persuaded that Iphigenia wants to die. And Iphigenia herself, far from being the inconsistent character Aristotle alleged, or driven virtually into psychosis as has often been claimed, proves herself a typical, well-acculturated Argive: she has internalized her community's behavioural patterns, becoming as morally unstable and vacillating in the face of well-tricked-out arguments as the strongest men in the Greek army, her father and uncle included.

Spin works best in a world with few external moral reference points, and insecurity about the nature or requirements of divinity. One strand in the play's reception since ancient times has been the view that it shows the evil effects of religious zealotry or superstition. This interpretation has an aetiology extending back to Lucretius, the ancient Epicurean polemicist, who after narrating the sacrifice at Aulis famously pronounced, 'so much evil can religion bring about' (*de Rerum Natura* 1.80–101). The absurd world depicted in *Iphigenia in Aulis*, relative even to the confused and disturbing metaphysical environments of most Greek tragedy, is astoundingly irreligious. Very little happens except that an oracular demand for human sacrifice, which was received, accepted and put into motion well *before* the beginning of the play, is actually carried out after the two key agents – the sacrificing father and the sacrificed daughter – talk themselves into it. The crucial transformations do not take place on the level of action, or weather, or even Iphigenia's body, but exclusively in the minds of the leading characters. *Peitho* ('Persuasion') of a particularly sinister kind is seen to take effect. There is little emphasis on the oracle delivered by Calchas (indeed it is only summarized in *oratio obliqua* at 89–91), no discussion of it, no further omen, no angry bird, no visible epiphany of a god, no inspection of entrails. There is no guidance from any priestly figure, no divination of the will of heaven. There is no new communication from the gods during the course of the entire play (a point well brought out in Foley's analysis[28]). Agamemnon even criticizes all seers as frauds, while failing to contest Calchas' faintly recalled pronouncement. This presentation of the myth implies that the suffering Iphigenia must undergo is not only entirely avoidable, but that it remains so until the eleventh hour.

The characters in *Iphigenia in Aulis* may be stranded in an absurdist ethical and metaphysical vacuum, with no way of discerning any meaning in their universe, but this does not mean that they need to *choose* to perform and suffer an inhumane atrocity. This is a play which will always speak loudest to an audience themselves characterized by intense, secularized moral *aporia*. No character can find a moral framework to help them identify and then adhere to their instinctive ethical reactions to what is happening – even Clytemnestra is ultimately persuaded out of her proposal to take a defiant last stand against Iphigenia's sacrifice (1459–60). The one exception is the old slave, an impressive individual who does seem to be capable of independent ethical intuition and steady resolve. It is very nearly true that in the world portrayed in *Iphigenia in Aulis* nobody does wrong with any great willingness (in ancient philosophical terms, half-heartedly demonstrating the truth of the Socratic principle that 'nobody does wrong willingly'), since, after reflection, both Agamemnon and Menelaus do think better of the sacrifice scheme. But they do not possess the moral vertebrae which would enable them to jeopardize their generalships in order to prevent it.

The devastation of mothers bereaved of their children presents an obvious link between *Iphigeneia in Aulis* and *Bacchae*, and if Manto played a role in *Alcmaeon in Corinth*, maternal misery may have featured there too. The parallelism between Clytemnestra and Agave's predicaments may have been further underlined if (as is likely) the two mothers were played by the same actor. The suffering portrayed in the closing episodes of *Bacchae*, when Agave comes to understand that she has brutally killed her own son, is in no way less intense than the suffering of Clytemnestra and Iphigenia in *Iphigenia in Aulis*. But the metaphysical basis for the suffering could not be presented more differently. We are left in considerable doubt about the divine endorsement of Iphigenia's sacrifice, and feel that Clytemnestra capitulates too quickly. In

Bacchae, on the other hand, Agave has no chance whatsoever to exercise free will or moral choice. The near-constant presence of Dionysus, his clear statement of his plan to wreck Thebes through its women, and the numerous miraculous 'signs and wonders' witnessed by the audience or reported to them, makes the divine control of events in *Bacchae* overwhelmingly explicit. The absolute inevitability of the suffering undergone by the Thebans, and the horror of the violence committed against Pentheus, the proof of the existence of god by signs and wonders experienced phenomenologically and sensually rather than through language, are closer to Antonin Artaud's 'Theatre of Cruelty' than to any version of the 'Theatre of the Absurd'. It is little surprise that practitioners of the 'Theatre of Cruelty' so often claim *Bacchae* as a linear ancestor, and indeed have sometimes staged pioneering performances of it.[29] The only Euripidean tragedy where characters have equivalently little room for manoeuvre is *Hippolytus,* in which the entire action is ordained by Aphrodite, as angry for being insulted by Hippolytus as Dionysus is angry for being denied by the Theban royal family in *Bacchae.*

The supernatural and miraculous element in the play is by no means confined to events which the spectators witness at first hand. Many marvels take place behind doors or outside the city walls on the mountains, but are described by awed reporters in awesome detail. The soldier who had first brought in the bound Dionysus, disguised as his own priest, reports that the women Pentheus had already imprisoned have miraculously escaped. Their fetters, apparently, fell spontaneously to the earth, and the bars keeping the prison doors closed slid back of their own accord: the soldier concludes, 'Yes, full of many wonders to thy land is this man come' (449–50).

In the first messenger speech Pentheus (who is already disoriented) hears what the Theban women have just been doing on Cithaeron (677–774). The narrative begins with strange and disturbing sights, although not supernatural ones, such as the live, hissing snakes the women used for girdles, and the breastfeeding of a fawn and a wolf cub by mothers of newborn. But then the miracles begin. At the touch of a thyrsus, fresh water spurts from rocks and wine from the earth. Milk is squeezed from the soil, and honey drips from thyrsuses. When the women sing, wild animals kneel in submission. The maenads acquire the supernatural strength to tear limbs from cattle with their bare hands. Then they attack a village, snatching children and carrying them, laughing, on their shoulders, with no need to hold them in place; they can break metal without incurring injury, and place flames in their hair without being burnt. The villagers find weapons useless against the bacchants: the thyrsus alone, in the women's soft white hands, proves sufficient defence. No wonder the messenger concludes, 'Sure some God was in these things!' The second report from the mountain is far more unnerving (1043–1152).

The grotesque, sinister key is struck by the petrifying picture of Dionysus seating Pentheus on the branch of a pine tree he has bent, with his supernatural strength, to the ground, before carefully releasing it to lift the cross-dressed king to his parody of a throne above the tree-tops. This is followed by the god's disembodied voice, a pillar of flame, and a terrifying, windless silence, before the maenads launch their assault.

The spectator who witnessed *Bacchae* in performance was regaled with these gruesome, uncanny narratives but also directly presented with an unrelenting series of visible and audible proofs of the existence and ineluctable will of the divine Dionysus. It is appropriate that this essay concludes with the emphatic onstage proofs of the power of Dionysus which the entire Athenian Dionysia was designed to celebrate. The young god's first words in the prologue proudly declare who he is – Dionysus, son of Zeus – now returned to his mother's homeland. The paranormal is already visible in the smoke which mysteriously never stops issuing from Semele's tomb. Dionysus has arrived in Greece, after teaching the rest of the world to celebrate the rites which prove and display him as 'manifest god'. He has already shown his power by sending the women of Thebes mad and sending them out from their homes to the mountainside. When he has proved to the doubting Pentheus that he is a god, Dionysus will proceed to other Greek cities to display the might of his godhead.

Cadmus and Teiresias, old men, feel the years melt away from them as they prepare to join the Bacchic rites – a magical rejuvenation which takes place before the audience's eyes (188–94). Dionysus is led off to the prison, and the maenadic chorus sing in his praise, but their ode is interrupted by the most spectacular miracle so far: a divine voice is heard from offstage, telling the maenads that it belongs to the child of Zeus and Semele; Dionysus' voice then calls for aid from the 'female spirit of the Earthquake' (585). And then an earthquake really does strike the palace, a seismic event somehow made apparent to the audience in the theatre, at the very least by sound effects and the reaction of the characters and chorus. This miracle is followed by the god's instruction to the fire on Semele's tomb to leap up, which it does (this would have been feasible with available stage technology in the late fifth century BC). Earthquake and flame are followed by the climactic third stage in this triple miracle. Dionysus, last seen bound and being led off to gaol, appears from the palace constrained by no fetters at all.

Dionysus, in the guise of his priest, now describes to the chorus how he has been mocking Pentheus inside. He has so altered the king's powers of perception that Pentheus bound a sacrificial bull, mistaking it for the priest. He also began to stab at the air with his sword, in a murderous rage, imagining he was attacking the priest: he was actually suffering a fit of psychotic delusion

(617–41). Dionysus' capacity to alter mental states at his will is best exemplified, however, in his two subsequent onstage scenes with Pentheus, first when he persuades him to inspect the Bacchic rites for himself, and secondly when he puts the finishing touches to Pentheus' 'disguise' as a maenad. Dionysus' sinister mind-altering power could not be more graphically illustrated than by Pentheus' own description of his (false) consciousness: double vision, the hallucinated bull, and his feeling that he suddenly possesses superhuman physical strength. Pentheus leaves for the mountain, but the same dreadful power of the god to transform human consciousness is redoubled with the subsequent appearance of the delusional Agave, holding a head in her hands which she believes belongs to a lion when in fact it is her son's.

At the end of the play (1330), Dionysus appears, almost certainly in the theatrical machine, to gloat in his full godhead over the humiliation of the Thebans. Although we have unfortunately lost the section of the play in which Dionysus made his epiphany, and pronounced his judgement on the daughters of Cadmus, the text does resume mid-speech, when he turns to address the aged founder of Thebes himself. Dionysus' predictions show how far detached is the world of *Bacchae* from the realm of discernible human experience – the only realm dramatized in the doggedly anthropocentric *Iphigenia in Aulis*. Cadmus is to be transformed into a serpent, and to take with him his wife Harmonia (herself a superhuman creature from Olympus, daughter of the war-god Ares). They will travel on a cattle-drawn chariot, through eastern lands, and gather an army to lead against Greece (this motif must have reawakened the audience's memories of the processions which opened the Dionysia), before being translated to the Islands of the Blest. Finally, Agave and Cadmus desperately plead for some softening of the god's vindictive plans, but to no avail. These events are what Zeus ordained long ago (1349), we have experienced them through our senses as well as through language in a performance which has undermined our very ability to rely on the truth of our sense-perceptions, and no human word or action can change them: this is Euripides' prototype of the Theatre of Cruelty indeed.

Notes

1 Hall (1989), especially Ch. 3.
2 Winnington-Ingram (1997).
3 Segal (1986) 268–93.
4 See further Hall and Wyles (2008).
5 Braund (1993) 468–9.

6 Hall (2002) and (2006) 311–12.
7 Dittenberger (1960) no. 648B. See Eitrem, Amundsen and Winnington-Ingram (1955) 27.
8 On which see Hall and Macintosh (2005) chs 11–13.
9 Jodrell (1781) vol. 2, 550.
10 Hall (2013) ch. 11.
11 Teevan (2004). On the process by which I translated the fragments and Teevan used them as a springboard for his new play, see my Introduction in that edition.
12 Haug (2012) 214.
13 Hall (2006) ch. 4, especially 105–11.
14 Hall (2006) 109, with further references.
15 See Michelakis (2002).
16 See further Pearson (1917) 69, 130.
17 See Webster (1967) 257–8.
18 Philemon fr. 118 and Axionicus fr. 3 *PCG*.
19 For English translations of the sources, a papyrus (*The Oxyrhynchus Papyri* 2737, fr. 1, col. ii), and a fragment of a comedy by Cratinus (*PCG* F 17) see Csapo and Slater (1995) 135 no. 71, and 108 no. 1.
20 The sources for this information, Aeschines, *Against Ctesiphon* 66–7, ancient scholars' comments, and Plato, *Symposium* 194, are translated in Csapo and Slater (1995) 109–10 nos. 4–7.
21 The source for this information, an ancient scholar's comment on Aristophanes' *Acharnians* 243, is translated in Csapo and Slater (1995) 110 no. 9.
22 See the sources as translated in Csapo and Slater (1995) 111–12 nos. 10–14.
23 Csapo and Slater (1995) 112–13 nos. 15–16.
24 See Goldhill (1987).
25 Hall (2013) ch. 4.
26 Reinhardt (1957). The best introduction to the 'Theatre of the Absurd' remains Esslin (2001).
27 I elaborate this interpretation further in Hall (2005).
28 Foley (1982).
29 The theoretical groundwork of the 'Theatre of Cruelty' is Artaud (1958); for the genealogy connecting *Bacchae* with this school of avant-garde theatre practice, see e.g. Sutherland (1968) 87–8 and Zarrilli (2010) 516.

2

Bacchae and Earlier Tragedy

Alan H. Sommerstein

Every surviving Greek tragedy was built around, or developed out of, a story which was known in outline to its audience; usually this story was part of the vast corpus of inherited myth, but in Aeschylus' *Persians* (as in a small number of earlier plays which have not survived) it was an event of very recent history. By Euripides' time the story of a new tragedy very often was, or was based on, a story that had been dramatized already. Famously Aeschylus, Sophocles and Euripides all wrote plays on the revenge of Orestes (and Euripides wrote another, *Orestes*, with a largely invented plot, on the aftermath of the revenge); but this trio is only unique because all three plays happen to have survived. Of Euripides' sixteen genuine tragedies (that means omitting *Cyclops*, which is a satyr-drama, *Alcestis*, which was produced in place of a satyr-drama, and *Rhesus*, which is not Euripides' work), at least nine run closely parallel to known plays of Aeschylus or Sophocles. *Bacchae* is one of these.

This was, of course, known to the ancient scholars who studied *Bacchae*, and one of them, in a headnote ('Hypothesis') which precedes the text of the play in one of our two medieval manuscripts, states that 'the storyline is found in Aeschylus' *Pentheus*'. That is actually almost all we know for sure about Aeschylus' *Pentheus*, at least under that name; only one line of text (Aeschylus fr. 183) is quoted from the play by an ancient author (the great medical writer Galen), in which someone is warned not to 'spill a gout of blood on the ground'. But the Aeschylean antecedents of *Bacchae* are much more extensive than that.

We can start in Aeschylus' *Oresteia* – to be precise, in the third part of that trilogy, *Eumenides*. The opening scenes of *Eumenides* are set at Delphi, and it begins with the prophetess of Apollo (the Pythia) making a prayer to all the gods worshipped at and around the great sanctuary, before entering the temple to give her inspired responses. In lines 24 to 26 she makes mention of both Dionysus and Pentheus:

Nor do I forget that Bromius ['the Noisy One', a common name for

Dionysus in poetry] has dwelt in this place ever since he led his bacchants
in battle and netted Pentheus in death like a hare.

On which an ancient commentator (scholiast) remarks:

Here he says that the events concerning Pentheus took place on [Mount]
Parnassus, but in *Xantriai* he says they took place on Cithaeron

– as, of course, they do in *Bacchae*. We have several ancient quotations from
Xantriai, one of which (fr. 169) comes from a speech by Lyssa, the goddess of
madness; the quoting author tells us that Lyssa was 'inspiring the bacchants',
and the goddess speaks of someone being torn in pieces from head to foot (or
rather from foot to head). So it looks very much as though the death of
Pentheus was the tragic climax of *Xantriai*. The title of the play gives us a
little more information: like most plural titles of tragedies, it evidently refers
to the chorus, and it means 'women carding wool', a typical feminine
occupation – unless, as has been suggested (rather improbably),[1] what they
were 'carding' was actually Pentheus' flesh.

What is going on here? Did Aeschylus deal with the same subject twice, as
Euripides famously dealt twice with the story of Phaedra and Hippolytus?
Were *Pentheus* and *Xantriai* perhaps successive plays of a trilogy? I have
discussed these and related questions elsewhere,[2] and will state only my
conclusion here, which is that *Pentheus* and *Xantriai* were simply alternative
names for one and the same play, which in that case will have both shown us
Pentheus' character and told us of his terrible death. I believe the play to have
been the third in a trilogy, and I will describe in detail what we know, or can
infer, about that trilogy, which makes contact with *Bacchae* at multiple points.

The first play was called (probably later) *The Archeresses (Toxotides)* after
its chorus, which will have consisted of nymphs attending upon the archer-
goddess Artemis. Its central character was Actaeon, a son of one of Cadmus'
daughters (Autonoe) and therefore a cousin of Pentheus (Actaeon's fate is
recalled twice in *Bacchae*, at 337–40 and 1291). In accounts later than
Aeschylus the savage death of Actaeon, torn apart by his own hunting dogs,
is regularly attributed to an offence against Artemis – in *Bacchae* he had
boasted that he was a better hunter than the goddess; in the most famous
version, that of Ovid,[3] she was angry with him because he had seen her
bathing; another account has him actually aspiring to become her lover.[4] But
the sixth-century BC lyric poet Stesichorus,[5] and also Acusilaus,[6] a compiler
and systematizer of myths who was Aeschylus' older contemporary, told a
different story, in which Artemis destroyed Actaeon as an agent of Zeus, who
was angry with him because he was courting Semele – Zeus, of course, having

earmarked Semele for himself. Aeschylus may well have used this version, which gives a neat link between *The Archeresses* and the next play, *Semele* – and, as we shall see, it may not have been the only link. In the few surviving fragments of *The Archeresses*, Actaeon comes across as extremely boastful: boastful about his prowess as a hunter of wild beasts (fr. 241: he never comes home empty-handed), and boastful also about his prowess as a hunter of women (frr. 242–3: he can tell at a glance, from a woman's eyes, whether she is a virgin or not). That sort of cocksureness will offer Artemis an easy way to trap him. All she would need to do is disguise herself as a mortal woman (as Aphrodite famously does when seducing Anchises in the *Homeric Hymn to Aphrodite*), give herself the sort of face that makes Actaeon say to himself 'here's a goer', and plant herself in Actaeon's path when he is out hunting. We cannot tell exactly how things developed from that point, but they certainly ended with a messenger, probably a slave of Actaeon, reporting how Actaeon had been turned into a stag and torn to pieces by his hounds (fr. 244 is a line from the messenger's narrative).

The second play goes by the name of *Semele or The Water-Carriers (Hydrophoroi)* – the latter being the women of the chorus. Its subject was the premature (first) birth of Dionysus and the death of his mother Semele. We learn from a scholiast on Apollonius of Rhodes' *Argonautica* (1.636) that Aeschylus 'brought Semele on stage pregnant and possessed (*entheazomenēn*), and the women who touched her belly also became possessed': Semele, after all, was *entheos* in the most literal sense – she had a god within her. The women were laying hands on Semele's belly probably as a ritual action to ease her labour pains.[7] The most memorable feature of the play, though, was the role played by Hera, who visited Semele in the disguise of a begging priestess of the river-nymphs of Argos (Plato, *Republic* 381d); the first few lines of her speech are quoted by Plato and two other ancient writers (one of whom, impossibly, assigns them to *Xantriai*), and we have a papyrus fragment (Aeschylus fr. 168 Radt = 220a Sommerstein) that includes these two lines and extends some way before and after them. From this we can see that Semele's relationship with her family was apparently under a cloud, presumably because they were reluctant to believe that the father of her unborn child really was Zeus. Then along comes the disguised Hera and tells her, among other things, that 'modesty . . . is by far the best adorner of a bride' (line 23) and that the nymphs can be 'harsh and hateful' to those of whom they disapprove (line 27) – words evidently designed to increase Semele's anxiety and embarrassment, if she is widely suspected of having allowed herself to be seduced by some mortal lover, and to make her receptive to a suggestion (of which we know from several other sources)[8] that she should ask Zeus to prove that *he* had been her lover by visiting her in his full divine glory. This, of course, proves fatal to Semele, and to that extent the jealous Hera has triumphed; but, as is well known, Zeus snatched the unborn Dionysus from the flames and sewed him up in his own thigh until he was ripe for birth (*Bacchae* 88–100).

We have already seen evidence of one close link between *Semele* and *The Archeresses* – the idea that Actaeon was punished by Zeus for courting Semele – and a four-word quotation by a scholiast on Homer (fr. 221) suggests another: 'Zeus, who killed him.' Who is this 'him' (*touton*)? One suggestion[9] has been that it is the unborn Dionysus, whom the speaker understandably believes to have perished with his mother; but would a foetus have been referred to in the masculine gender? The only other possible candidate is Actaeon; and the fact that he is spoken of as *touton* ('this man') rather than *keinon* ('that man') suggests that his tomb may have been part of the stage setting, like the tomb of Darius in Aeschylus' *Persians* or the tomb of Agamemnon in his *Libation Bearers*. In both these plays one or more women bring liquid offerings to the tomb, and it was a brilliant suggestion of the nineteenth-century scholar Johann Gustav Droysen that that is the explanation for *Semele*'s chorus of 'water-carriers'.[10]

About the third play, *Pentheus/Xantriai*, which we would love to be able to compare closely with *Bacchae*, we know irritatingly little. Since bacchants do not spend their time carding wool, the women of the chorus must have been either Theban wives or else palace slaves (like, say, the chorus of Aeschylus' surviving *Libation Bearers*). The latter is the more likely alternative. For one thing, the Theban wives ought to be bacchantizing on the mountains (otherwise how could Pentheus have been killed there?); for another thing, wool-working is an indoor occupation, and women congregating away from their own homes would not be engaged in it. In early tragedy, before the *skene* building existed, the audience were sometimes expected to imagine (usually, it seems, with the aid of appropriate furniture) that the action was set indoors: in two of the three plays of Aeschylus' trilogy based on the *Iliad*, Achilles was shown sitting silent, in anger or grief, *inside* his hut,[11] and in *The Persians* the councillors at one point (140–3) decide to sit down and deliberate 'in this ancient building'. Probably the same thing was done in *Pentheus/Xantriai*.

If there are no bacchant women on stage, Pentheus of course cannot display his impiety by persecuting them. His victim would have to be an individual devotee, very likely the disguised god himself (which would complete a hat-trick of disguised deities in the trilogy). Meanwhile the free women of Thebes would be away on Mount Cithaeron. In Euripides they are led by Pentheus' mother Agave and her sisters Autonoe (the mother of Actaeon) and Ino (*Bacchae* 681–2, 1227–32). Jenny March[12] argued that this was not the case in Aeschylus, in which case this would be another, and a very profound, innovation by Euripides. There is a vase-painting from the late sixth century BC,[13] when Aeschylus was a child, that shows the killing of Pentheus, gives the name of one of his killers, and calls her not Agave (which was probably the name of Pentheus' mother as far back as Hesiod)[14] but Galene. It is a very plausible supposition that it was a tragic poet who first thought of having Pentheus killed by his mother: tragedy is extraordinarily fond of killings of close family members, whether actually perpetrated (as in four of the six genuine surviving plays of Aeschylus) or narrowly avoided (as in Euripides' *Ion* and *Iphigeneia in Tauris*). But for that very reason, it is at least as likely that Aeschylus was responsible for this change as that Euripides was.

How did Pentheus get to Cithaeron? Our best clue comes from the *Eumenides* passage, in which Dionysus is described as having 'led his bacchants in battle', or more literally as having been their general (*estratēgēsen*). That suggests a military confrontation, in which the bacchants, probably armed only with their *thyrsoi* (and inspired by Lyssa), defeated a conventional army; a view perhaps supported by a fragment I have already quoted (fr. 183), in which someone (presumably Pentheus) is warned not to spill blood. Pentheus' soldiers would have been routed, and he himself surrounded and slaughtered.

This was a trilogy, then, in which three deities, all using disguise, caused the destruction of three mortals – one of Cadmus' daughters and two of his grandsons (Dionysus himself, of course, is a third grandson of Cadmus). Semele, to be sure, was much less culpable than her two nephews, and was destined for a magnificent rehabilitation and ultimately to attain divine status herself; but the three plays as a whole would constitute an impressive display of the power of the gods and the folly of defying them – and Pentheus, in the climactic play, showed the greatest folly, because he should have taken warning from the fate of other members of his family.

This was not the only production in which Aeschylus presented a human ruler in conflict with Dionysus. He also composed a tetralogy that came to be known as the *Lykourgeia* (Aristophanes, *Women at the Thesmophoria* 135). Its action was located in Thrace, and its principal character was Lycurgus, king of the Edonians.

The first play of the series, *The Edonians*, is the one about which we are best informed. At the beginning of the play, Dionysus had just arrived in Thrace, with a band of followers of both sexes;[15] they did not, however, form the chorus of the play, which (as its title indicates) consisted of male citizens of Lycurgus' kingdom, who in a surviving quotation (fr. 57) vividly describe the newcomers and especially their wild music. Lycurgus arrested the disguised Dionysus and the women bacchants; he cruelly mocked the effeminate-looking god (frr. 59, 61, 62), and then imprisoned him in the palace, but his prisoner miraculously escaped in a convulsion comparable to an earthquake and attended by an epiphany of Dionysus (fr. 58). Whether in revenge for his imprisonment or for further insults, Dionysus drove Lycurgus mad, and he killed his own son Dryas in the belief that he was cutting a vine branch ([Apollodorus], *Library* 3.5.1). One of the ancient quotations (fr. 60) has Lycurgus asking after the identity of someone whom he describes as 'a musical prophet, another soft-stepping one'; the word 'another' implies that this is not the disguised Dionysus but someone else, and Martin West[16] has conjectured that it was Orpheus, who certainly fits the bill as a 'musical prophet' and who we know appeared in the second play of the series. We do not know what role he had in the first play; West suggests that he warned Lycurgus, in vain, of the danger of defying a god. This might seem a little surprising, given that in the next play Orpheus himself defies Dionysus with fatal consequences, but we shall see that Aeschylus had an explanation for his change of heart.

This second play did have a chorus of female bacchants; they apparently wore the *bassara*, an outer garment of Asian (Lydian) origin (as Dionysus himself had probably done in the first play: fr. 59), and the play came to be called *The Bassarids* (it may also have had an alternative title *Bacchae*). We have what appears to be a synopsis of it in a work called the *Catasterisms* and attributed (wrongly) to the great Alexandrian scholar Eratosthenes. ('Catasterism' means 'being turned into a star or constellation'; Orpheus wasn't turned into one, but his lyre was.) This is what we are told:

> Orpheus, after going down to Hades in quest of his wife [Eurydice] and seeing what things were like there, ceased to honour Dionysus, by whom he had been glorified, and regarded the Sun (whom he also called Apollo) as the greatest of the gods; he would rise before daybreak and await the sunrise on the mountain called Pangaeum, so as to be the first to see the Sun. Dionysus was angry at this and sent against him the Bassarids ... who tore him in pieces and scattered his limbs far and wide; but the Muses collected them together and buried them at the place called Leibethra [in Macedonia].

Evidently what turned Orpheus against Dionysus, in favour of Helios-Apollo, was the experience of what it was like to be in the underworld, cut off from sun and daylight, which made him feel that the Sun was the greatest benefactor of the world. But he was making the classic mistake of imagining that he could honour one god and ignore another – like the Euripidean Hippolytus, who honours Artemis and despises Aphrodite. That Orpheus was torn apart by Thracian women was the standard myth, but we do not normally hear elsewhere of their being devotees of Dionysus, and this important detail may have been Aeschylus' invention. We may note for future reference that the Muses, who collect Orpheus' scattered limbs, are his mother and aunts, for Orpheus was the son of the Muse Calliope.[17]

There must actually have been *two* bands of female bacchants involved in the action of *The Bassarids*. Since by the conventions of Greek drama it would be impossible to show the killing of Orpheus on stage, the 'Bassarids' who killed him cannot have been the 'Bassarids' who formed the chorus of the play. Instead the chorus, like that of *Bacchae*, will have commented from a distance. Two fragments, both brilliantly reconstructed (by Richard Kannicht[18] and Martin West[19] respectively) from lines quoted separately by different ancient authors, give us glimpses of a key moment in the play. One,[20] significantly in the lyric metre known as 'bacchiac', goes like this:

> The bull seems about to charge me! What peak,
> what shore, what wood can I flee to? Where can I go?

Orpheus, evidently, has been driven mad, and is under the delusion that he is confronted by an angry bull, no doubt a hallucination sent by Dionysus. From this hallucination he flees, as Orestes flees at the end of Aeschylus' *Libation Bearers* from the Furies whom, at that point, only he can see. He flees to some remote spot – where his killers await him. And the other Bassarids, the ones on stage, sing – again in bacchiacs – anticipating his destruction:[21]

> Though he has got a start, the ivy-crowned destroyer,
> the Bacchic god, the seer, will leap forth upon him for his crimes.

Which the Bacchic god duly did. Ironically, by the way, the word translated 'destroyer' is *apollōn* – the name of the god to whom Orpheus was too exclusively devoted.

About the third play, *The Young Men (Neaniskoi)*, we know very little, but with both Lycurgus and Orpheus now dead, its tone may well have been rather different, and it has more than once been suggested[22] that this play presented some kind of reconciliation between Dionysus and Apollo and their followers; both of them, after all, were held in equal honour by the Greeks of Aeschylus' time, and they actually shared possession of one of the greatest of all Greek sanctuaries, that of Delphi. I shall later make a speculative suggestion as to how this theme may have been reflected in *Bacchae* in a distorted and sinister form.

It is now time to look at Euripides' *Bacchae* in the light of these Aeschylean precedents. Readers, I am sure, will already have noticed that many events and ideas in the two Aeschylean trilogies reappear in *Bacchae*, some of them in interestingly modified forms. *Bacchae* is in fact a blend of motifs derived principally from *Pentheus/Xantriai* (hereafter *PX*), *Edonians* and *Bassarids*, with a few features from *The Archeresses*, *Semele* and possibly *The Young Men*, and with the addition of some important elements which are entirely new.

Let us begin at the beginning. Dionysus arrives at Thebes from abroad, disguised as a mortal: the Theban setting is parallel to *PX*, the arrival from abroad corresponds to *Edonians*, the disguise featured in both. He draws attention to the tomb of Semele (6–12); we do not know whether this tomb was part of the setting of *PX*, but we have seen that there may well have been an onstage tomb of Actaeon in *Semele*. Dionysus is accompanied by his female worshippers (in *Edonians* he had a retinue of both sexes), and these worshippers form the chorus of the play (as in *Bassarids*). He says (35–8) that he has driven the women of Thebes mad and they have gone to Mount Cithaeron, as in *PX*, and he threatens (50–2) that if Pentheus continues to resist him, he will lead his maenads in battle, also probably as in *PX*. Teiresias and Cadmus try to persuade Pentheus to relent (266–369), as Orpheus (an Apolline prophet, like Teiresias) may have tried to persuade Lycurgus in *Edonians*, and Cadmus reminds him (337–40) of what happened to his cousin Actaeon (a reminiscence of *The Archeresses*); but Pentheus is adamant and orders the destruction of Teiresias' place of augury, a site sacred to Apollo (346–51); this last is a new feature so far as we know, though it is noteworthy that in *Edonians* Lycurgus seems to have spoken mockingly about Orpheus as well as about the disguised Dionysus, and it is quite possible that he ventilated his dislike of Orpheus by some punitive act that constituted an insult to Apollo.

Then, in a sequence closely mirroring *Edonians*, the disguised Dionysus is arrested, taunted, and taken off to prison in the palace complex (434–518); in the course of this scene (511–14) Pentheus also declares his intention to enslave the female devotees (he cannot imprison them, as Lycurgus did in *Edonians*, because they could not then function as chorus). Next, still following the precedent of *Edonians*, the voice of Dionysus is heard, the palace is shaken, and the disguised god escapes (576–656). A herdsman arrives from Cithaeron and reports the activities of the bacchants there, including a quasi-military attack on some nearby villages (660–774); there was probably some comparable messenger-speech in *PX* to motivate Pentheus' determination to lead a military expedition against the bacchants, though some features of the account of the village attacks (748–64), for instance the invulnerability of the maenads, may be based rather on a narrative of the final battle, which *PX* certainly must have contained.

Despite all this warlike action, no human being has yet been killed (only animals: 735–47), and Pentheus can still, if he wishes (as the messenger points out: 769–74), accept the Dionysiac cult into Thebes without Thebes suffering any really serious harm. Pentheus does nothing of the sort: he immediately orders a muster of all arms – heavy infantry, light infantry, cavalry and archers (780–5). The disguised Dionysus, as apparently in *PX*, tries to dissuade him (787–99) and even promises to bring the women back to Thebes peacefully (802–7). After a little verbal sparring Pentheus brusquely puts an end to the conversation (809): 'Bring my armour out here – and you, stop talking!' We can see that he is about to walk straight into the same fate that befell his Aeschylean equivalent in *PX*.

But the god does not stop talking, and his one-line reply (810–11) turns the action on to a completely new track:

Ah! Would you like to see them sitting together in the mountains?

To which Pentheus responds, 'Yes, indeed, I'd give any amount of gold to be able to', and from that point the military expedition is replaced by an unarmed spy-mission which eventually delivers Pentheus – now himself dressed up as a female bacchant – helpless into the rending hands of the real bacchants. This, we can be pretty certain, is all Euripides, though there are still one or two echoes of earlier dramas, particularly *Bassarids*: Pentheus, not for the first time (cf. 618–622), has a hallucination of Dionysus as a bull (920–2), as Orpheus did, and after his final exit the chorus sing exultantly of his coming destruction (977–1023) as did the chorus of *Bassarids*.

It is not till about line 1077 that the storyline more or less returns to the beaten track. Pentheus has gone with the stranger to Cithaeron, and finding himself unable to get a good view of the bacchants' supposedly obscene behaviour (1059–62) he has suggested climbing a tree; the stranger miraculously helps him to do so – and then vanishes. Suddenly the voice of Dionysus is heard urging the bacchants to attack Pentheus, as the goddess Lyssa had inspired them to do in *PX*; they first throw missiles at him, then uproot the tree, and finally, led by Pentheus' mother (as may or may not have been the case in *PX*), they tear him into pieces (as the Bassarids did Orpheus), imagining him to be a wild beast (as Lycurgus killed his son in *Edonians* thinking he was a vine branch).

Agave returns to Thebes carrying Pentheus' head, a *coup de théâtre* that is surely new. She is followed by Cadmus, who has collected his grandson's scattered limbs – the task that in *Bassarids* was performed by Orpheus' mother and aunts, whereas this time Pentheus' mother and aunts were his killers. For the rest of the ending we know no clear precedent, though we must remember that two substantial passages are missing from the surviving text (after 1300 and 1329) and that we know very little about the final scenes of the relevant Aeschylean plays. Cadmus brings Agave back to her senses; she laments her son (grieving over each separate body part);[23] Dionysus appears to vindicate his divinity, justify his punishment of Pentheus and his house, and decree that all the survivors, including Cadmus himself, must leave Thebes; and the tragedy ends with the break-up and exile of the family. It is striking that in these final scenes Actaeon is mentioned at least twice (1227, 1291) and possibly a third time (after 1371, where the name of his father Aristaeus appears in an incomplete sentence): Pentheus' fate is being implicitly compared to his, as it doubtless was towards the end of *PX*.

One subject that is not mentioned in the surviving text, and probably was mentioned in one of the missing portions, is the burial of Pentheus. Orpheus in *Bassarids* was buried by his mother and aunts (the Muses); Agave and her sisters, as Pentheus' murderers, are in no position to do likewise, and perhaps she asked Cadmus, as the only other relative available, to perform this duty, just as it had been Cadmus who collected Pentheus' limbs. She may have done this in a speech of which only the first line (1329) survives. For what it is worth, the Byzantine drama *The Passion of Christ*, built up of lines from various Euripidean plays including prominently *Bacchae*, has the Virgin Mary asking (1123–4) 'In what tomb shall I lay your body, and with what garments shall I cover your corpse?' If Agave said something like that in Euripides' play, she would have been saying in effect 'I am unable to do either.'

There may possibly be one further distorted echo of Aeschylus at the end of *Bacchae*. We have seen that there is a case for the view that the *Lykourgeia* ended with a reconciliation, in the play *The Young Men*, between Dionysus and Apollo. The most notable feature of the relationship between these two gods in classical times was their amicable time-share arrangement at Delphi. This is mentioned earlier in *Bacchae*, appropriately by the Apolline prophet Teiresias (306–9):

> One day you will see him [Dionysus] on the Delphian rocks, leaping with his pine-torches over the high plain between the two peaks, shaking and brandishing his bacchic wand, exalted throughout Hellas.

But Delphi is mentioned again in the concluding (and only surviving) portion of the one major speech that Dionysus makes in his own divine person, and in a very surprising way (1330–9). Dionysus is addressing Cadmus:

> You will change shape and become a serpent, and your wife too – Harmonia, daughter of Ares, whom you, mortal though you were, were

given in marriage – will be turned into a beast and take the form of a snake. And, so an oracle of Zeus foretells, you and your wife will drive an ox-cart at the head of a force of barbarians, and with a horde beyond number you will sack many cities. When they have pillaged *the oracular shrine of Loxias,* they will have a miserable return home; but you and Harmonia will be rescued by Ares, who will settle you in the land of the Blest.

This refers to an invasion of Greece by the Encheleis from the far north-west.[24] It had nothing directly to do with Dionysus, but nevertheless it is Dionysus who is made to predict this sack of Apollo's sanctuary by a barbarian army. If the *Lykourgeia* ended as West and Seaford think it did, the Euripidean play is going to end (or rather *almost* end) with a jarringly discordant reminiscence of it; so horrible does the prophecy seem to Cadmus that even the promise of immortality with which it concludes is distasteful to him:

And, wretched that I am, there will be no end to my troubles, nor will I sail the infernal lake of Acheron and find rest below (1361–2).

We see, then, that the greater part of *Bacchae* consists, as it were, of recycled material, blended, rearranged and sometimes modified from at least three older plays to produce a new one. There are probably only two major portions of the drama that Euripides has freshly invented, but they are crucial. Instead of going out confident and well-armed to war, and being defeated and killed by ill-armed women, Pentheus goes out confident, unarmed and feminized to spy, and is easy prey for the Dionysiac forces; he has, in fact, been defeated psychologically before he ever gets to Cithaeron, and he who mocked a 'womanish' priest, not knowing that he was actually mocking a god, is turned into a woman himself. And in the end, Cadmus and Agave come to learn what they have done, and how they will suffer for it – except that that is not in fact the end of the play. While Dionysus shows us what the world of the gods is like – a world that knows no tears, no compassion, nothing but 'looking after one's honour' (the literal meaning of Greek *timōria,* which in practice means 'revenge') and demanding obedience – we also see at work the sublime power of human love, the love of Cadmus for Agave and of both of them for Pentheus; and the play ends not with the despairing cry of Cadmus that I quoted above, but with the poignant parting of a loving father and daughter who know they will never meet again (though Agave will at least have her sisters to give mutual support: 1381–2). Dionysus came to Thebes to establish his cult there; he may or may not have done so in his lost big speech – what we do know is that the sisters who had denied his divinity still want nothing to do with his worship:

> May I go where filthy Cithaeron may never <see me> nor may I set eyes on Cithaeron, and where there resides no memory of the *thyrsos*; let them be the concern of *other* bacchants!

(1383–7)

We can be pretty sure that neither Aeschylus' *Lykourgeia*, nor his Actaeon–Semele–Pentheus trilogy, ended on that kind of note.

Notes

1 First by Butler (1816) in volume viii of his edition of Aeschylus.
2 'Aeschylus' *Semele* and its Companion Plays', in G. Bastianini and A. Casanova (eds) *I papiri di Eschilo e di Sofocle* (Florence, 2013) 81–94.
3 Ovid, *Metamorphoses* 3.138–252.
4 Diodorus Siculus 4.81.4–5.
5 Page (1962) fr. 236.
6 Acusilaus fr. 33 in Fowler (2000).
7 Compare Soranus, *Gynaecology* 2.4.1.
8 Diodorus Siculus 3.64.3–4; Ovid, *Metamorphoses* 3.256–315; [Apollodorus], *Library* 3.4.3.
9 Made by Dodds (1960) xxix n.4.
10 Droysen (1894) vol.ii, 84 n.3 (originally published in 1841).
11 This is said explicitly in Aeschylus fr. 131 (the opening lines of the first play, *The Myrmidons*), and can safely be assumed also for the third, *The Phrygians*, in which Achilles likewise sat silent for a long time (so the scholia to Aristophanes, *Frogs* 911, and the ancient *Life of Aeschylus*).
12 March (1989) 33–65.
13 Boston, Museum of Fine Arts 10.221.
14 Hesiod, *Theogony* 975–8, though he does not mention Pentheus, gives the names of Cadmus' four daughters exactly as Euripides does: Ino, Semele, Agave and Autonoe.
15 Male devotees are mentioned in Aeschylus fr. 57.1–6, females in [Apollodorus], *Library* 3.5.1.
16 West (1990) 29–30.
17 Asclepiades fr. 6 Jacoby (from his *Tales Told in Tragedy*).
18 'Zu Aeschylus fr. 23 und trag. adesp. fr.144 N2', *Hermes* 85 (1957) 285–91.
19 West (1990) 46.
20 Aeschylus fr. 23 Sommerstein (= Aeschylus fr. 23.1 Radt + *tragica adespota* 144 Snell-Kannicht).

21 Aeschylus fr. 23a Sommerstein (= frr. 23.2 + 341 Radt).
22 West (1990) 46–7; R.A.S. Seaford, *Classical Quarterly* 55 (2005) 605–6.
23 Apsines, *Art of Rhetoric* 401–2, in Spengel and Hammer, *Rhetores Graeci* (Leipzig, 1894).
24 For the story of an attack on Delphi by the Encheleis from Illyria, see Herodotus 9.43.1.

3

Family Reunion or Household Disaster?
Exploring Plot Diversity in Euripides'
Last Production

Ioanna Karamanou

This chapter sets out to investigate crucial aspects of the plot structure of the three tragedies belonging to Euripides' last production (*Iphigenia in Aulis*, *Alcmeon in Corinth* and *Bacchae*) and their possible implications for the meaning of the 'trilogy' as a whole (the term 'trilogy' is used here conventionally and put in quotation marks, as it is not a connected trilogy of an Aeschylean kind).˙

The three tragedies were evidently written shortly before Euripides' death in 406 BC during his stay at the court of King Archelaus in Macedonia, where he spent his final years (probably from 408 BC onwards; see *TrGF* V1 T1 IA 6, IB 3, 2.9, 3.4, 4.25–7). The scholiast on Aristophanes' *Frogs* 67 reports that the three plays were staged in Athens posthumously by his son and namesake, Euripides the Younger. According to the Byzantine Lexicon of Suda (ε 3695 Adler), this production was awarded the first prize.

Before exploring the plot patterns upon which each of the three tragedies has been constructed, it is useful to recount their intriguing transmission history, which has shaped what we know of their dramatic plot. It is worth bearing in mind that the nine annotated Euripidean tragedies (*Alcestis*, *Medea*, *Hippolytus*, *Andromache*, *Hecabe*, *Trojan Women*, *Phoenissae*, *Orestes* and the Pseudo-Euripidean *Rhesus*) formed a 'selection' of plays belonging to the school syllabus probably by the end of the first century BC; it is then that Didymus wrote the first commentary on Euripides, which formed the basis for the ancient scholia on these tragedies. This 'selection' was consolidated in late antiquity, and the text of these nine tragedies was transcribed into minuscule in about the tenth century AD. It is thanks to good fortune that a copy of nine 'non-select' plays arranged in alphabetic order (from E to K: *Helen*, *Electra*, *Heraclidae*, *Heracles*, *Hiketides*, *Iphigenia in Aulis*, *Iphigenia in Tauris*, *Ion* and *Cyclops*) was discovered in the fourteenth century by Demetrius Triclinius, who made a copy which became the model of manuscript L forming subsequently the basis of the text of these plays in manuscript P. *Bacchae* has a singular place in the history of the text of Euripides. Oddly enough, it is preserved only in the two aforementioned manuscripts (L and P) comprising the so-called 'alphabetic' plays, though it is evident from the first letter of its title that it did not form part of the 'alphabetic' group of tragedies. The fact that the unknown author of the Byzantine drama *Christus Patiens* draws heavily upon *Bacchae*, as upon other tragedies of the 'selection' (though not upon any of 'non-select' plays), may suggest that *Bacchae* was transmitted alongside the annotated tragedies of the 'selection', though no scholia on this play have come down to us.[1]

As mentioned above, *Iphigenia in Aulis* has fortuitously been preserved in the 'alphabetic' group of plays outside the 'selection'. Its transmission, however, has been problematic ever since antiquity. It is likely that Euripides died leaving this tragedy incomplete and, therefore, its text was supplemented presumably by his son, who staged the production. Moreover, the text has been extensively interpolated by actors mostly during the fourth century BC; it is this practice of interpolating dramatic texts that led the Athenian statesman Lycurgus (in about 330 BC) to order that an official copy of the plays belonging to the theatrical repertory should be made and kept in the state archives (Pseudo-Plutarch *Lives of the Ten Orators* 841F). One of the most challenging passages is the prologue (1–163), which as transmitted seems to result from the fusion of two alternative openings. Furthermore, the ending of this tragedy comprising a messenger-speech that reports Iphigenia's miraculous disappearance (1578–1629) is clearly spurious, being most probably composed in late antiquity; the preceding lines (1510–77), as well as a short fragment probably including a speech by Artemis *ex machina* foretelling that a deer will be sacrificed instead of Iphigenia (fr. inc. 857 K.) seem to be similarly inauthentic.[2] Hence, there is no way of restoring the original Euripidean ending of the play – if the dramatist indeed managed to write the closing scene before his death.

The lost *Alcmeon in Corinth* was the least favoured by fortune of all the three tragedies of this production. The fact that even a few fragments of this play (frr. 73a–76 K.) have been preserved presupposes its survival in antiquity, which primarily emerges from the citation of excerpts from this tragedy by later authors. In more specific terms, we know that the Alexandrian edition of Aristophanes of Byzantium towards the end of the third century BC comprised the surviving 78 out of the 92 plays of Euripides' production arranged alphabetically. This edition probably relied on the aforementioned state copy made according to Lycurgus' decree. Had this tragedy not been included in the Alexandrian edition, it would not have stood any chance of being cited in later works. *Alcmeon in Corinth* shared the fate of the Euripidean tragedies which were not selected for school use and came down to us in a fragmentary state, with the exception of the aforementioned nine unexpectedly discovered 'alphabetic' plays. Many 'non-select' tragedies continued to be performed at least until the end of the second century AD and were still obtainable among literary circles. In late antiquity the establishment of Christianity probably led to the consolidation of the 'selection', as the parts of pagan tradition standing any chance of long-term survival were only those included in the school syllabus. Moreover, the trend of excerpting literature for educational purposes and the compilation of gnomic anthologies presenting passages arranged by subject eventually resulted in only indirect access to plays outside the 'selection'.[3]

Naturally enough, *Alcmeon in Corinth* is the least studied play of the three, owing to its fragmentary state. The basic source for its plot outline is the account provided in Pseudo-Apollodorus' *Library* (3.7.7):

> Euripides says that in the time of his madness Alcmeon begot two children, Amphilochus and a daughter Tisiphone, by Manto, daughter of Teiresias, and that he brought the babies to Corinth and gave them to Creon, king of Corinth, to bring up; and that on account of her extraordinary beauty Tisiphone was sold as a slave by Creon's spouse, who feared that Creon might make her his wedded wife. But Alcmeon bought her and kept her as a handmaid, not knowing that she was his daughter, and coming to Corinth to get back his children he recovered his son also. And Amphilochus colonized Amphilochian Argos in obedience to oracles of Apollo.
>
> (transl. Frazer 1961–3, I 387–9 with minor adjustments)

The play enumerates only five certain fragments: one from a papyrus commentary (fr. 73a K.), two quoted in Ioannes Stobaeus' gnomic anthology dating to the fifth century AD (frr. 75 and 76 K.), another one by the twelfth-century Byzantine scholar Ioannes Tzetzes (fr. 74 K.) and a single-word fragment attested in the Byzantine Lexicon of Hesychius (fr. 77). The possibility that more lines of this tragedy could have been preserved is open to speculation, since another group of fragments (frr. 78–87 K.) is vaguely ascribed to an *Alcmeon* play by Euripides without any specification as to whether they derive from *Alcmeon in Corinth* or the earlier *Alcmeon in Psophis* produced by the dramatist along with *Cretan Women*, *Telephus* and *Alcestis* in 438 BC.

Despite the small number of lines preserved, most of the available fragments are quite informative. Fragment 73a K. is delivered by Apollo, who was evidently the prologue-speaker. The god is reporting that Alcmeon begot twins, Amphilochus and Tisiphone, by Apollo's priestess Manto:

And I myself was childless by her;
but the unmarried girl bore Alcmeon two children.

(transl. Collard and Cropp 2008, I 91)

Strangely enough, these lines attest that a god's union with a mortal woman
failed to produce offspring; these words contradict the traditional rules of
mythical theogamy (marriage or intercourse between a god and mortal),
according to which a woman being seduced by a god always conceives (see,
for instance, Homer's *Odyssey* 11.248–50). This has to be a Euripidean
deviation in the treatment of the legend, considering that mythographic
sources, such as Pseudo-Apollodorus (3.7.4), attest that Apollo actually begot
a son by Manto named Mopsus. A similarly desacralized treatment of
theogamy was provided by Euripides in *Auge*, in which the princess bears a
child not to a god, but to Heracles presented as a humanized hero. In the
present case, however, the dramatist goes as far as presenting a god's union as
barren and a mortal's union with the same woman as fertile. This situation
may well be interpreted in the light of the scepticism often expressed by
Euripidean characters towards divine births. This critical approach of
theogamy is prominent in *Bacchae*, being articulated in the disbelief of
Pentheus and his family towards Dionysus' divine origin (26–31, 245), and
constitutes a sub-topic in *Iphigenia in Aulis* (794–800) with reference to
Helen's divine descent (see also *HF* 353–4, *Ion* 338–41, 436–51, *Hel.* 17–21).
In several of these cases, especially in *Bacchae*, the woman's assertion of her
divine union is disparagingly interpreted as a way of her justifying her illicit
sexual intercourse.[4] It is noteworthy that this fragment indicates that the
scepticism towards theogamy was a shared theme in all three tragedies of this
production. Sadly, the scanty evidence for *Alcmeon in Corinth* does not give
scope for a further investigation of the specific reasons for this divergence.

As in all divine prologue-speeches, Apollo must have set out the
background of the story, that is, Alcmeon's separation from his offspring and
Tisiphone's reduction to slavery. The god is expected to have identified
Alcmeon's children from the very beginning, as Hermes identifies the temple
boy as the son of Apollo and Creusa in *Ion* 78, so that the spectators have a
superior knowledge of events to that of the stage characters and can clearly
discern the instances of tragic irony.

We are informed by fr. 74 K. that the chorus consisted of Corinthian
women asking for the provenance of a stranger who has just arrived at
Corinth:

Friends, friends,
come forward, do come! Who is this stranger here, from what country

has he come to Corinth by the sea?

(transl. Collard and Cropp 2008, I 91)

On the basis of the available evidence, the stranger of this fragment cannot be anyone other than Alcmeon. Stylistically and thematically speaking, these lines closely resemble the beginning of the *parodos* in *Heraclidae* 73–4 and in Sophocles' *Oedipus at Colonus* 118–22 (probably also in Euripides' *Aegeus* frr. 1 and 2 K.) presenting the chorus as entering 'on the run' and asking about the identity of a dramatic character or about a particular situation.[5] If this fragment indeed preserves the beginning of the *parodos*, the chorus' 'discovery' of Alcmeon would also indicate that the hero is already onstage (as the characters in *Heraclidae* and *Oedipus at Colonus*), having entered most probably in the course of the prologue after Apollo's monologue; as a rule, gods deliver their detached prologue-speeches and then leave upon the appearance of an incoming mortal (see *Hipp.* 51–3, *Hec.* 52–4, *Ion* 76–8).[6]

Fragment 76 K. describes King Creon as a childless old man being punished for his arrogance with exile:

See how the king is fleeing into exile, childless in old age;
one who is mortal should not think proudly.

(transl. Collard and Cropp 2008, I 93)

On the other hand, fr. 75 K. involves an address to someone as 'son of Creon':

Son of Creon, how true then it has proved,
that from noble fathers noble children are born,
and from base ones children resembling their father's nature.

(transl. Collard and Cropp 2008, I 91)

The latter reference clearly clashes with Creon's description as childless in fr. 76 K. The reasonable inference is that Amphilochus is the person regarded as the king's son in these lines and that Creon naturally remains childless after Alcmeon's recognition with his children. Fragment 75 K. comprises a comment on heredity of character; due to its gnomic nature and the loss of context we cannot recover the exact tone of these lines, but, in any case, the misconception of Amphilochus' paternity involves a strong tragic irony. Fragment 76 K. referring to Creon's sentence to exile must be placed towards the end of the play. Its strongly didactic tone makes it likely to have been delivered by a *deus ex machina*. The same concluding divine speech could have comprised the foundation myth of Amphilochian Argos, which is attested by Pseudo-Apollodorus to have derived from the Euripidean play;

this would be consistent with the dramatist's predilection for aetiologies at the epilogues of his plays connecting the tragic legend to the contemporary world of the audience. This fragment explicitly attests that Creon is an unsympathetic character punished with exile at the end of the play. He could have played a malicious role, perhaps by preventing Alcmeon from getting his children back; he would not like to lose Amphilochus, whom he raised as his own son, and could wish to regain Tisiphone, who was sold as a slave by Creon's jealous wife because of the king's desire for her.[7]

  Overall, the dramatic plot is expected to have had several complications, the details of which cannot be restored, until Alcmeon's final recognition of his twin children and Creon's punishment. On the basis of its plot structure, *Alcmeon in Corinth* is a play of mixed reversal ending in good fortune for sympathetic characters and in misfortune for the unsympathetic ones. This double structure is not commended by Aristotle, who nevertheless admits that it corresponds to the tastes of the audiences (*Poetics* 1453a.30–5). In view of its plot patterns, *Alcmeon in Corinth* is generically affiliated with other Euripidean plays treating the motif of 'family reunion', which consists in the recognition between long-separated close kin and the restoration of their household after a major crisis threatening their *oikos* (*Iphigenia in Tauris, Helen, Ion, Antiope, Hypsipyle, Captive Melanippe*). The approximate dating of this group of plays indicates that the development of this typology occurs in later Euripidean production from 415 BC onwards. It does not seem to be a coincidence that all these plays were staged in a period of socio-political crisis in Athens culminating in the last decade of the Peloponnesian War. The aforementioned penchant of the spectators for plays of mixed reversal could quite reasonably have emerged from their preference for 'mild' plays inspiring optimism, which were, nonetheless, staged alongside tragedies ending in misfortune, as in the case of the present production.[8]

  The Euripidean typology of the complex plot involving an effective recognition-scene between separated kin, coupled with a reversal of action and leading to a happy ending repeatedly provided a thematic and structural model for the poets of New Comedy. In an earlier paper I argued that *Alcmeon in Corinth* could have been a source text for Menander's *Periceiromene*. To put it very briefly, both plays are set in Corinth and treat the specific theme of the exposure of a pair of twins by their father, in view of a particularly difficult situation. In both cases the twins are split and have divergent fates. The boy grows up in wealth, while the girl is raised humbly. Moreover, the recognition-scene in the fourth act of *Periceiromene* is written in tragic diction and shares the particularity and distinctiveness of the *anagnorisis* in the Euripidean play, in that three parties, a father and his twin children, are all recognizing each other. Hence, the tragic forerunner, the value of which had already been successfully tested on stage, as it belonged to a prize-winning Euripidean production and was expected to have been appreciated by later audiences at its revivals, seems to have been creatively assimilated by Menander and refigured to enrich his comic plot.[9]

On the other hand, *Bacchae* is a typical tragedy in which the tragic *pathos* culminates in a violent act of murder unwittingly committed between close kin. A tragic deed between blood-relatives constitutes the core of *Iphigenia in Aulis*, as well. So far as the genuinely Euripidean parts of this tragedy can be recovered (as designated in Diggle's Oxford edition), they indicate that the theme of a youth's sacrifice for victory in war, which had constituted a sub-topic in earlier Euripidean tragedies, as in *Heraclidae* (474–607), *Phoenissae* (977–1018) and the fragmentarily preserved *Erechtheus* (fr. 360 K.), was reiterated in this dramatic plot and brought to the fore. As mentioned above, the closing scene of the play is spurious, therefore we are not in a position to know whether Euripides wished to inform the dramatic characters and the audience of Iphigenia's rescue or let them imagine that she is going off to die. The former possibility could raise issues of dramatic coherence and characterization, especially if Clytaemestra was the recipient of the messenger-speech (or of a *deus ex machina* speech, as in the aforementioned fr. inc. 857 K.). A self-evident implication would involve the serious inconsistency in the treatment of the theme of her resentment against Agamemnon. Her grudge towards her husband for his decision to sacrifice their daughter is repeatedly stressed (874–88, 898, 912–13, 1138–1208), and her future revenge on him is foreshadowed (1180–5, 1454–7). These hints would be meaningless if she was informed that Iphigenia has been rescued.[10] Moreover, Clytaemestra's character-sketching in this tragedy justifying her ill will towards Agamemnon accounts for the events taking place in the subsequent phases of the Atreidae-myth treated in earlier plays, as in Euripides' *Electra* (as well as in Aeschylus' *Agamemnon* and Sophocles' *Electra*). In all these plays the sacrifice of Iphigenia by Agamemnon constitutes Clytaemestra's strongest argument when stating her reasons for murdering her husband (see Aeschylus' *Agamemnon* 1412–20, Sophocles' *Electra* 528–48, Euripides' *Electra* 1018–29). Accordingly, this tragedy has justifiably been described as a 'prequel' (to quote Griffith and Most 2013, 89–90) to the plays dealing with Agamemnon's murder and its repercussions, and it is no coincidence that in modern performance *Iphigenia in Aulis* has repeatedly been paired with these tragedies, as in Ariane Mnouchkine's *Les Atrides*.[11]

On the basis of the aforementioned remarks, this production displays a notable plot diversity, which is indicative of the variety and multiformity of Euripidean tragedy. I shall attempt to provide a reading of the plot structure of the three tragedies from the viewpoint of the fate of the household (*oikos*) in each play and its possible implications for the city-state (*polis*). According to ancient political theory, the *oikos* was an essential component of the *polis* (Aristotle's *Politics* 1252a.24–1253b.23). The household was protected by Athenian law as a constituent element of the city-state and as its economic and social foundation ever since Solon (Solon fr. 4 West). The association of the *oikos* with the *polis* is regularly represented in fifth-century drama, often as reciprocal, but also in certain cases as oppositional, being suggestive of a tension between the private and the public sphere of action.[12]

In *Bacchae* King Pentheus is eliminated due to his impiety, imprudence and injustice. Throughout the play he is accused of irreverence towards god Dionysus (490, 502, 613, 859–61, 1042, 1080–1, 1293, 1325–6). His attitude is explicitly defined as *hybris*, which denotes a serious attack on the honour of another (in this case expressed as an assault against a god) committed for the pleasures of superiority and arousing the offended party's wrath and desire for revenge:[13]

> look upon
>   pentheus
>   all he has done
>
> his malice
>   blasphemy
> his sacrilege
>   against
>   the thunder god
>   (373–5: translated by David Stuttard; see also 515–18,
>   553–5, 1297, 1347)

Because of his impiety Pentheus is forcefully termed as 'god-fighter' (44–46, 635–36, 1255–56), which is also suggestive of his futile resistance to an overwhelming power. Piety (*eusebeia*) reflects the religious feeling and the respect towards the sanctions which the gods are believed to uphold. This virtue is related to *sōphrosynē*, which is a moral value encompassing in Euripides the ideas of good sense, self-control and moderation and preventing one from transgressing human limits and committing *hybris*. Pentheus is constantly reproached for lack of *sōphrosynē* in his attitude towards Dionysus and the expansion of Bacchic cult (268–71, 310–12, 325–7, 332, 358–9, 367–9, 386–401, 504, 640–1, 1150–2). Most importantly, in late fifth-century ethics moderation alongside justice constitute the features of a quiet moral behaviour, which assists in the good administration of one's household and renders the citizen useful to the city-state. Pentheus is also prone to injustice

(516–18, 1042), and his transgression of values leading to his downfall is eloquently encapsulated in three words: 'godless, lawless, unjust' (995).[14]

Pentheus fiercely opposes Dionysiac cult, regarding it as a disruptive force and as a threat to the integrity of Theban households (215–25, 352–4, 487), which are essential units of the city.[15] Nonetheless, this disruption of the household is clearly attributed by Dionysus to the irreverence shown towards him and his mother Semele by Pentheus' mother Agave and her sisters, who challenged his divine origin (26–31, cf. 1249–50, 1341–7). It is for this reason that they have been goaded from their houses in frenzy and dwell on Cithaeron (32–4). Likewise, the city of Thebes is presented at the start of the play as unwilling to be initiated into Bacchic rites (39–42, 47–52, 195–6), and therefore its womenfolk have been driven to the mountain (35–8), so that Dionysus' divine power is demonstrated (39–42, 47–52). Due to his lack of sound judgement King Pentheus misuses his power to repress Bacchic cult. His imprudence is disparaged by Teiresias as harmful to the *polis* (266–9), as well as to his *oikos* (367–8).

The death of Pentheus, who is the head of the royal household of Thebes, and the absence of a male heir designate the collapse of his *oikos*. It is made clear that this household is condemned to extinction as a result of Pentheus' violation of the cardinal virtues of piety, moderation and justice. The repercussions of this transgression and of the irreverence shown towards Dionysus' divine birth by Cadmus' family are stressed in the closing scene (1301–15, 1341–51, 1374–6), but they have already been foreshadowed earlier in the play:

> rough unchecked tongues
> rough uncurbed ignorance
>   dies in disaster
>
> a gentle rhythm
>   mind in harmony
>   unruffled
>   keeps the house secure
>
>   (386–92: transl. D. Stuttard)

Pentheus is an errant ruler of his *oikos* and of the *polis*. He unwittingly becomes the scapegoat (*pharmakos*) being ritually driven out of the community, so that the city of Thebes is spared:

> You are the only man. The only man. The weight of Thebes is on your shoulders, and the trials that lie ahead are all for you.
>
>   (963–4: transl. D. Stuttard)

Pentheus is isolated as the rejected 'other', becomes the victim of stoning (as part of the *pharmakos* ritual) and is subsequently a sacrificial victim through scattering dismemberment (*sparagmos*). In that scene Dionysus assumes the role of an escort bringing salvation (965), which might be suggestive of the redemption of the city through the expulsion of the scapegoat and the establishment of Dionysiac cult ensuring communality and cohesion.[16]

Iphigenia in Aulis similarly foreshadows the disaster of Agamemnon's household. It is one of those plays in which the clash between the private and the public spheres of action is most eloquently articulated. Agamemnon wavers between guilt and public commitment, between sacrificing his own daughter and opposing the will of the army that demands Iphigenia's sacrifice. 'Am I not to be allowed to rule my own *oikos*?' (331), he bursts out. The particular features of this dramatic situation may be grasped in the light of the effects of radical democracy, which promoted the development of the ideology of the citizen's strong commitment to the city-state and of the necessity to comply with the power of the *dēmos*, thus creating tension in the relation between the *oikos* and the *polis*. These circumstances led to the rise of the demagogues, furthering their own ambitions by trawling for popular favour, which caused a gradual degeneration of democratic politics in Post-Periclean Athens. The type of the demagogue seems to be represented by Odysseus manipulating the masses and rousing their bloodlust (524–35, 1362–8). Agamemnon is unable to execute effective policy and to control the army, thus succumbing to the rioting shouts of the mob pressing for the sacrifice (450, 514, 1259–63).[17] Although this play is not Athens-centred (as compared, for instance, to *Heraclidae, Hiketides* and *Ion*), Euripides' configuration of this dramatic situation apparently arises from his experience of late fifth-century Athenian public policy and ethics.

Agamemnon displays weakness and inefficacy in the management of his household and of the community. Clytaemestra disparages his lack of sound judgement and the injustice done to Iphigenia, who was lured to Aulis by ruse (1166–79). She pleads with him to show *sōphrosynē* by sparing their daughter's life (1206–08). His lack of wisdom emerges from Clytaemestra's description of her husband as 'mad' (876) and as possessed by a vengeful spirit (878: *alastōr*). The latter reference may well involve an intertextual allusion to this avenging spirit presented as being embodied in Clytaemestra after Agamemnon's murder in Aeschylus' *Agamemnon* (1501); this allusion could provide a causal connection between the two actions in both stylistic and conceptual terms, by presenting Agamemnon's death as retribution for Iphigenia's sacrifice through the representation of *alastōr*. As already mentioned, the future disaster of Agamemnon's *oikos* is foreshadowed in

Clytaemestra's resentful statements about her husband's decision to sacrifice their daughter. In this play the tension between private and public also takes the form of a gender conflict between Clytaemestra defending the integrity of her household and Agamemnon as leader of the military community. In my view, the resolution of the plot involves an inversion of the *pharmakos* motif represented in *Bacchae*: the role of the scapegoat is undertaken by Iphigenia, who, unlike Pentheus, is an innocent victim voluntarily giving her life for the community and for the sake of Hellas.

Alcmeon in Corinth also dramatizes the breakdown of the royal *oikos*. In the aforementioned fr. 76 K. King Creon of Corinth is presented as a childless old man fleeing into exile. This penalty is clearly imposed because of the king's haughty behaviour. The phrase *mega phronein* employed in this fragment denotes 'to be haughty'/'to be presumptuous' (*LSJ*[9]), having a negative nuance in tragedy from Sophocles onwards and conveying lack of moderation and impiety (see Sophocles' *Oedipus Tyrannus* 1078, *Antigone* 479, 768, Euripides' *Heraclidae* 979, *Hippolytus* 6, 445, *Hiketides* 862–3). Stylistically speaking, it is a synonym of *hyperphronei* employed in *Bacchae* 1325 to convey Pentheus' disdain for Dionysus. Although we cannot recover the particular dramatic circumstances of Creon's misconduct, it is safe to observe on the basis of this fragment that he is punished for his lack of moderation. It is because of his violation of *sōphrosynē* that he is sentenced to exile, and his household is condemned to extinction being deprived of a male heir. Sadly, no evidence has been preserved with respect to any possible implications that the downfall of the royal household may have had for the city of Corinth.

As argued above, the disaster of the royal household in all three tragedies results from the transgression of cardinal moral virtues, especially of moderation, by the errant head of the *oikos*. At the same time, in *Alcmeon in Corinth* the collapse of Creon's household designates the rescue of Alcmeon's *oikos* through the reunion of the missing male heir with his natal family. The recovery of Alcmeon's son ensures the continuity of his household. As with the rest of the aforementioned 'family reunion' plays of later Euripidean production, which were staged in a critical period of socio-political dissolution and moral uncertainty caused by the War, the resort to and protection of the wisely ruled *oikos* as an essential unit of the *polis* seems to contribute to the restoration of social order. In these plays (especially in *Ion*, *Antiope*, *Hypsipyle* and *Captive Melanippe*) the management and continuity of the restored household is undertaken by righteous young men ensuring the integrity of the domestic hearth, which could serve as the backbone of the *polis*. This sense of continuity is further enhanced through the foundation myths systematically introduced in this group of tragedies.[18]

In the particular case of *Alcmeon in Corinth* Euripides assigns the colonization of Amphilochian Argos to Alcmeon's son Amphilochus, deviating from the historical tradition which attributed this foundation to Alcmeon's brother (Thucydides 2.68.3, Ephorus *FGrH* 70 F123). According to this divergence, Amphilochus as the legitimate heir and continuator of Alcmeon's household is assigned the further role of the founder of a new community. In this light, the preservation of the *oikos* seems to represent a prerequisite for the establishment of a collective, political entity.

Consequently, despite their evident plot diversity the three tragedies seem to be conceptually interrelated with regard to the fate of the household and its possible effects on the community/*polis*, as defined by moral behaviour and the exercise of co-operative excellences, such as *sōphrosynē*. This production provides an eloquent example of the manner in which the political and the ethical element are intrinsically interwoven in Greek tragedy. The theoretical foundation of this interrelation is provided by Aristotle (*Politics* 1288b.1, *Rhetoric* 1356a.26), suggesting that fifth-century tragedy displays a conjunction of politics with ethics (*Poetics* 1450b.7).[19]

It is noteworthy that these three plays do not seem to have an obvious Athenian focus. Given the probable Macedonian context of their composition, this comes as no surprise. Moreover, the extant *Bacchae* and *Iphigenia in Aulis* convey a strong sense of communality extending far beyond the Athenian borders. The notion of Dionysiac cosmopolitanism and the collective character of this cult permeate *Bacchae*, and it is no coincidence that Bacchic cult was particularly popular in Macedonia. Likewise, *Iphigenia in Aulis* is imbued with the concept of Panhellenism being probably influenced to some extent by the Hellenizing policy of King Archelaus of Macedonia.[20] We are in no position to know whether the same could hold true for *Alcmeon in Corinth*, though its ending does appear to have conveyed the notion of collectivity through the aetiology for the foundation of a new social entity. At the same time, it is worth bearing in mind that these tragedies were staged in Athens *post mortem* in a prize-winning production. The universal value of this pervasive sense of communality along with the aforementioned cardinal virtues of private and civic behaviour propounded in these plays may have served as instruction to the audience – conveyed, as always, in the allusive manner of tragedy – at the climax of the socio-political crisis towards the end of the War.

On the whole, these tragedies seem to offer a broad, conceptual approach of late fifth-century ethics and political thinking, which, albeit stemming to a certain degree from the Athenian political experience, is raised to a theoretical level and is imbued with notions of a wider, even Panhellenic interest. This reading of Euripides' last production has suggested that the dramatist's experimentation with different types of plot structure leading either to household disaster or to family reunion displays the complex dialectical relationship, as well as the tension between *oikos* and *polis*, and articulates aspects of his political thought. At the same time, it should be stressed that in each of these plays the fate of the household and, in certain cases, of the community is defined by the dramatic characters' attitude towards the cardinal virtues shaping private and civic conduct, which sets the stage for ethical consideration. Euripides thus conjoins the political with the ethical, setting forth instruction of universal significance.

Notes

* I am indebted to David Stuttard for valuable suggestions.
1 Manuscript L: Laurentianus 32.2; Manuscript P: Palatinus gr. 287 and Laurentianus conv. soppr. 172. For more detail on the transmission of *Bacchae*, see Zuntz (1965) 110–25, Seaford (1996) 52–54, Carrara (2009) esp. 496–97. For the papyri preserving certain parts of the play, see Diggle's Oxford edition (*OCT* III).
2 The abbreviation K. is henceforth employed to refer to the numbering of Euripidean fragments in Kannicht's edition (*TrGF* V). On Lycurgus' decree, see Hanink (2014) 60–91. For the series of problems concerning the text of *Iphigenia in Aulis*, see Page (1934) *passim*, Stockert (1992) I 64–87, Kovacs (2003b) 77–103, Gurd (2005) esp. 61–72, Michelakis (2006) 105–14.
3 Zuntz (1965) 254–56, Reynolds and Wilson (2013⁴) 53–4, Easterling (1997c) 225.
4 For Euripides' critical approach to divine births, see especially Huys (1995) 90–2, 120–1.
5 See Kannicht (2004) I 213 on this fragment; Wilkins (1993) on *Heraclidae* 73–4.
6 For this conventional practice, see for instance Halleran (1985) 8 and n. 18.
7 For this dramatic plot, see Collard and Cropp (2008) I 87–89, Jouan and van Looy (1998–2003) I 98–100, Webster (1967) 265–68 and van Looy (1964) 103–31, also providing a critical approach of Zielinski's (1922, 309–23) highly conjectural reconstruction. For the reception of the play in modern performance, see Hall (2010) 341–3.
8 The term 'mixed reversal' was established in Euripidean criticism by Burnett (1971). *Helen* was produced in 412 (see the scholium on Aristophanes' *Frogs* 53 in combination with the scholium on *Thesmophoriazusae* 1012); for the dating of the rest of the 'family reunion' plays, see for instance Diggle (1981–94) II 242 (*Iphigenia in Tauris*), II 306 (*Ion*), Collard and Cropp (2008) I 175 (*Antiope*), I 589 (*Captive Melanippe*), II 254 (*Hypsipyle*). *Alexandros* (dated with certainty to 415) also shares this plot-pattern, but the hero's reunion with his natal family has, in this

case, sinister repercussions, as it leads to the Trojan War. For the spectators'
predilection for this type of plot towards the end of the fifth and during the
fourth century BC, see Easterling (1993) 562, Green (1994) 49–56.

9 Karamanou (2005). For Menander's use of tragic style in this
recognition-scene, see Katsouris (1976) 128–30, Hunter (1985) 133–4,
Zagagi (1994) 51–2; on his wide reception of Euripidean drama, see further
Hurst (1990), Gutzwiller (2000), Cusset (2003).

10 For these implications, see Stockert (1992) I 80–3 and Kovacs (2003b) 98.

11 For further examples, see Michelakis (2006) 125–7.

12 On the *oikos–polis* relation, see Nagle (2006), Patterson (1998) 85–91,
Hansen (2006) esp. 109–12, Pomeroy (1997) esp. 36–9. For its representation
in tragedy, see for instance Hall (1997) 104–10 and Goldhill (1986) 114.

13 For the definition of *hybris*, see Fisher (1992) 1–6 and on Pentheus' *hybris, op.
cit.* 443–52, Winnington-Ingram (1948) 60–1, Seaford (1996) 182–3.

14 On Pentheus as 'god-fighter' (*theomachos*), see Kamerbeek (1948) 271–83,
Dodds (1960²) 68, Mills (2006) 58. In Plato's *Phaedrus* (237E–238A)
sōphrosynē is explicitly defined as the opposite of *hybris*. On this virtue as an
essential feature of the good citizen, see North (1966) 69–84 and for its
conjunction with justice, cf. Adkins (1960) 177–8, 195–8, Balot (2009)
282–300. For Pentheus' lack of moderation, see Winnington-Ingram (1948)
19–21, 42–4, 75–6, 145–6, Seaford (1996) 47–9, 229.

15 Cf. Seaford (1994) ch. 8 arguing extensively for the disorder caused to
the household by Dionysus. See also Segal (1997²) ch. 4 and Fisher (1992)
444–5.

16 The idea that the city of Thebes is finally rescued by means of this scapegoat
ritual was first proposed by Burnett (1970) 28–9 and further developed by
Seaford (1994) 311–18. For the cohesion provided by Dionysiac cult, see
Segal (1997²) 391–2, Seaford (1994) 238–51 and (1996) 44–52.

17 See Michelakis (2006) 33–5, 80, Luschnig (1988) 111–14, Markantonatos
(2012) 193–4. For the degeneration of democracy after Pericles, see
Thucydides 2.65.7–10; on the shortcomings of radical democracy, see for
instance Ober (1989) 92–4, 122–4 and Rosenbloom (2012a) 408–16 with
further bibliography.

18 For the righteousness and worth of these young men, see *Ion* 56, 247–380,
429–51, 585–647, *Antiope* fr. 223.127–28 K., *Captive Melanippe* fr. 495.40–43
K. Hypsipyle's twins (Euneos and Thoas), like Antiope's offspring (Amphion
and Zethus), present 'an ideal combination of practical and intellectual
accomplishments' (see Collard, Cropp and Gibert 2004, 181). Ion will be
the eponymous ancestor of Ionia (*Ion* 74–75, 1573–88), Melanippe's son
Aeolus will colonize the Aeolian Isles north of Sicily (Diodorus of Sicily
4.67), Hypsipyle's son Euneos will establish the Attic family of Euneidae
(Hesychius ε 7007 Latte) and Antiope's sons will undertake the fortification
of Thebes (*Antiope* fr. 223.115–26 K.). On the socio-political resonances of
Euripides' 'family reunion' plays, see Karamanou (2012).

19 See the interpretations of this Aristotelian passage by Else (1957) 265–6 and Lucas (1972²) 106–7; for Euripides' conjunction of the political with the ethical, see Gregory (1991) esp. 1–12.

20 See Michelini (1999/2000) 54–6, Rosenbloom (2012b) 374–9, Markantonatos (2012) 205–18, Michelakis (2006) 84. On Archelaus' Hellenizing policy and the Macedonian context of the composition of these tragedies, see for instance Revermann (1999/2000) 454–67 and most recently Moloney (2014) 234–40, both with rich bibliography.

4

Staging in *Bacchae*

Rosie Wyles

Euripides' *Bacchae* is one of the most exciting, yet also one of the most problematic tragedies when thinking about fifth-century staging. It is already clear from Euripides' much earlier play, *Medea* (the second earliest fully extant play by Euripides, performed in 431 BC), that he had a flair for spectacular, innovative and dramatically effective staging. In *Bacchae*, one of his latest plays to survive, we can see this interest culminating in the creation of an intensely self-conscious tragedy which puts Dionysus, god of drama, centre stage. Staging in *Bacchae* is used to reinforce the play's thematic engagement with ideas of illusion and reality, confinement and release, the disruptive inversion of norms, and power (both positive and destructive). At the same time, it is possible to read the play's staging as making a broader contribution to the fifth-century BC critical discourse on theatre (developed within the text, subtext and stage action of both tragedy and comedy). While there has been controversy in scholarship over whether a ritual or metatheatrical lens is a more fruitful way of interpreting the staging in the play, I am entirely in agreement with Segal, who suggests that one need not detract from the other (though, as will become clear, my own approach privileges a metatheatrical interpretation).[1]

Dionysus sets the scene

The figure of Dionysus is key to understanding the meaning of the staging in *Bacchae*. As Helene Foley has brilliantly argued, Euripides presents Dionysus as a director who constructs his own play within a play.[2] This role is already clear in the prologue. While in broad terms the appearance of Dionysus at the beginning of the play – alone, explaining the dramatic situation and predicting the suffering which he will cause – may be compared to, for example, the role of Aphrodite at the beginning of the earlier Euripidean tragedy *Hippolytus*, there is an important difference: Dionysus, unlike Aphrodite, does not appear as himself but is disguised. He draws particular attention to this as early as line 4 of the prologue (just after he has said who he really is): 'I've changed my form, shape-shifted, god become flesh'. He returns to this nearer the end of the prologue and comments again on his changed appearance (52–3). This is the first hint to the audience that rather than simply a tragedy of divine revenge, this will be a play which also engages in the examination of the nature of theatre (since the use of disguise is, after all, a close analogy for the use of theatre costume and therefore may invite reflection on the theatrical process). As the prologue develops Dionysus offers further potential indications that this play, which is on one level about him bringing his ritual to Thebes and the punishment of Pentheus, will also offer 'metatheatrical resonances'[3] (that is, it will invite the audience to reflect on the nature of theatre). The term that Dionysus uses to refer to the clothing of his worshippers, for example, *skeuē*, is also the standard word for theatre costume. This is an ambiguity that we will see is exploited within the stage action of the tragedy. The emphasis on the clothing and accessories of bacchic worshippers in the prologue is used to prefigure this. Finally, at the close of the prologue, Dionysus 'directs' the *parodos*, entrance song, of the chorus (58–61), instructing them on stage action:

> beat the rhythms of the east
> my rhyming rhythms
> rhea's rhythms
> beat the rhythms loud
> for pentheus to hear
> for thebes to hear
> loud
> loud
> and louder still

These comments distance Dionysus (and perhaps the audience) from the dramatic illusion: he is not a character experiencing the chance arrival of friends (as is often the situation at the *parodos*), but he takes the role of director in control of the *parodos* and how it will happen. This distancing from convention is an example of one of the 'metatheatrical resonances' (or theatrically self-conscious moments) that may be detected throughout the play and which are frequently achieved in relation to staging. Another example of Dionysus acting as director (and creating a self-conscious distance from a theatrical convention) is offered at the arrival of the messenger after Dionysus' (still in disguise) escape from the palace (657–9):

> But there's someone coming for you now – down from the mountains – listen to their news. And don't worry about me. I won't go away.

The prologue, therefore, does not only explain the dramatic situation, but is also used to prepare the audience for Dionysus' role in the staging of the play and the play's engagement, through this, with ideas about theatre. In the following discussion, I have selected some of the key aspects of staging to demonstrate Euripides' creation of dramatic meaning through this element of his craft in this play.

The tomb and the palace

Apart from setting the tone for the play, the prologue is also important as it informs the audience's understanding of elements of staging, preconditioning the way in which it should be understood by encoding symbolic meaning through Dionysus' words. In particular, the tomb of Semele and the palace (which are the only things on stage apart from Dionysus at this point) are invested with specific meaning through what he says about them. Firstly, the tomb of his mother, Semele (which we might imagine in front of the palace perhaps to one side) is given special attention early on (6–9) as Dionysus draws attention to it and explains what it signifies. His description of his mother's death through Hera's anger and Cadmus' respectful behaviour towards his daughter's tomb ensure that the tomb stands as a constant visual reminder throughout the play both that Dionysus really is a god and that Cadmus, at least, had behaved correctly towards him.

The potential impact of the tomb's symbolism should be kept in mind as the play's action unfolds. The dramatic effect of this might be felt, for example, during the discussion of the nature of Dionysus' birth. Cadmus' cynical reasons for believing in Dionysus (333–6), juxtaposed with the outward sign of his belief (i.e. his respectful treatment of Semele's tomb), either draws attention to his clever use of rhetoric in trying to persuade Pentheus (by adopting an argument which will appeal to him) or it undermines the value of his action in respecting the tomb. Meanwhile Cadmus' extraordinary exchange with Dionysus at the end of the play (1344–9) takes on a different resonance when imagined taking place in the presence of Semele's tomb:

Cadmus   Dionysus, we did wrong! Forgive us!

Dionysus   No. You learned too late. And when you should have known me, you rejected me.

Cadmus   I know now. But to punish us like this – it's more than we deserve.

Dionysus   I am a god and you insulted me.

Cadmus   Gods should not have the passions that men do.

Dionysus   This has long been the will of Zeus my father.

Since Semele's tomb, thanks to Dionysus' words in the prologue, can be seen as a symbol of Cadmus having done the right thing in relation to Dionysus, Cadmus' complaints here seem all the more justified and Dionysus' revenge (not just on Pentheus but on the entire household) seems all the more unfair. Semele's tomb adds to the *pathos* of Cadmus' weakness before a wrathful god. At the same time, the detail in the prologue about the destruction of Semele being caused by Hera but executed through the thunderbolt of Zeus (with whom we might say ultimate responsibility lay for the entire sorry affair) perhaps enables this reference to the destruction of the household being the will of Zeus to resonate differently. Certainly the clear reference in the prologue to the tomb as the ruins of the house enables it to operate prefiguratively and as a constant reminder through the play of the power of the gods. Given this symbolism, the tomb is capable of heightening the tension as the audience watch Pentheus vehemently refusing to worship Dionysus in the presence of a visual symbol of divine power.

The effects of the tomb discussed so far relate to its potential as a constant visual presence in the staging, in effect as a backdrop. It is given prominent attention, marked by comments in the words of the play, in a second place, after the prologue. During the 'palace miracle' or earthquake, it is said that its flame flares up. Before considering this spectacular moment in stage action in more detail, it is worth exploring the meaning that has been constructed for the palace before it is shaken.

It is first mentioned at line 7, when Dionysus notes that the tomb of his mother is beside the house. For the audience, though, the palace, as the building that is the constant backdrop to the action, would already be prominent through its visual dominance at the back of the performance space (all the more marked at the opening of the play before the chorus take up their position in the *orchestra*). Its symbolism is made clear by Dionysus' instruction to the chorus, at the end of his prologue (60–1), to beat their drums around the royal house of Pentheus. As Seaford observes, 'this relates the central conflict of the drama, between Dionysiac cult and the royal power, to the physical arrangement which so perfectly expresses it.'[4] The palace's symbolic connection to the royal household is reinforced by Cadmus' emergence from it (178–80), wearing the clothing and accessories of bacchic worship (on which see below) and Pentheus' arrival, along one of the side entrances to the performance space, explicitly racing towards the palace

(212). This association of the palace and household is important to the meaning of the 'earthquake' which shakes the house. A further layer of meaning for the house, created by the first exchange between Dionysus, in disguise, and Pentheus, is also significant to understanding the 'palace miracle'. In the stichomythic exchange of one-liners between these characters, a recurrent theme is Pentheus' wish to bind Dionysus. He tries to counter the bacchic worship (493–7) of the other 'man' by attacking the outward symbols of it, the long hair and thyrsus (wand), and by locking him up. In other words, Pentheus is opposed to the liberty (physical and, as he supposes, sexual) that bacchic worship invites and he tries to use the enclosure of the palace to limit the practice of this worship. The palace represents 'inside' and constraint and therefore, symbolically, it embodies the assertion of royal authority and an anti-bacchic stance.

The shaking of the palace and Dionysus' escape from it, on the other hand, represents the exact opposite: the assertion of bacchic authority and liberty from constraint. The question of how exactly the earthquake and flaming tomb were staged is open to interpretation.[5] At its core, of course, is the extent to which the theme of illusion and reality is prominent at this moment in the play. If Euripides wanted to heighten the audience awareness of how bacchic worship distorts perceptions of reality, then an effective way to do it would be to offer no attempt at the visual representation of the effects (earthquake, lightning, flame on tomb, destruction of house?) described by the chorus and Dionysus. The disparity between the chorus' and audience's experience and perception would therefore be reinforced by the staging. Alternatively some attempts to represent the shaking of the palace, sound effects and fire on the tomb could have been made. The 'special effects' would not have had to be particularly sophisticated, as the nature of tragedy with its use of theatrical conventions demanded a generous audience in this respect. Indeed the reference to the potential jerkiness of the stage crane in Aristophanes' *Peace* (173–5) suggests not only self-consciousness about this but also acceptance of it.

In whatever ways these effects were represented on stage, we know that the voice of Dionysus is heard from offstage directing events. The impact of this is close to that of a *deus ex machina* (appearance of a god) although of course Dionysus is not physically present. The staging here and the threatened destruction of the house prefigures its final symbolic destruction through the death of Pentheus and departure of both Agave and Cadmus (leaving the palace empty by the end of the play). It also operates more specifically to prefigure the death of Pentheus through the use of the offstage voice of the god, since in the messenger's description of Pentheus' death it is a voice which instructs the maenads (frenzied worshippers of Dionysus) to take revenge on the 'spy' (i.e. Pentheus, 1078–9). The audience can only appreciate this prefiguration retrospectively. The staging of this earthquake scene, however, changes the audience experience of the messenger speech. As they have witnessed the destructive power of the dislocated voice enacted before them in this scene, the description of that same voice by the messenger is made all the more real and powerful.

The tension builds after this physical threat has been made to the household, and a further visual demonstration of Dionysus' power has been added to Semele's tomb. The house is transformed by this scene from a symbol of royal authority to a symbol of Dionysus' power. In a piece of visual mirroring and inversion, typical of this play, the next person to enter it will be Pentheus and when he comes out of it he will be totally under the control of Dionysus.

Dressing up for Dionysus

Dionysus' eventual power over Pentheus is symbolized through the king's appearance when he emerges from the palace (918): he is dressed as a woman and carries bacchic accessories. Before entering the palace, audience expectation over his change in appearance on re-emerging had been informed by Pentheus' prediction (845–6) that he will come out either armed or following Dionysus' advice (i.e. cross-dressed). The line potentially alludes to an alternative version of the myth in which Pentheus battled with the bacchants armed, and therefore it toys with the audience's expectations by hinting at the possibility of this alternative being followed. The earlier references to perhaps doing battle with the bacchants seem to lend weight to this possibility. Dionysus' own predictions (857), however, that he will go in and dress Pentheus in clothing appropriate for death, set up another expectation. But in order to appreciate the layers of symbolism within this scene, it is important to consider the meaning already established for bacchic clothing and accessories within the play.

In the prologue Dionysus establishes bacchic clothing and accessories, i.e. dappled fawnskin, thyrsus (wand) and ivy crowns, not only as symbols of his worship but also as symbols of his power. He describes how he has 'forced' Pentheus' aunts to wear these accessories (34); his control over them is demonstrated by these elements of their outfit. By the same logic, Pentheus, when he encounters Cadmus wearing these signs of bacchic worship but also Dionysian control, pleads with his grandfather to remove the thyrsus and ivy crown.

This scene with Cadmus and Teiresias, however, does more than simply reinforce the idea of control. Seaford argues that the presentation of Cadmus and Teiresias with these symbols of worship is used to prefigure elements of mass participation in the cult of Dionysus (adopted by the end of the play by Thebes).[6] The idea that these bacchic accessories, and by extension worship of Dionysus, empower their wearer is also explored in this scene as both Cadmus and Teiresias claim to feel rejuvenated. There is a potential inter-performative allusion here to Aristophanes' comedy *Acharnians* (435f) in which the comic hero puts on the tragic costume of Telephus and instantly feels its effects, beginning to talk and act like the tragic hero. If some audience members made this connection, then it would invite them to compare the transformational powers of Dionysian ritual clothing and theatre costume (since in the passage from *Acharnians* it is explicitly a 'theatre costume', rather than everyday clothing, which is borrowed and put on). Both types of *skeuē* (the ambiguous term used for bacchic kit and theatre costume) have the power to enable someone to become someone else. The analogy allows us to understand the effect of worship that is being represented here. What is striking, in this respect, is that Cadmus, despite saying that he feels the effect of Dionysian worship, betrays the limits to his transformation by his query: 'Do you think we should drive to the mountain?' (191). This, I would suggest, might hint at the limits to Cadmus' own belief. The potential slippage between ritual wear/theatre costume in this scene (invited by the terminology *skeuē* as well as the possible inter-performative allusion) also reinforces the idea (already explored) of the play being directed by Dionysus as god of drama – his actors are dressed up to play their parts.

Pentheus' dressing up incorporates both the idea of bacchic accessories as signs of Dionysian control as well as its transformational powers. While Pentheus' outfit may be read as alluding to ritual clothing (see Seaford), it also has the potential to be read as theatre costume. This reading is invited by status of Pentheus' outfit as disguise (which, as I suggested above, is analogous to costume) and is reinforced by his questions about how to seem more like a bacchant. Also, just like Teiresias' *skeuē*, the clothing and accessories prove transformational (affecting more than physical appearance) to the wearer; Pentheus reveals his sense of power, for example, when he asks whether he can lift the mountain on his shoulders.

At the same time, the appearance of Pentheus cross-dressed and with bacchic accessories offers a visual representation of Dionysus' full control over him. The battle of power, and conflict of Dionysian ritual and its refusal, which runs through the play and has several permutations between Pentheus and Dionysus, culminates in the scene before this in the closely debated dispute over whether Pentheus will put on this attire. The theatrical exploration of power dynamics through one character imposing a change of clothing on another had already been explored in a comic way in Aristophanes' *Wasps* (1122f). Here the consequences of the change are far more serious as Dionysus' ominous reference to clothing for death (857) has made clear.

When Pentheus emerges from the house dressed as Dionysus wished, under his control, and suffering transformational delusions, the audience knows that it means his death. It is extraordinary, therefore, that at this point there is a clear inter-performative allusion to Aristophanes' *Women at the Thesmophoria* (249f), a comedy in which a man is persuaded to cross-dress in order to spy on a female-only festival. The general situation of one male character's concern over another's cross-dressed appearance, as well as the specific detail about arranging the pleats properly (Ar. *Thesmo.* 256 cf *Bacchae* 935–6), make the allusion clear. The effect of this is to invite a comparison of the scenes and to draw attention to how much more sinister Dionysus' concern over Pentheus is: he is preparing his victim for death (this is reinforced through ritual detail).[7] In the comedy, the Kinsman, who is the cross-dressed spy, despite being discovered by the women at the festival will not suffer death. In the tragic frame, the scene is transformed and this perhaps enables the audience to appreciate Euripides' dramatic mastery (he can even make cross-dressing, which had proven comic potential, tragic).

Denouement

While the death of Pentheus is in some respects handled in an entirely conventional way through the use of a messenger speech reporting the off-stage action, the manipulation of staging in this part of the play makes the revelation of the death (which the audience has, after all, sensed was inevitable) particularly powerful. Firstly the chosen internal audience for the messenger's speech and the response his news engenders add to the horror of the events. The chorus of 'barbarian' bacchants are the ones to receive the news from the messenger and their ecstatic joy in response to it is chilling, while heightening the *pathos* for the circumstances of Pentheus' destruction. The messenger's failure to understand their response and their reiteration of it in even starker terms encapsulates the dramatic effect of the juxtaposition offered here (1032–4):

Messenger   What are you saying? How can you speak like that? How can you gloat at the news of his suffering?

Chorus   its
          the cult cry of bacchus

> the song of the foreigner
> sweet liberation
> an end to our fear

The difference in emotional response to the news of the death is reminiscent of the moment in *Medea* (1132–5) where the heroine, on hearing that the princess and king are dead, asks the messenger for the details saying that her pleasure will be twice as great if they died most horribly. In *Bacchae*, however, the effect of the staging, with the messenger physically outnumbered by this band of fifteen ecstatic barbarian women, breaking into ritual cry, is arresting. It is *their* emotional response which is the overwhelming force. Even if the messenger is able to take centre stage (metaphorically) as he relates the events which led to Pentheus' death, the emotional impact of these words is disrupted by the staging of the chorus response immediately after the end of the speech as they break into dance (1153):

Chorus dancers
>>> soar high
>>> in the dances
>>> of bacchus

In fact the use of the chorus in the staging of this scene is the culmination of Euripides' exploitation throughout the play of the chorus' dramatic power as a group symbolizing the disruptive force of this newly arrived religion. This is, as Seaford points out, neatly expressed in the staging of their *parodos* (discussed above) which sets them up as the embodiment of the threatening cult.[8] Part of the sense of threat is in the explicit emphasis on their status as outsiders: the audience is not allowed to forget that these women are not from Greece. They themselves draw attention to this in their response to the messenger quoted above, but it has been prominent from the very beginning of the play. Dionysus in his prologue refers to them as his *thiasos* (band of worshippers) from Lydia (modern-day Turkey) and later he refers to them as 'barbarian women' (604).

It seems likely to me that the costumes of the chorus offered a visual indication of their homeland and, more importantly, that they contrasted with the Greek female bacchants (of whom Agave is the only one to appear on stage). Even if they all carried the same ritual accessories of bacchic worship, the fabric of the chorus' robes could be far more elaborate (in both patterning and richness of dyes) to indicate that they are from Lydia (renowned for its wealth and dyes; for its elaborate clothing, see, for example, the seventh-century BC poet, Sappho fr. 39, which refers to beautifully

Looking at Bacchae

decorated Lydian sandals). Such patterning would not only add to the visual richness of the play and its choral dances, but it would also clearly express the Greek and barbarian distinction. Furthermore, the alignment in Greek thinking between barbarian ways and effeminacy means that as a physical presence in the performance space with the effeminate Dionysus, the chorus are an overwhelmingly feminine presence – a force to which Pentheus eventually gives way symbolically through cross-dressing.

Finally the chorus' barbarian status also offers the opportunity for an eye-catching stage effect (in addition to those already noted above) during the palace miracle. The chorus, in response to the offstage voice of Dionysus and the palace miracle, throw themselves on the ground trembling (600–1). Hecuba (another female barbarian), in one of Euripides' earlier plays, *Trojan Women*, similarly (though through grief rather than awe) falls to the ground (462) during the play's action (in fact, she is also on the ground at the opening of the play, 98). The visual effect, however, of fifteen chorus members in the orchestra of the theatre of Dionysus suddenly prostrate must have outdone this and made for a powerful theatrical moment. Seaford argues that this staging offers an allusion to mystic initiation.[9] The gesture, however, is given a specifically barbarian association in Aeschylus' *Agamemnon* (920), so this staging may also reinforce the association of this chorus, and by extension the cult, with Asia Minor.

Perhaps the most shocking moment of staging in the entire play is the appearance of Agave carrying the decapitated head of Pentheus (1168). Some argue that the head is on the end of her thyrsus at this point, but later in the scene, at least, it is in her hands. The focus on this prop allows for the development of an extended period of painful dramatic irony while everyone except Agave can see that it is the head of Pentheus (and not, as she thinks, of a lion or a bull). Therefore it represents the final engagement through staging with the theme of illusion and reality which pervades the play. In addition to the horror of a mother carrying her son's decapitated head without realizing it, the dismemberment, so graphically described by the messenger, is again brought to mind through its symbolic representation in the corpse (such as it is) that Cadmus has hunted out and brought with him (1216–21 and 1299). There is some evidence to suggest that even more was made of this in the staging, with Agave lamenting over each limb, although the gap in the text as we have it is an obstacle to detailed knowledge or analysis of this moment in the play.

On another level, the use of Pentheus' mask as the prop for the head (which would be the most effective means of staging this) also allows for the final symbolic representation of the god of drama's triumph. It also, I would suggest, allows, on another level, for a self-conscious moment of reflection on the nature of theatre, through the juxtaposition of a masked actor and this mask. Agave (represented by a male actor dressed in female mask and costume) faces the mask from the costume of a male character who had dressed up in female disguise and is explicitly described as looking just like his mother or one of his aunts (i.e. one of Cadmus' daughters, 917). At a glance this could look like the artistic representation of an actor or poet holding a mask (of which there is at least one example surviving from this period and more from just after). Since it is a female character holding the mask it perhaps invites some of the audience, at least, to reflect on the feminine nature of the tragic art. This is just one potential additional layer of meaning created here. The visual double created by Agave facing the mask aligns with the recurrent 'doubling' or 'mirroring' in the staging of this play.

The textual gaps in the final section of the play limit our knowledge of its finale and specifically the nature of Dionysus' appearance. A spectacular appearance as a *deus ex machina* using the stage crane would have been dramatically effective: demonstrating Dionysus' triumph and proving that he really *is* a divinity. The spatial dynamic of this would also work well to reinforce the references to Cadmus' fate of becoming a snake; Dionysus suspended on high would draw attention to Cadmus' apt closeness to the ground. The surviving text can tell us that Cadmus and Agave part and therefore the palace, which has been a focus of attention for Dionysus since the very opening of the play, will be left empty.

Final thought

One final consideration affecting the dramatic impact of the staging of this play is its performance date. A *scholion* (marginal comment added by an ancient scholar beside a text) on Aristophanes' *Frogs* 67 informs us that according to the ancient performance records (*didascaliai*) Euripides' son produced the Euripidean plays *Iphigenia at Aulis*, *Alcmaeon* and *Bacchae* at the City Dionysia after Euripides' death. Since Euripides died in 407–406 BC, *Bacchae* is sometimes assumed to have been performed in 405 BC. If this is the case, or even if it were in a subsequent year, then Aristophanes' *Frogs* had already appeared on stage at the Lenaea fesitval (held in January) in 405 BC. *Frogs* also features Dionysus as a central character, and while Euripides could not have planned *Bacchae* as a response, since he was dead before its production, the performance experience of the audience meant that they would bring the memory of Aristophanes' comic treatment of Dionysus with them as spectators of *Bacchae*. Therefore while Euripides deliberately creates meaning in the staging of *Bacchae* through allusion to Aristophanes' *Women at the Thesmophoria*, there is also potential for an unintentional interplay (created through the order of performance) with Aristophanes' *Frogs*. This might not only affect the audience response to Dionysus appearing in disguise, as he does after all in *Frogs*, where he sports an unconvincing Heracles disguise, but might also, for example, invite an added pleasure to the prologue (since Euripidean prologues are parodied in *Frogs*). The experience of *Frogs*, which offers an explicit exploration of the nature of theatre (expressed not only through the *agon* but also through the staging, such as the use of disguise), may also have primed the audience to interpret *Bacchae* through the metatheatrical lens suggested here. The final effect, even if he could not know it, was that Euripides would be able to share the triumph of Dionysus at the end of *Bacchae*, since he had not only successfully made *Women at the Thesmophoria* into tragedy but also, in a sense, *Frogs* as well.

Notes

1 Segal (1997) 374–8. Seaford (1996) privileges ritual. My discussion owes much to both of these works and to Foley (1985).
2 Foley (1985) 205–58.
3 The phrase is used by Segal (1997) 376.
4 Seaford (1996) 28.
5 See Goldhill (1986) 277–84, for a more detailed discussion of the possibilities and their meaning.
6 Seaford (1996) 166.
7 On ritual detail in this scene, see Seaford (1996) 222.
8 Seaford (1996) 28.
9 Seaford (1996) 200 and in his essay for this collection.

Looking at the Bacchae in *Bacchae*

Chris Carey

Whether we look at a Greek play from inside or outside, the chorus is at its core. Looked at from the outside, from the organization of the festival, the chorus is central in the fundamental sense that permission to compete is expressed in terms of the chorus; playwrights make their pitch to the archon at the beginning of the administrative year and the archon grants or withholds a chorus at the expense of a wealthy backer.[1] Within the play, in simple arithmetic choral song makes up a significant proportion of the words heard and its dance is the most significant visual spectacle in a theatre which does not usually go in for elaborate stage action. This is not just crude arithmetic, however. Looked at from the perspective of the dramatic action the chorus is the only personality in the play who remains with the audience for the whole of the performance; while characters, human and divine, come and go, only very rarely in surviving tragedy does the chorus leave the theatre space. It is therefore the most persistent voice heard by the theatre audience. At the level of genre its constant presence shapes the fabric and tone. Combined with a backdrop (the stage building) which locates action outside, it makes Greek tragedy a very public art form, in which even the most personal exchanges take place in front of a group.

So when you sit down to write for the theatre of Dionysus and see the play in your mind, one of the most important decisions you make is the choice of the chorus. When we encounter a Greek play, the chorus is a given, not least because it often gives the play its title. But this play could have looked very different. For Euripides all the identity markers of the chorus (age, gender, status, ethnicity) were negotiable according to his conception of (this version of) the story. There were good intertextual/metatheatrical reasons to opt for the chorus identity we now have. Aeschylus had written a *Bacchae*. Whether this was the title used by Aeschylus or was imposed by the later tradition is immaterial; it points to the sex and identity of the chorus (though not necessarily the ethnicity). To a greater degree than almost any other Euripidean play *Bacchae* engages in intertextual dialogue with the earlier dramatic corpus, involving a sustained and close interaction with the Aeschylean corpus of

Dionysiac-themed plays.[2] And this in turn fits within a larger Euripidean tendency to compete overtly with specific plays by Aeschylus.[3] The chorus of *Bacchae* is part of that engagement, great and small, though unfortunately our ignorance of the specifics of the earlier play makes it impossible to trace the relationship with the Aeschylean *Bacchae* at the level of detail we would like. But intertextuality is for Euripides merely one aspect of the creative process; it never drives the whole plot and cast list. So this chorus was not inevitable to Euripides or his audience, as it is now for us.

It is therefore worth pausing to ask 'what if?' The gender of a chorus often mirrors that of the (human) protagonist. So an obvious choice for this play was a group of males. And in a civic context in which the king's authority is tested or contested one choice which lay very near to hand was a group of mature Theban citizens, like the chorus of *Oedipus Tyrannus* or *Antigone*. The implications for the tone of the play and our response to it are enormous. As the only vocal group within the play the chorus are the dramatic character which most resembles the theatre audience. And in a world, like that of archaic and classical Greece, where the chorus in a whole range of performative (usually cultic) contexts is the voice of the city it is an important compass point for audience reaction. It can no more control audience response than any other character in the play.[4] But as commentator on the action it can suggest a way of evaluating what we are seeing, even if that view is, like everything else in a forward-moving performance, provisional. There is no simple correlation between gender and utterance.[5] But a male citizen chorus would have presented us (like the *Edonians* of Aeschylus, which also dealt with Dionysiac myth)[6] with an externalized view of the god and his cult. The myth which provides the storyline of *Bacchae* precludes a fully sympathetic treatment of Pentheus. He fits too well the mythic model of the *theomachos*, 'god-fighter', the human who contests or insults the power of a god. The root occurs only four times in Euripides and interestingly three of those four occurrences are in *Bacchae* (45, 325, 1255).[7] But a male citizen chorus might have dulled the edges of his strident opposition to the god by surrounding him with a group potentially sympathetic to some of his anxieties about the cult, or at least aware of the burden of responsibility he carries and more inclined to see resistance to the order of the *polis* as subversive and dangerous.[8] Certainly we would have lost not just the ecstatic presentation of the cult but also the exquisite beauty of the lyric account of the delight of service to the god. Euripides instead has opted for a female chorus, a chorus of initiates of Dionysus who see the cult from the inside, and a chorus not just of outsiders but of non-Greeks.

The implications of the choice of chorus for focalization are fundamental. Unlike Greek epic with its third-person narrator external to the action, a play lacks a controlling voice; any appearance to the contrary (such as a divine prologue) is illusion. The result is greater polyphony within the text and commensurately greater audience autonomy. But within that polyphony both sympathy and sense of fact can be shaped by the sequence of events and the interaction between event and utterance, by the frequency, convergence, divergence and sequence of views expressed. The text exerts its control, even if the control is not absolute. But within the text Pentheus is for most of the play a lone voice. He is alone in opposing the cult and equally alone in his illusions about the behaviour of the Theban women. All the individuals he encounters: his grandfather Cadmus, Tiresias (the nearest thing in the play to the voice of – human – religious authority), his own subordinates; all urge him to abandon his resistance to the god, either to share the joys of the experience the god represents or simply to protect himself from inevitable destruction. And above all this the collective voice in the play like a sounding board amplifies both the positive and negative messages, the benefits of the cult and the criminality and folly of resistance. The positive aspect is given exquisite expression in the *parodos*, which offers an account of the joys of the cult of Dionysus, embodied in the *oreibasia*, the ritual of running wild in the mountains which formed part of the worship of Dionysus in some parts of Greece well into the Roman period. The account is designed to draw the hearers in and sweep them along, with the urgency of its repeated calls (82, 'go bacchae, now bacchae', 116, 152–3 'to the mountains, the mountains'), the hypnotic power of its emphasis on plenty (143–4 'and the earth flows with milk, and the earth flows with wine, and the earth flows with honey and nectar'), the frenetic movement and the recurrent stress on pleasure. At the same time the insistence on blessedness and purity remove any element of self-indulgence from the expression of delight. At the level of plot structure the internalized view of the cult from the chorus makes for a text in which information available is carefully skewed. The joys of the cult are presented in terms of innocuous and pious absorption into the natural world. Many of these ingredients surface again in the first *stasimon* but in a different form. The first word of the song (370) is *hosia* (sanctity, holiness), personified as a goddess and claimed for themselves, while Pentheus is presented as offering a direct affront to the goddess through his assault on the god's cult; again Pentheus is a generic *theomachos*. The song stresses the disastrous end which comes from uncontained impiety such as his, and the hostility of the god to those who resist his simple pleasures (386–9, 424) in contrast to the security of those who adhere to the simple good sense of the ordinary man. But there is no hint of the form of Pentheus' punishment nor any sense of a desire to see him suffer. Their desire is only to escape (401–16). The frenzied aspects of the cult are accordingly played down here and the pleasures brought by the god are the simple (and civilized) joys of the banquet, wine, song and love. The sense of the chorus as victims re-emerges in the second *stasimon* (520–25), where the chorus express puzzlement at the failure of Thebes to accept them and their cult. The criticism of Pentheus becomes more strident (737–55) and culminates in a desire for his punishment, but again without any hint at the awful form it will take. There are hints in the text which point toward other more unsettling aspects of bacchic experience. The description of the ritual hunting and rending of the animal victim in the *parodos* hints at a propensity for violence within the cult and its followers. The same applies to the mention of Orpheus in the second *stasimon*. Orpheus features there (561–3) in a motif common in Greek hymns, the listing of locations favoured by the god; the mention elides the fact that in a well-known version of his myth Orpheus was torn apart by the bacchants of Thrace. The capacity for violence remains only implicit and fleeting until it erupts explicitly once Pentheus is ensnared in Dionysus' plan, but it is there waiting in the text. The link between the capacity for violence in the idyllic account of the cult and the brutality of the god and his worshippers when opposed is made almost explicit when the ritual cry of 'to the hills' is used to urge on the killing of Pentheus in the fourth *stasimon* (977, 986).

The denial of a supporting voice (it is not until Pentheus is dead that we hear anything said in his favour) means that Pentheus is isolated within the plot. While being the secular and central power in Thebes he becomes within the community of the play the outsider, a man whose acts and ideas are alien, shocking and often inexplicable to the other human characters around him, an effect exacerbated by his tyrannical behaviour, which removes him from normal collective experience. The effect, increased by the sequence of events which demonstrate his inability to control the god, and ultimately even to control himself, is an unsettling mixture of untrammelled authority and impotence. In contrast the god Dionysus, who as a figure who can control both the natural world and the human psyche needs neither support nor sympathy, receives (within the play) both sympathy and support.

But focalization is not the only issue in the choice of chorus. *Bacchae* is not alone in having a chorus of foreign females. And it is not the only surviving Euripidean play to do so. Nor is it the only play to have a chorus of foreign women in Greek space. But foreignness is no more an absolute than any other characteristic, in tragedy or anywhere else. Proximity and distance are managed according to the needs of the plot, for the chorus as for other characters. The chorus of Aeschylus' *Suppliants* are simultaneously Greek and non-Greek, refugees from Egypt and visibly outsiders from their costume but claiming kinship by descent from Argos. His chorus of Trojan slaves in *Choephori* are fully absorbed into the house of Atreus, loyal servants of the king who sacked their city and made them captive (however implausible this might be in the real world). The same applies to the chorus of young Phoenician maidens in *Phoenissae*, who have a natural link with Greece through their backstory as worshippers of Apollo[9] and to Thebes though their kinship with Cadmus.[10] The bacchants in *Bacchae* in contrast are linked to Greece only by the god; like the chorus in *Phoenissae* they identify their place of origin in Asia (64–5) but claim no kinship with Thebes. They reflect in this respect only one aspect of the twin personality of the god, who is simultaneously a member of the Theban ruling family (and cousin to Pentheus) and an arrival from the east. Unlike Dionysus they are completely alien. The Theban dimension is left to the bacchants in the mountains. This dimension of alienness was enhanced by costume and dance. We can be reasonably sure of the costume worn by the chorus, at least in broad outline. Firstly, props. Dionysus reifies his introduction of his worship to Thebes in the *thyrsos*, the wand carried by the devotee of Dionysus (25). It is associated constantly both with bacchants and with the god in iconography. The sheer persistence of the mentions in the play[11] makes little sense unless this object is reflected in the outfitting of the chorus, as it is in the props carried by his local worshippers, Cadmus and Tiresias (176). The other item associated with bacchic revels both in iconography and in this play is the tambourine (*tympanon/typanon*). Dionysus actually calls on the bacchants to raise their tambourines (58–9) in announcing their entrance song; and the bacchants in response bid themselves sing Dionysus to the accompaniment of the tambourine (156–7). The second of these passages could theoretically refer to accompaniment by musicians offstage or even mute actors at the edge of the performance space, but the former only makes sense as a reference to instruments carried by chorus members. So probably we have a chorus with two sets of props, some, probably the majority, with the *thyrsos*, some with tambourines. They are also garlanded; their garlands are either worn on top of or are built into the masks. Throughout the play ivy garlands are associated with the god's worship,[12] including the chorus in what looks like a self-reflexive gesture:

Chorus   blessèd is he
            the initiate
            god-kissed
        walking the path
            of the mysteries of god
        soul joined with gods soul
        and high in the mountains
        worshipping

> bacchus
> the lord dionysus
> in ritual
> purity
> worshipping
>   cybele
>   mother god
>   earth god
> beating the thyrsus
> embraced in the ivy
> for bacchus.

The local worshippers are wearing fawnskins to worship the god, as they tell us (176) and as Pentheus confirms in his shocked response (249). The Theban women in the wild wear the same (697). The fawnskin is combined with the *thyrsos* in the outfit of Dionysus himself in Euripides fr.752 (from *Hypsipyle*). In *Bacchae* line 24 it is again associated with the *thyrsos* as part of the costume which he has imposed on Thebes. It is the archetypal outfit of the ecstatic worshipper (137, 835) and the garment which the chorus urges Thebes to adopt in the *parodos* (111). Though the way the old men wear the skins may add a slightly comic feature to their appearance in line with the overall tone of their entrance scene, the general agreement between character and choral costuming in other details and the iconic status given to skins in the text suggest (as does the intrinsic implausibility that the Asiatic worshippers are more soberly dressed than the elderly Thebans) that this too mirrors the costume of the chorus. We need not suppose a full outfit of skins in the manner of Robinson Crusoe. The visual effect needs only an animal skin worn round the shoulders on top of a *peplos* in a way we find illustrated in iconography (as with the front cover of this collection). But the presence of the skins is important. The physical accoutrements of the chorus are more than just stimulating visual effects. They are also a visual expression of their nature and the nature of their cult. Already in l.25 the *thyrsos* is presented as a weapon ('missile matted green with ivy shoots'), a role it plays literally in the encounter with the rustics and then with Pentheus later in the play (733, 762, 1099).[13] The skin combines within it the key ideas of freedom and the hunt. The freedom is expressed not only in the narrative of the Theban women running free on the mountains but also in the simile of the colt running free beside its mother used to describe the exultation of the bacchic dance (163–5):

Chorus and
> like a colt

straining its limbs
its swift hooves
in the meadows
galloping close
to its mother
exultant

like a colt
all exultant
the dancer leaps high

The hunt[14] is already present in the *parodos* in the account of the joys of the Dionysiac ritual of *omophagia*, the ritual of eating the raw flesh of an animal victim:

Chorus it is good to be on the hillside with the hunting pack
it is good to let yourself fall naked
  only the deerskin to clothe you

and you're blooded with the goats blood you've been hunting
and its flesh is quivering and warm
and you taste it
and you tear it

Hunting language underlies the ambiguous and confused relationship between the king and the devotees of Bacchus. Pentheus threatens to hunt down the women loose on the mountains and bring them back in chains, termed by Pentheus 'nets of iron' (231). In his febrile fantasies the women 'hunt' not Bacchus but Aphrodite in the wild (688), as does the enigmatic stranger (459). Pentheus' agreement to spy on the women instead of taking them by force is approved ironically by Dionysus with the remark that it is better not to hunt ills with ills (839). As the women on the mountain are (disastrously) 'hunted' by the rustics (718–9, 731) in their desire to ingratiate themselves with the king by bringing back his mother, so the chorus of bacchants compare themselves to a vulnerable young animal which has outrun the pursuing hunters (963–76):

Chorus will i
  pound my feet hard
  on the earth
    in the

    night
       dance
    and
    throw back
       my head
       in the
    cool
       mountain air

      like
    a fawn
    leaping high
       in the
    lush
    meadow grasslands

       ecstatic
       alive

    and the hunt's
       far behind now
    the beaters
    the terror
    the hunting nets
    cleared

The image does, however, reflect the ambiguous nature of the chorus and the emotional experience they espouse. For they too are hunters (1005). And like hunters they urge on 'the dogs of Frenzy' (977) to drive Pentheus to his death in the hills. The bacchants in the hills too are hunters as well as hunted and their eventual prey is Pentheus, who is repeatedly (like the god he resembles without realizing – 436) described in terms of wild beasts, both when he is at his most menacing (361, 539–42) and when he is hunted down and destroyed (1020–3, 1108). His mother brings his head back like a successful hunter who has killed a lion (1139–47), an idea she repeats in her own celebration of her success (1169–1215, 1233–43, 1255).

    As noted above, the ethnicity of the chorus mirrors one side of the god, who is simultaneously Theban and foreign; it also as the ecstatic alien mirrors the psychological experience of bacchism, in which the individual becomes possessed by something outside himself. This must also have been reflected in sound and movement. Dance and music are lost. But the *parodos*, with its syncretic absorption of Dionyisac mysteries within a large amalgam of orgiastic cults,[15] calls for lively movement. The same applies to the highly emotional tone, reflected in the urgent repetitions in the commands and entreaties to follow the bacchic cult. We can also interpolate from the iconographic images which show at least in some cases a dervish-like movement in which the body seems to be thrown around. This is of course tendentious. But it is supported by the repeated presence of the term *mainas/maenad* ('frenzied women') for the devotees of Dionysus in the play.[16] This is a god who does not simply exist at a remove, to be placated by sacrifice and other formal ritual, but one who possesses and becomes one with his worshippers, as he will possess Pentheus later in the play. In the process they are temporarily metamorphosed and become one with the god. The effect is a rapture which brings with it a loss of individual consciousness. At the level of language we are constantly reminded that these women are maddened. And the dance must at least intermittently reflect this. The choral songs show a preference for ionic rhythms (based on the sequence u u – – u u – –), which are associated not only with worship, and Dionysiac worship, but also with Asia.[17] The association with the east is not inevitable, but in the mouths of a chorus which is repeatedly associated with Mount Tmolus (modern Bozdağ) in Lydia (55, 65, 154) the rhythms are heard as not merely non-Theban but emphatically non-Greek. The chorus is not merely the voice of bacchism but also its visual manifestation. The combination of visual (both in costume and movement) and aural aspects of the chorus (not just what they sing but how they sing) creates some paradoxical effects in performance. Like many other tragic choruses this one moralizes extensively, expanding outward from the events in the play to provide a generalizing frame for its evaluation. It calls for piety, moderation, good sense rather than cleverness (386–401, 427–31, 882–96). It locates itself very firmly within the Greek ethical tradition. Much of their moralizing would sit comfortably in the mouths of the maiden chorus of Alcman or the singers of the cult songs and epinicians of Pindar and Bacchylides. Especially appealing within the specific context of democratic Athens is the emphatic statement of the chorus that they align themselves with the collective values of the mass of citizenry (430–1):

Chorus   the common way
            that's best for all
         is best for me.

This is not the smug smartness of the intellectual but the good sense of the ordinary person, the very basis of democratic thinking. But when this chorus approximates most to the sober norms of non-dramatic choral song, the conventional wisdom of typical tragic chorus or the common sense of the man in the street, the words come from a source whose very appearance is an enactment of ecstasy and wildness. The performative paradox does not undermine what they say, for what they say is not just unexceptionable but actually admirable in terms of conventional Greek values. And their insistence on the need for piety and restraint is fully justified in context by the behaviour of Pentheus. But the mismatch between medium and message serves (like the hints of violence noted above) as a constant low-key reminder to the audience that there is another, more brutal, side to this chorus and what they stand for, a side which emerges when Dionysus finally moves to destroy Pentheus. At this point the language of wisdom does not change but the definition of wisdom changes radically. They consistently ask what constitutes wisdom. But where before it had consisted in remaining pious, remembering the limitations of mortal life and enjoying the moment, now it amounts to putting one's foot on the neck of one's foe: revenge, violence, victory over the enemy (877–81, 896–901). In a sense nothing has really changed; capitulation to the passion of the moment is as likely to be hideous as it is likely to be beautiful. All that has changed is that we have a better perspective.

The wild side of the chorus gives them a binding role. They are the main link with the 'offstage' world. Other characters come from the mountain: the herdsman who reports on the first encounter with the Theban bacchants, which illustrates both their pacific and chaste activities in the hills which refute (if only he would listen) the prurient fantasies of the king, and later the messenger who comes to report the king's death. But the chorus bring the mountains into the theatre space. Though Greek tragedy operates within very tight constraints on seen space, it extends the physical confines of the theatre with a panoramic imagined space. It relies heavily on the ability of its audience to respond to narrative and description in order to create a mental image of the world beyond the theatre building and the side *parodoi* continuous with the seen world of the theatre space.[18] *Bacchae* relies very heavily for its themes on a contrast between the settled world of the *polis*, the world which Pentheus is desperately but misguidedly trying to protect, and the wild world outside represented by Cithaeron, which is a constant unseen backdrop to the seen action.[19] The cult of Dionysus by encouraging its worshippers to abandon temporarily the rigid disciplines of everyday life blurs the boundaries between these worlds of experience; and for Pentheus that means the loss of all moral restraint. Within the play the opposition between the *polis* and the wild mountain turns out to be a fragile one. It has already broken down for the women of Thebes before the play begins; they have been driven mad and sent to run wild on Cithaeron (32–8). It is also broken down by the presence of the wild bacchants in the heart of

Thebes. The Asiatic females whom we see in the orchestra are one of two groups of bacchants in the play, the other being the Theban women running wild in the hills. At a very superficial level their relationship is one of opposition. The women from Asia have given themselves voluntarily to the god, while for the women of Thebes bacchic frenzy is imposed as a punishment for resistance to his cult and rejection of his divinity. Yet at a more profound level they resemble each other closely. Though they do not meet until Agave enters at the end of the play after the killing, they are brought together spatially by convergence of the projected experience of the chorus with the reality of the Theban bacchants. A persistent theme in the *parodos* is the yearning of the chorus, confined in Thebes, to run wild in the mountains (76, 116, 135, 163), as the Theban women do on Cithaeron. They have in a sense exchanged places, as the Theban women have abandoned the confines and everyday activities of the home (32, 36, 1236–7). The choral account of the bacchic ritual which they both remember and crave is the reality for the Theban women in the hills (73–87, 677–711). But the shared experience goes beyond the physicality of rite and location, real or imagined. The chorus also both mirror and predict the emotional responses of the Theban women in the imagined space of Cithaeron, showing the same mood swings between beatitude and bestial violence. As the women in the hills turn violent when the herdsmen seek to capture them and when Pentheus spies on them, so the chorus in the orchestra move from the language of innocuous pleasure to the language of revenge and force. The link between the maenads onstage and off is at its closest in the fourth *stasimon*, when the chorus urge on the 'dogs of Frenzy' (976). It is almost as if they are addressing the Theban bacchants in the hills, who had themselves been called hunting dogs by Agave (731). The bacchants in the orchestra act as a bridge between the seen and imagined worlds of the play, between the city and the countryside which lies beyond one of the *parodoi*. They bring both the beauty and the violence of the world outside into the orchestra. But the two worlds of the play, the seemingly secure but ultimately fragile *polis* and the liberating but uncontrolled and destructive world of the mountains, are not just topographical entities. They are experiential and psychological entities. Dionysus as a god of emotional and physical liberation is part of the world of nature. Humankind too is part of that world of nature and that world is part of mankind. Dionysus himself is a psychological experience and not just an anthropomorphic divine being. This duality of Dionysus is clearest in the chilling scene where he plays with the deluded Pentheus after the latter has given himself over to the god. As he converses with the god in a quasi-drunken delusion, we have the uncanny sense that the god is simultaneously beside him and within him. This is not just a play about cult and its acceptance or resistance. It is about the duality of human nature. In helping to articulate the fluid binary division in the topography of the play the chorus also help to articulate the fragile world within the human psyche and the coexistence of order and reason on the one hand with passion and disorder on the other. The beauty and liberation of surrender to passion and the senses which the chorus describe in the *parodos* is very real. And their hostility to a narrow focus on reason is persuasive. A life lived wholly rationally without passion and without a degree of surrender to transient sensory experience is arid. But surrender to passion comes at a risk, in that emotion once released is difficult to confine and can as easily be a destructive as a life-enhancing force.

Notes

1 See Carey (2013) 155, Roselli (2011) 23–5, Wilson (2000) 6, Cartledge (1997) 18, Csapo and Slater (1995) 100, 108.
2 For the intertextual dimension of the play see Hall, Karamanou and Sommerstein in this volume.
3 E.g. *Electra* 508–76, which revisits elements of Aeschylus' *Choephori, Orestes* 866–935, which reprises the trial of Orestes in *Eumenides, Phoenissae* 103–201, 737–53, 1104–40 (if genuine), which revisit the dialogue between Eteocles and the scout in *Seven against Thebes*.
4 Easterling (1997b) 163–4.
5 Swift (2013) 132–3.
6 Fragment 57.
7 The last instance, however, is ironic; by this time he has died horribly and his mother is holding his head in her hand as she complains about his poor hunting skills.
8 Cf. Sophocles, *Antigone* 471–2, 853–6.
9 *Phoen.* 205–7.
10 *Phoen.* 218–20.
11 Twenty-one times, as against five occurrences in the rest of the plays and fragments.
12 81, 106, 177, 702–3.
13 Finally in 1141 the *thyrsos* becomes the spike on which Agave carries her son's head on her return from the hunt.
14 For the ubiquity of hunting in *Bacchae* and its association with the duality of Dionysus see Segal (1997) ch.2.
15 Cf *Cretans* fr.472.
16 For choral mainadism in the play see Bierl (2013).
17 West (1987) 61–3.
18 For the role of narrated space in Greek tragedy see Kampourelli (2015).
19 62, 661, 751, 797, 1045, 1142, 1177, 1219, 1292, 1384, 1385.

6

Mysteries and Politics in *Bacchae*

Richard Seaford

The idea that the ancient Greeks have much to tell us can shade into the idea that 'they were just like us'. But of course, if they really were just like us, there would be no point in studying them (other than as self-legitimation). In fact Greek culture was – unlike some cultures – similar enough to be comprehensible to us, but at the same time very different in a way that justifies efforts to understand it.

This point applies with particular force to the modern staging of ancient Greek drama. It can be – and generally is – staged so as to express something within the mainstream range of our preoccupations. Alternatively, a brave director might attempt to stage a production which contributes to *expanding* the range. In one sense such an attempt should be easy, given the narrowness of our mainstream: from within any culture (including our own) the mainstream looks much broader than it really is. But on the other hand such an attempt is risky, and requires a special kind of effort on the part not only of the translator, director and performers, but also of the audience.

Consider, from this perspective, the problem of staging *Bacchae*. There is at the heart of the play a mystery. Dionysus is bringing to Thebes something mysterious, and Pentheus wants to know what it is. We have the vague sense that just beneath the surface there is something profound, even though it is never made clear *what it is*. Mysteries can of course be solved. But our culture also equips us with the idea of a mere *atmosphere* of mystery, mystery without content, and this is what is generally conveyed by productions of *Bacchae*.

The ancient Greeks would not have understood this. Our word 'mystery' derives from a Greek word (*musterion*) which refers to a kind of *ritual*. There were various Greek mystery-cults, notably those celebrated in various places in honour of Dionysus and those celebrated in honour of Demeter and her daughter Korē at Eleusis near Athens. These cults are sometimes called simply 'the mysteries' (Dionysiac or Eleusinian). But they were not about – or not just about – creating a mysterious atmosphere. They had a specific purpose. Mystic initiation was a rehearsal for death, which subjected the initiands to individual suffering, to the fear of death, and then to a joyful conclusion. The point of this was that they would subsequently, at their real death, be confident of experiencing the transition from suffering to joy that they had experienced in the mystic rehearsal. And it is mystery-cult that Dionysus in *Bacchae* is bringing to Thebes. But none of all this has played any part in the attempts to interpret *Bacchae*, whether by scholars, translators or theatre directors. This makes *Bacchae* the least understood of all ancient dramas. There are three reasons for this failure of understanding.

The first is the secrecy surrounding mystic ritual. It had to be kept secret, because if the initiands had known beforehand of the joyful conclusion, they would not have been sufficiently terrified in the initial stages of the ritual. Aeschylus was prosecuted for profaning secrets of the mystery-cult in his dramas. Euripides in *Bacchae* could not make explicit the joyful outcome of the mystic ritual. The narrative of the *Homeric Hymn to Demeter* concludes with the goddess saying 'blessed is he of men on the earth who has seen these things, but he who is uninitiated and portionless will never have a share of such things when dead below in the dank darkness'. This refers to initiation into the Eleusinian mystery-cult, but the content of the ritual cannot in the (narrated) myth be made explicit. Similarly in *Bacchae*, the chorus of Dionysus' female followers, once arrived in the theatre, sing 'blessed is he who, *eudaimōn* (in right relation to the gods), knowing the *teletas* of the gods, is pure in life and joins his soul to the *thiasos* (sacred band) . . .'. *Teletas* refers to the Dionysiac mystery-cult, but – here again – the content of the ritual cannot in the (dramatized) myth be made explicit. Nevertheless, there are in both *Homeric Hymn* and *Bacchae* strange events which undoubtedly reflect the content of the mystic ritual. Such reflection is typical of the kind of ('aetiological') myth that explains how a ritual came to established. Both *Bacchae* and the *Homeric Hymn to Demeter* embody an aetiological myth of mystic ritual: both deities after long wandering arrive in disguise at a place (Thebes, Eleusis) where they manifest themselves in an epiphany and establish their mystery-cult. Despite the secrecy, we do know a certain amount about what occurred in the ritual, for instance from Christian writers, who did not respect the secrecy, or from some gold strips that were inscribed with mystic formulae and then buried with the initiated dead.

The second reason for the general failure to understand *Bacchae* is more fundamental. With the triumph of Christianity, mystery-cult disappeared from Europe, leaving a large and permanent gap in religious imagination and practice. Because mystery-cult is so alien to our culture, we do not notice the indications of it in *Bacchae*. Mystery-cults of various kinds controlled the passage to the afterlife, and so were of vast significance to many ancient Greeks, and could not fail to be serious rivals to Christianity. An example of this rivalry is provided by Clement of Alexandria (*c*. 150–*c*. 215 AD), a church father who had almost certainly been initiated into pagan mystery-cult before his conversion to Christianity. As a result of his conversion, he did not feel obliged to respect the secrecy of the pagan mystery-cult. And he was aware – unlike all subsequent commentators – of the mystic content of the *Bacchae*. In the last chapter of his *Protrepticus* ('Exhortation') he describes being guided by god as being 'initiated into those holy mysteries' (i.e. Christianity), and then launches an attack on various cult actions depicted in the *Bacchae*, comparing them unfavourably to corresponding elements in what he calls the mysteries of the Word (*tou logou ta mustēria*), the 'truly sacred mysteries' of Christianity. 'These', he says, 'are the bacchic revels (*baccheumata*) of *my* mysteries.' Conversion to Christianity is mystic initiation that is superior to the mystic initiation in *Bacchae*. In its elimination of the mystery-cults, Christianity claimed to be the true mystery.

The third reason for the failure to understand *Bacchae* is this. It is emphasized in the play that the cult that Dionysus brings to Thebes is for *everybody*. 'He wants to have honours from all' (208). This universal participation was a general feature of Dionysiac cult. Such universal accessibility seems to contradict the confinement of secret knowledge to a few in mystery-cult. However, there is less contradiction than it may seem. At the heart of the Dionysiac festival we sometimes find a secret ritual performed by a small group on behalf of the whole *polis*. An example is the Athenian festival called Anthesteria. And I suspect that it was secret ritual of this kind that, at the City Dionysia towards the end of the sixth century BC, was intriguing enough to develop into the public spectacle of tragedy. Moreover, at Eleusis large numbers were initiated every year, with the result that probably most citizens were initiates, and the secret initiation ritual together with its splendid public procession were regarded by the Athenians as important for the well-being of their *polis*. Dionysus in *Bacchae* (39–40) insists that the *polis* must be initiated. The emotion of a ritually enacted transition from the *individual* suffering of death to *collective* joy in the afterlife was of *political* significance. Modern democracy is an arrangement between autonomous individuals, whereas Athenian democracy was reinforced by – perhaps even dependent on – the collective emotion of spectacular rituals.

The mystic transition from suffering to joy, and from individual isolation to joyful community, emerges clearly from what is – though brief – perhaps the best ancient account of mystic ritual, in a fragment (178) of Plutarch. The soul on the point of death:

has an experience like that of those being initiated into the great mysteries ... At first wanderings and tiring runnings to and fro and anxious journeys without completion through darkness; and then before the completion itself all the terrors, shuddering and trembling and sweat and awe. But from this a wonderful light met (him), and pure places and meadows received (him), having voices and choral dancings and solemnities of sacred sounds and holy visions, among which he – now complete and initiated, become free and moving around at large, and crowned – celebrates rites and is with holy and pure men, looking down on the uninitiated and impure mob here (on earth) in mud and darkness trampled by itself and driven together, in fear of death clinging to sufferings through their disbelief in the good things there (in the next world).

Now consider the passage in *Bacchae* in which Pentheus is described as trying to imprison Dionysus (not realizing that he is the god) within his house. I have shown in my Commentary on *Bacchae* how the whole scene reflects in numerous details the ritual of mystic initiation. Here I confine myself to the very strange behaviour of Pentheus. He tries to tie up a bull, and as he does so pants, sweats and bites his lips. Dionysus then creates an earthquake, thunder and lightning, and ignites the tomb of Semele. Pentheus, thinking that the house is on fire, rushes here and there until – thinking that Dionysus has fled – he seizes a sword and rushes into the dark house, whereupon the god makes in the courtyard a light,[1] which Pentheus attacks 'as if slaughtering' the god. The god then brings the house crashing to the ground, and Pentheus collapses exhausted.

Commentators have not thought that this odd behaviour requires a specific explanation. After all, people in tragedy often behave oddly. But the oddity of Pentheus' behaviour and experiences is very specific, both here and elsewhere in *Bacchae*, for instance when he dresses as a maenad and sees two suns and two cities of Thebes. In every case there is – as I show in my Commentary – correspondence with what we know about the experience of mystic initiation. The strange behaviour of Pentheus within the house corresponds in various respects with the account of initiation in Plutarch: the sweating, runnings around vainly, anxiety, exhaustion, darkness and then the miraculous light.[2]

There is more. While Pentheus is trying to imprison Dionysus within the house, the chorus of maenads, followers of the god, are in despair, fearful that they will 'fall into the dark enclosures of Pentheus' (611–12) and fall to the ground. But Dionysus creates the earthquake, and appears to his terrified followers, telling them to stand up, take courage and stop trembling. They respond thus: 'O greatest light of the joyful-crying bacchanal. How I rejoiced to look on you in my lonely desolation' (607–9).

This gives us a contrast between the chorus and Pentheus. The chorus pass

– as in the Plutarch description – from fear, the threat of darkness, falling to the ground, trembling and individual isolation to joyful salvation in which they greet Dionysus as a light. Pentheus too suffers – as an isolated individual – the sufferings of initiation, but when he identifies the miraculous light with Dionysus he does not greet it as his salvation (as the chorus do Dionysus as 'greatest light') but rather attacks it. Pentheus, here and throughout the play, is imagined as the anxious and isolated mystic initiand who *resists* the transition to salvation and community. As is often the case with the aetiological myths of rites of passage, the experience of Pentheus is confined to expressing the negative phase of the ritual. Two necessary secrets of mystic ritual are that the 'death' of the mystic initiand is entirely fictional and that his fearful isolated resistance is in the end followed by the transition to communal joy. But the myth, being public, must not reveal anything that precludes the initial fear that must be created in the intitiand: it describes the death as real, and can do no more than hint at the transition and incorporation into the group. So it is in the myth dramatized in *Bacchae*: Pentheus does in a sense abandon his resistance and dresses as a maenad, but is horribly killed.

I will now say more about two themes that I have only touched on: firstly the identification of the deity with light, and secondly an aspect of the transition that accompanies the appearance of the light, namely replacement of individual isolation by community.

The identification of the deity with light in mystic initiation is not confined to *Bacchae*. For instance, in the *Homeric Hymn to Demeter*, which we saw reflects mystic initiation, Demeter appears in an epiphany in which light shines from her body and the house is filled with light 'as with lightning' (278–80). There is evidence to suggest that the mystic vision at Eleusis might include statues of deities illuminated *from within*. And the mystic Dionysus in Sophocles' *Antigone* is called 'chorus-leader of the fire-breathing stars' (1146–7).[3] Scholars have been so puzzled by the attack made by Pentheus on the light (why attack a light?) that they have changed the Greek text, replacing the word for light with a word for apparition. This completely misses the point. Pentheus is right to identify the light with Dionysus (just as the chorus have called Dionysus in his epiphany a light), but rather than accepting this mystic epiphany as the cause and expression of his salvation (as the chorus do), instead he attacks it: in this persistence of isolated resistance to his own salvation there is something supremely horrific.

It is worth adding that the experience of mystic initation resembles in detail – and seems to have been influenced by knowledge of – the so-called Near-Death Experience (NDE) that has been extensively recorded over the last thirty years or so.[4] Most NDEs exhibit a typical sequence of features that is found in different cultures. A central feature is transition from fear and suffering to bliss, a transition that is often associated with the appearance in the darkness of a wonderful light, which often takes the form of the so-called Being of Light – a light that is also somehow a person. A small minority of NDEs are recalled as unpleasant throughout: they consist of some of the same elements as the positive NDE, which are, however, resisted; and the resistance may end – like Pentheus' – in exhaustion.

Another feature of the blissful conclusion of the NDE is the loss of ego and sense of harmony. In Plutarch's account the transition is from individual isolation (running around vainly in darkness, people trampling on each other) to the company of 'holy and pure men' in a place where there is choral dancing. In *Bacchae* each member of the chorus had fallen to the ground in 'isolated desolation' that was joyfully ended by the mystic epiphany of the god. Notice how, when a goal is scored in football, one team comes joyfully together while each member of the other team is in isolated desolation. Pentheus, in his resistance to the god, maintains through most of the drama an extraordinary degree of individual isolation. Those with whom he comes into contact – Dionysus, the chorus, the servant, Teiresias, Cadmus and the messenger – all try to dissuade him from resisting the new cult, but in vain. The power of the god manifest in the collapse of Pentheus' house, and in the miracles performed by the maenads, makes no difference. When Pentheus does agree to dress as a maenad, this results from a sudden personality change that we feel has been induced by the god. Pentheus is an extreme example of one of those people with whom we are all familiar, stubborn to the point of seeming trapped in himself. He embodies – among other things – the isolated and anxious resistance of the mystic initiand taken to an extreme.

The chorus of maenads, on the other hand, embody the solidarity of the initiated group. For them mystic initiation means 'joining the soul to the *thiasos* (sacred band)'. They dance and sing in unison, as do the *thiasoi* of maenads on the mountainside (725), whose movement is compared to a rising flock of birds (748).

This opposition between the stubborn isolation of the 'tyrant' (775–6) Pentheus and the solidarity of the anonymous chorus members has – we have seen – a ritual dimension. But it also has *political* significance. The Athenians regarded mystic ritual as important for their *polis* (for instance in Aristophanes' *Frogs*). And the opposition is also to be found in a whole number of Athenian tragedies. Think for instance of the ignorant isolation (leading to downfall) of Agamemnon in Aeschylus' *Agamemnon* or of Creon in Sophocles' *Antigone*.

As for the political significance of the opposition, this is something that we can and should appreciate – in our age of destructively acquisitive hyper-individualism. It is a feature of *Bacchae* that is easier to convey in our theatre than is mystery-cult. And so I end with an aspect of Pentheus' destructive hyper-individualism that has special resonance for us. I mean his obsession with money. When urged by Teiresias to accept the god, Pentheus accuses him of being motivated by the prospect of fees for performing the new rituals (255–7). That says more about Pentheus than it does about Teiresias.[5] When Pentheus is asked by Dionysus whether he would like to see the maenads sitting together on the mountains, he replies that he would. This introduces Pentheus' sudden strange compliance and eventual death, and is the turning point of the play. What Pentheus actually says is 'Yes, I would give an enormous weight of gold to do so' (812).

Pentheus sees the motives of Teiresias, and even the sight of secret Dionysiac cult, in terms of money. Such a sad state is – two and a half millennia later in the history of money – well known to us. We are reminded of another Greek myth – of Midas, whose touch turned everything to gold, with disastrous consequences. The chorus of *Bacchae* ask what is the best thing, and answer by comparing the uncertainties of wealth and power unfavourably with the permanent happiness of the here and now bestowed by mystic initiation.[6] Midas is a man of money who puts the same question – 'what is best?' – to another follower of Dionysus, Silenus, and receives the answer that best for humankind is never to have been born, second best to die as soon as possible. From the perspective of the ancient wisdom of nature embodied in Silenus, the man of money is pitiful. But one version of the Midas story has a happy ending: he is initiated into Dionysiac mystery-cult, recognizes Silenus as a fellow member of the *thiasos*, is saved from his own monetary power by Dionysus, and thereafter dwells in the wild.[7] In the highly political genre of tragedy, on the other hand, Pentheus is killed and his family exiled, but all the other citizens receive the benefit in perpetuity of the cult that in the prologue Dionysus promised to establish in Thebes.[8] As so often in Athenian tragedy, the demise of the powerful individual or family is accompanied by new and lasting benefit for the community.

Notes

1 I read in 628 *kelainōn* (genitive plural) and in 630 the manuscript reading *phōs*: see my Commentary.
2 If Plutarch's account is drawn specifically from the Eleusinian mystery-cult, then either the Eleusinian and Dionsyiac experiences of initiation were similar, or the *Bacchae* passage conflates the Dionysiac with the Eleusinian experience – as does Plato's *Phaedrus* and Aristophanes' *Frogs*.
3 See my *Cosmology and the Polis* (Cambridge University Press 2012) 41–2.

4 See my *Cosmology and the Polis* 277.
5 Creon in Sophocles' *Antigone* and Oedipus in his *Oedipus Rex* also accuse
   Teiresias of being motivated by money. To Creon Teiresias responds that he
   (Creon) is *projecting* onto him (Teiresias) the typical preoccupation of the
   tyrant with money (*Antigone* 1062, a line always mistranslated): i.e. he accuses
   Creon of being the one preoccupied with money.
6 897–912, a passage misunderstood by Dodds: see my Commentary.
7 For references see my 'Dionysus, Money, and Drama' in *Arion* 11.2. (2003),
   17 n. 5.
8 The passage in which Dionysus presumably announced its establishment has
   been lost from the manuscript. But of course Dionysus had no reason to
   suddenly change his mind.

'A Big Laugh': Horrid Laughter in Euripides' *Bacchae*

James Morwood

If I'd known what I was laughing at when I was laughing, I wouldn't have laughed.

(overheard by Alan Ayckbourn after a performance of
one of his darker plays)

In one of his Elizabethan essays published in 1934, T.S. Eliot suggested that we should take Christopher Marlowe's grisly *Jew of Malta* 'not as a tragedy, or as a "tragedy of blood", but as a farce'. He went on to say that he was talking of 'the farce of the old English humour, the terribly serious, even savage comic humour ...' (p. 28). In a famous Royal Shakespeare Company staging of the play by Clifford Williams in 1965, I recollect the audience falling about with laughter as it responded with horror to the hellish cosmos which Marlowe was exploring. Then in 1979 Nicholas Brooke developed Eliot's insight – though strangely without acknowledgement – in his *Horrid Laughter in Jacobean Tragedy*. He justly remarks that 'Lear's fool should be funny if he can, but his jokes do not relieve – they aggravate the tension. The Gravedigger in *Hamlet* is lighter, but he is light about death, just as Macbeth's Porter is about Hell. And so on ...' (p. 4).

Michael Silk, in his *Aristophanes and the Definition of Comedy* (2000), clearly believed that the appreciation of the profoundly serious jesting which tragedy can so eloquently exploit had not meaningfully spread to students of Greek tragedy. He remarked that 'it is easy to point to amusing scenes or characters in tragedy, even if the amusement often has a black edge: the porter in *Macbeth*, the foot-shuffling guard in *Antigone*, the cross-dressing in *Bacchae* are cases in point' (p. 59); but he still felt the need to conduct an extended discussion to break down unreal oppositions between comedy and tragedy (pp. 42–97).

As Silk pointed out, Euripides' *Bacchae* contains one scene with obvious comic content. In this essay I shall look at that episode and three others in an attempt to show how 'horrid laughter' is evoked and ultimately suppressed to supremely tragic effect in this tremendous play.

The drama gets off to a forceful and alarming start with the appearance of Dionysus; it is possible that the potential for a comic undertone to the play's development is suggested if the character wears a smiling mask; we shall return to that later. Then, in the first episode, a charming if poignant tone pervades the tragedy as the two old men, the blind prophet Tiresias and the formerly heroic ex-king Cadmus, enter in Bacchic attire: they carry *thyrsoi*, the Bacchic wands; they are wearing fawnskins; their heads are crowned with ivy shoots (176–7, 180); and they are planning to dance and shake their grey heads in worship of Dionysus (184–5). It is, of course, important to acknowledge a deeply serious function of the scene: it emphasizes that Dionysiac worship is open to everybody, old as well as young, and male as well as female (we have just met the female chorus of Bacchae and all the women of Thebes are already out on the mountain celebrating the god). In Aristophanes' contemporary comedy *Frogs* the old men dance off their age in the Bacchic procession (345–50) and Plato's *Laws* makes clear the importance of the rejuvenating dance of old men at Dionysiac state festivals (666b). Indeed, in his stimulating edition of the play, Richard Seaford disavows any comic element in this scene (note at 170–369). Yet the visual effect of the two doddery old men in festive garb surely cannot be so easily ignored; though he immediately rejects it, Cadmus certainly raises the possibility that he may be viewed as shaming his old age by his Dionysiac behaviour (204–5); and the cynicism with which he suggests to Pentheus that, even if Dionysus is not a god, it would be advantageous to buy in to the lie (333–6), suggests that his worship of the divinity is less than totally sincere. Later Tiresias will add to this sense of ebbing optimism when he says that 'it is shameful for two old men to fall. Still, let come what will come. Men [*or* we] must be slaves to the Bacchic god, the son of Zeus' (365–6). Pentheus' reaction to the sight of the two men, a big laugh (πολὺν γέλων, 250), is, of course, crudely one-dimensional, a key to his unsympathetic characterization at this point of the play. The humour is gentle and yet at times the episode carries an intense emotional charge which is anything but funny (e.g. 278–83, 306–9). The laughter does not in fact subvert the serious purport of the scene, as Seaford seems to fear it would. Indeed, by locating it in a broader range of human emotions, it validates it.

Dionysus now makes his first appearance in his human form. The messenger who brings him in tells Pentheus that he was laughing (γελῶν, 439) as he handed himself over to the king's men. This is often taken to indicate that the actor wears a smiling mask (see above) and there is no strong reason to disbelieve this: the god is portrayed as 'smiling in his dark eyes' in the Homeric hymn where his capture by pirates is described (6–15) and his mask-like face is sometimes depicted in vase painting with a smile. However, while it would make good dramatic sense if the god who presides over the play were to be represented as smiling coolly and quizzically each time he appears, we must bear in mind that the word applied to him in 439 tells us that he was not smiling but laughing. As well as amusement, his laughter denotes contempt for the human efforts to control him. There is also a latent sense of danger which will explode with terrifying power at 1020–3 when the chorus call upon him to destroy Pentheus:

> Come, o Bacchus, as a wild beast, and with laughing (γελῶντι) face throw your deadly noose around this hunter of the Bacchae when he has fallen beneath the maenads' herd.

I am reminded of another play from the Elizabethan/Jacobean period, John Webster's *The Duchess of Malfi*, in which one courtier remarks, 'The Lord Ferdinand laughs' and another adds, 'like a deadly cannon' (3.2.54). Not only does Dionysus play a verbal and psychological cat-and-mouse game with Pentheus, but still more alarmingly he submits him to abject humiliation (616, 632) in the palace miracle episode. He describes his victim as he engaged in frantic, indeed in laughable activity which proved totally futile, and then dropped his sword in exhaustion (616–35).

The degradation of Pentheus will be re-enacted on stage, far more devastatingly and to far more blatant comic effect, when, after the famous ἅ (810), which serves as a kind of hinge on which the play revolves, Dionysus offers to take Pentheus to see the women on the mountain and persuades him to put on female dress, supposedly to spy on the Bacchae in safety. Despite feeling shame at the thought of donning women's attire (828) and being alert to the comic potential of his cross-dressing ('γγελᾶν, 842 – though it is possible that he is here referring to the Bacchae laughing over him in triumph more generally), the king, now pathetically under the god's control, falls in with the proposal. We must imagine Dionysus dressing him offstage, and then he appears in drag, hallucinating that he can see two suns and two cities of Thebes and that Dionysus has assumed the form of a bull (918–22); but the tone changes with Pentheus' insistence on getting the details of his Bacchic dress correct (925–44).

How precisely can we identify this new tone? One possible clue lies in the fact that the scene may well owe something to the episode in *Thesmophoriazusae*, Aristophanes' uproarious comedy of 412/411 BC (only a few years before the composition of *Bacchae*) in which Euripides himself is shown shaving, singeing and putting women's clothes on a character called Inlaw so that the latter can escape detection at the women's festival identified in the play's title (213–68). Inlaw's instruction to Euripides to 'sort me out around the legs' (256) is echoed in *Bacchae* in the following exchange:

> **Dionysus**   . . . the pleats of your dress do not hang evenly to below your ankle.
>
> **Pentheus**   I think so too, at least by my right foot. But on this side the robe is straight at the tendon.

(935–8)

The dramatic durability of this cross-dressing scene is evidenced by the riffs the anarchic playwright Joe Orton played upon it in his 1960s farce *What the Butler Saw*; a stage direction even specifies a 'leopard-spotted dress'.

Seaford, however, is deaf to the invitation to a comic reading of the *Bacchae* scene, arguing that transvestism was a feature of the Dionysiac ritual as a means of detaching the initiand from his previous identity and that Pentheus' linen dress is also his funerary dress, linen being the cloth in which Egyptians and 'those who are called Orphics and Bacchics' bury their dead (Herodotus 2.81, Seaford n. at 912–76). Insisting thus on the fundamental seriousness of the scene, he denounces as misleading Bernd Seidensticker's view, expressed in his book on comic elements in Greek tragedy, that Euripides is here exploiting the comic possibilities of this classic theme of comedy. It may be that Seidensticker is somewhat rash to invoke Brandon Thomas's farce *Charley's Aunt* as a parallel, but I for one feel that he hits the nail on the head when he quotes Bernard Shaw's reaction to Ibsen's *Wild Duck* as an apt way of regarding this episode: 'to look on with horror and pity at a profound tragedy, shaking with laughter all the time at an irresistible comedy . . .'.[1] To Shaw's remark, we might add the further horror of our sudden realization of exactly what we are laughing at. We are surely responding to the kind of 'terribly serious, even savage comic humour' which Eliot found in *The Jew of Malta*, the 'horrid laughter' that Nicholas Brooke identified in Elizabethan/Jacobean tragedy more generally. To view Euripides' scene in this light will enable it to allow scope for multiple responses, including Seaford's.

After Pentheus and Dionysus have left for the mountain, the chorus erupt in a racing dochmiac rhythm in a terrifying song urging the Bacchae to kill the Theban king. Then a messenger enters to tell how Pentheus, after recognizing his errors (*hamartiai*, 1121), has been torn to pieces by the women:

One of them carried an arm, another a foot still in its shoe, his ribs were laid bare as they tore him apart, and with their bloody hands they all played ball with Pentheus' flesh.

(1133–6)

Agave now comes on carrying the head of Pentheus and is followed later by Cadmus, who is probably accompanied by attendants bringing on the dismembered remains of Pentheus on a bier. After Cadmus has led his daughter to a full awareness of what she has done, there is clearly a gap in the text. A third-century AD writer called Apsines tells us that here Pentheus's mother, 'taking each of his limbs in her hands, laments over each of them'.

How are we to respond to this grisly sequence? There is manifestly horror here; there are pity and terror aplenty. But with the profusion of body parts we must also come to terms with an element of the grotesque and macabre, possibly even the blackest of black humour. A scene from Webster's *Duchess of Malfi* may help us to locate our reactions here. In Act 4, Scene 1, the Duchess's deranged and incestuous brother appears to touch her hand with his in the dark. In fact, he leaves the hand behind and when the lights go up the Duchess discovers that she is holding a dead man's hand. This is immediately followed by the display of wax figures of her husband and their children 'appearing as if they were dead', and the despairing Duchess duly believes that they are so. Bernard Shaw dubbed Webster the 'Tussaud laureate' (after the celebrated waxworks, no doubt specifically its notorious chamber of horrors) but his implication of scary sensationalism on Webster's part is surely unjust. The playwright is risking the danger of tumbling into the luridly macabre in order to emphasize the terror of the Duchess in her isolation from her loved ones and the appalling psychological pressures to which she is being subjected. With his waxworks display, is he daring us to laugh? We are certainly skirting grotesquely comic territory. But any laughter will stick in our throats. The tension between our emotional responses will take us to the heart of Webster's universe in which, as Rupert Brooke said, 'human beings are writhing grubs in an immense night' (1956: 136–7). In *Bacchae* the temptation to laugh at this scene will of course have been exacerbated by what we have witnessed earlier in the tragedy; but, as in *The Duchess*, we choke back our laughter and in doing so we come closer to a full realization of how horrifying the episode actually is. The play's progress from the affectionate comedy of Tiresias and Cadmus in the first episode through the black humour of the cross-dressing scene to the extinction of laughter in the Cadmus/Agave scene is a journey into the heart of darkness. 'The horror! The horror!'

Note

1 Seidensticker (1982) 214–16. In his justly admired edition of *Bacchae*,
   E.R. Dodds remarks, 'As Hermann said, the groundlings will laugh and are
   meant to laugh; but for the sensitive spectator amusement is transmuted
   into pity and terror.' The invocation of the groundlings, a feature of the
   Elizabethan theatre, is interesting but the distinction between reactions
   from different parts of the audience seems forced. (Hamlet's well-known
   aspersions on the groundlings were, I take it, intended to get a rise out of
   them.) Shaw's formulation is to be preferred.

8

New Religion and Old in Euripides' *Bacchae*

David Kovacs

One of the reasons why *Bacchae* has seemed such a difficult play to interpret is that it has seemed to be at variance with what its scholarly interpreters thought they knew about Euripides' religious views. It was natural for scholars intent on understanding ancient writers to turn for help to what those writers' contemporaries said about them. In the case of Euripides the principal contemporary witness was the comedies of Aristophanes. In some of these (*Acharnians, Thesmophoriazusae, Frogs*) Euripides appears as a character; in others he comes in for mention, mostly of a mocking kind. From the sum of these comic references scholars from the beginning of the nineteenth century concluded that to his contemporaries Euripides appeared, in his artistic aims, as a wayward modernist, bent on lowering the tone of tragedy by taking the heroic figures of myth down to the level of ordinary mortals, bringing on adulterous women and other morally dubious characters, and leavening its heroic grandeur by introducing loquacious slaves and untransmuted lumps of quotidian life. Likewise, Aristophanes seemed to be saying, the divine dimension, which bulks so large in the tragedies of Aeschylus and Sophocles, was deliberately undercut by Euripides, who, it was alleged, was an associate of various radical philosophers of the late fifth century who denied the reality of the Olympian pantheon.

Since there is little else by way of contemporary evidence for Euripides' aims (but some important exceptions are noted below), it is not surprising that these scholars took Aristophanes' presentation seriously. In the early decades of the nineteenth century it was customary to set this evidence down to Euripides' discredit. Euripides' artistic and theological waywardness was regarded as proved. His work was contrasted with the classical perfection of Sophocles, whose theological orthodoxy and artistic propriety were regarded as unassailable.[1] By the last quarter of the nineteenth century, however, many scholars converted what was a damning verdict into a commendation: Euripides' work, in criticizing received notions of the gods and morality, represented an advance of the human spirit. The greatest German Hellenist of his day, Ulrich von Wilamowitz-Moellendorff, chose Euripides as the subject of so much of his work in part because he regarded him as in advance of his time. (His almost total neglect of Sophocles seems to have had its cause in the general perception of Sophocles as an unreflectively pious poet.) Gilbert Murray, Regius Professor of Greek at Oxford and a supporter of various liberal causes such as the League of Nations, saw Euripides as a champion of the human spirit against the narrowness of inherited and unexamined religious views.[2] Thus, whether they damned him or praised him for it, scholars were agreed that Euripides' plays offered a challenge to his countrymen's view of the gods.

Some of the extant plays seemed easy to interpret along these lines. Thus *Medea* seemed to many a purely human drama without any theological dimension at all (Medea's miraculous escape at the end was discounted as a contrivance to permit her a more complete revenge). And the divine figures in *Hippolytus* – the spiteful Aphrodite callously ruining Phaedra, and Artemis promising to destroy Aphrodite's favourite mortal by way of revenge – have been read as a satirical treatment of conventional myth.

But *Bacchae* puzzled many who were convinced that Euripides was a sceptic. Here was a play in which the god Dionysus is shown from the first both as a powerful divinity, able to work his will in the world, and as a giver of an ecstatic bliss that the Chorus of his Asian worshippers describe in terms that are not obviously satirical and that some have found quite attractive and even moving. By contrast, his opponent Pentheus is portrayed as a narrow-minded man who believes that this religion is merely an excuse for sexual licence on the part of the women of Thebes and who reacts with contempt to people such Cadmus who take a different view. He is also shown to have a weakness in him that that allows his divine adversary to persuade him to spy on his female subjects, an act that leads to his death at their hands. There is little here to tempt anyone to regard Pentheus as the portrait of a heroic champion of rationalism or a martyr of the Enlightenment. And the attractiveness of the picture of Dionysiac bliss in the work of someone thought to be a determined sceptic has seemed rather hard to explain.

Bacchae, as we know from a scholiastic notice on Aristophanes' *Frogs*, was written at the end of Euripides' life (it was produced only after his death). The last year or so of Euripides' life, we are told, was spent in Macedonia at the court of Archelaus, who invited a number of prominent poets and other artists to take up residence in the Macedonian capital of Pella.[3] Some scholars have proposed that Euripides, in the hinterlands of Macedonia, somehow underwent a conversion and came to understand the value of the religious beliefs of the majority of his fellow Athenians.[4] This colourful idea, unfortunately, has very little to recommend it, being mere speculation designed to bring *Bacchae* into some kind of relation to the (presumed) tenor of Euripides' other works.

In fact, the consensus that saw Euripides in those terms was based on only one witness, a comic poet, whose business was not to render nuanced judgements on his contemporaries but to be amusing at their expense. (In most cases where we can judge, Aristophanes had no genuine animus against those he lampoons: they were merely convenient targets for his comic muse.) If we look at the comments his characters make, it is unmistakable that truth is among the last and least of his concerns. It cannot even be maintained that the picture he gives differs from the truth only by comic exaggeration: sometimes there is no truth to it at all.[5] Those who think that Euripides as presented in *Frogs* is a comic exaggeration of reality, rather than something quite untethered from it, should consider whether the same could be maintained for his Aeschylus. In that play 'Aeschylus' is presented as always grand, one who never introduced the lowly and everyday in his plays, but see *Choephoroe* 753–62, Greek tragedy's only discussion of toilet training.[6] He claims (1018–22) that his plays encouraged his countrymen to be brave soldiers, but the play he instances is *Seven Against Thebes*, where the war in question is a fratricidal strife unlikely to serve as anyone's model. He claims (1043–4) that *he* in contrast to Euripides never put wicked women on the stage (Clytaemestra?). He claims that he never dressed his noble characters in rags, but see the end of his *Persae*, where Xerxes enters in ragged clothing. In fact the main determinant of an Aristophanic portrait is that it be both amusing and 'comically colourable'.[7] The traits given to 'Aeschylus' and 'Euripides' are amusing, and the contrast between them makes comic sense, but they are without value as an index of how either Aristophanes or his contemporaries really regarded them.

In addition, however, to the inherent unreliability of a comic witness, we have other indications that Euripides was not regarded as a determined outsider and critic of Athenian beliefs.[8] First, during his lifetime he was permitted to put on his plays (at public expense and at the City Dionysia, a highly visible public venue) seemingly whenever he had plays to put on.[9] Secondly, when prose sources mentioning Euripides begin to appear, as they do in the fourth century, it is noteworthy that orators such as Demosthenes and Lycurgus quote Euripides, as they do other poets, for sentiments they expect their audiences to accept. (By contrast, they do not quote philosophers, Sophists, or anyone whose views could be regarded as radical.) Furthermore, when Plato's Socrates in the *Republic* criticizes tragedy for its harmful and benighted view of the gods, he considers Euripides to be as harmful as the rest and not in any way an enlightened thinker. There is no reliable evidence that Euripides was seen as a Sophist or as anti-religious or as anything other than a respected tragic poet. We need not reconcile the presentation of Dionysus and the Dionysiac religion in *Bacchae* with beliefs about Euripides the evidence for which is so tenuous. A better idea might be to look at the text of the play and see how this religion is presented.[10]

The first thing to notice is something that so much of earlier scholarship tried to explain away, that the play exhibits the religion of Dionysus as a phenomenon whose divine warrant as the action proceeds is rendered more and more unmistakable. Though Dionysus is disguised as a mortal hierophant and appears as a divinity only at the play's end, the run of the action shows his power: the Servant's account of the fearlessness of the Stranger during his unresisted capture and of the miraculous escape of his bacchants, Dionysus' eerie calm in the face of Pentheus' questioning, his effortless escape from imprisonment in the palace, the report of Pentheus' servant, who describes the benign miracles of the maenads' worship followed by their miraculous routing of the Theban men arrayed against them – all these attest to something superhuman. This power is all the more impressive for the placidity – the languor, even – of the god in his human disguise, who shows not the slightest effort as he works miracles that impress everyone on the stage except Pentheus.

Throughout all this part of the play, Dionysus is mighty also in another sense in that his worship is described as powerfully attractive and a source of great bliss, a point made from their respective angles of vision by the Servant (436–48), the Messenger (680–713) and not least by the Chorus, who extol it as combining union with nature and union with one's fellow worshippers. Their words also provide a large dose of what Greek poetic and prose sources regard as basic sound sense, for example that chasing after what is impossibly distant is foolish, but that putting away care and taking joy in the present moment is the formula for such happiness as mortals can attain to. This presentation is made all the more attractive by the high poetry in which it is expressed.

There is a complementary truth, the reverse side of the tapestry, that is expressed in the last third of the play: what happens when the giver of such bliss is rejected and vilified. We must admit – indeed I would insist – that Dionysus in his revenge is devastating, and that the list of his victims includes not only Pentheus and Agave, who both denied his godhead, but also Cadmus, who did not. But the revelation of this other side would not, I would argue, have alienated an ancient audience or made them think that the bliss portrayed in the early part of the play was somehow unreal or unworthy. In the Greek poetic tradition the gods are not forgiving: those who diminish their *timê* (honour) are punished without mercy.[11] And collateral damage to the associates of those who offend them is not something they take pains to avoid.[12]

The second point to be noticed is a contradiction – at the very least we must call it a tension – that Euripides has installed in the heart of his play. When a playwright shapes his story in a way that violates realism and consistency, interpreters had better pay close attention since this will be a strong clue to the way the poet intends his audience to understand the story. Contradictions, after all, ought not to be gratuitous but to have some explicable purpose, and if we pay attention to them, we get a clue to the poet's aims. The contradiction is that the Dionysiac religion is presented as both new and old. Pentheus, like the Thracian king Lycurgus and other opponents of Dionysus, is resisting the introduction of a new god into his city. Dionysus is not only new to Thebes but was also born only a short time before the play's dramatic date: his grandfather, who made a shrine of the place where Zeus's lightning burnt up the god's pregnant mother, is still alive and fairly vigorous. So Dionysus is a newcomer and a young god. Yet, on the other side, those who speak in support of him make statements that identify his worship with 'what over length of time has always been customary and is grounded in nature' (the Chorus at 895–6).[13] In the dialogue between Cadmus and Teiresias we find warnings, directed implicitly to Pentheus, against 'despising the gods, when one is a mortal', 'playing the sophist where the gods are concerned', and ignoring 'the traditions we have received from our fathers, old as time itself', traditions 'no argument will overthrow, whatever subtleties have been invented by deep thinkers'. How can the religion of a god born within living memory be recommended on the grounds that it is the 'faith of our fathers' and a faith that has existed from time immemorial? Surely Euripides could have had Cadmus and the Chorus recommend this worship without applying to it a form of praise that is manifestly at variance with the facts of the play. If so, he must have had a reason for violating ordinary realism here.

There is a further fact to explain: from Pentheus himself we never hear that it is the newness of maenadism to which he objects, and he says nothing in defence of more established religious practices that might be thought diminished or threatened by the introduction of the new. The only thing he says about rites or practices already in use in Thebes is that Teiresias in attempting to introduce a new divinity is merely trying to increase the income he derives from augury, which rather implies that both old religion and new are motivated by profit.

Resistance to a new god might be a matter of mere conservatism, of clinging to the old ways and old worship. It might be a matter of mere ignorance that the new god is a god. A play on these lines would have an effect quite different from *Bacchae*, where Pentheus is not demonstrably pious toward the old gods and where his disbelief in Dionysus flies in the face of his servants' evidence and is therefore not merely ignorance. Furthermore, the worship of Dionysus is several times described in terms that equate it with religion *tout court*, that whole aspect of human life that is regarded as both immemorially old and worthy of veneration. The conclusion is hard to escape that Euripides intended his audience to regard Pentheus as emblematic not of religious conservatism but of a stance of general disbelief, an unwillingness to revere what the majority of people revere. In mythical terms, a person like Pentheus is a *theomachos*, a fighter against a particular god. But Euripides has broadened *theomachos* so that it means a man at war with religion in general.

Why did the poet do so? I think that there is only one plausible answer. Pentheus is made into an opponent of religion in general – and Cadmus and the Chorus are made to praise the religion of Dionysus as religion *tout court* – because Euripides means to turn this story of long-ago resistance to a new faith into a fable for his own time. The play is not an antiquarian piece about what may have happened in the distant past when Dionysiac religion struggled for acceptance in Greece. It is a piece designed to resonate with the controversies of the poet's own day.

The principal themes touched by the defenders of maenadism in the play read like a response to the writings and teachings of the Sophists. The Sophists, Greece's first professional educators, taught young men, among other things, the skill in speaking that was necessary for success in public life. Some of them engaged in interesting speculation on such things as the origins of human culture or wrote engagingly on what is involved when we experience the fictions of poetry. But some of their other themes, to thinkers such as Socrates and Plato, wore a more disquieting and destructive aspect. Several Sophists were either cool or hostile to the idea of the divine. Prodicus of Ceos suggested that the individual gods were simply names for beneficent features of the phenomenal world, Hephaestus for fire, Dionysus for wine, etc. And Critias, who was one of the Sophists' most gifted pupils and became the ruthless leader of the Thirty Tyrants, who ruled Athens after her defeat in the Peloponnesian War, appears to have put forward the argument that the gods are merely the invention of some clever man who wanted to frighten people into obeying the law even when no one was looking.[14] A current of thought sceptical vis-à-vis religion is discernible in the last third or so of the fifth century. When Cadmus and the Chorus, speaking in defence of maenadism, offer a defence of religion in general, it is hard not to suppose that this is a reply to contemporary speculation, inserted into the play at the cost of a noticeable contradiction.

Another and more specific point of intersection with contemporary

intellectual debates is discernible in the following string of passages, some
already cited in part:

> Unbridled tongues and lawless (*anomos*) folly end in misery. But the life
> of peace and of wisdom remains unshaken and holds houses together.
> For the gods in heaven, though they dwell far off, look down on mortal
> doings. To be clever is not wisdom, and it is not wise to think thoughts
> not mortal. The span of our life is short: this being so, who would pursue
> vast designs but then fail to win present happiness? Only madmen and
> fools have a character like that.
>
> (386–401)

> (Dionysus) hates the man who does not make this his aim, by day and
> through the sweetness of night to live a life of bliss, and to keep his heart
> and his thoughts wise, far from men of excess. What the multitude of
> ordinary men believe-and-practice (*enomise*) and make use of, that will
> I accept.
>
> (424–31)

> Though it moves slowly, yet the strength of the gods is sure. It brings to
> book those mortals who honour heedlessness and in their maddened
> hearts do not exalt the divine. The gods in various ways hide from view
> the footfall of Time; they hunt down the impious man. Never is it right
> to think and to act above the laws (*nomôn*). It costs but little to believe
> that this has might: the divine, whatever it may be, and what has always
> been lawful (*nomimon*) over the length of time and is grounded in
> nature (*phusis*).
>
> (882–95)

In making these defenders of Dionysus speak thus the poet seems to be
taking a stance on the issue, constantly aired in the late fifth century, of the
nature of *nomos* (law or custom) and its relation to *phusis* (nature). The
distinction between *nomos* and *phusis* is an obvious one to make: travel and
familiarity with foreign cultures made the Greeks aware that in one society it
may be customary to do A and in another society to do B or even the exact
reverse of A. But it was not inevitable that custom or law should be thereby
discredited and nullified. The historian and ethnographer Herodotus, whose
familiarity with the non-Greek world was greater than perhaps anyone else's
in his day, still ascribes an undeniable power to the *nomos* that obtains both
in Greece and elsewhere. A salient example of this comes from a famous
digression in the *Histories* (3.38) and its immediate context. The digression

concerns Darius, king of the Persians. Darius' entourage contained both
Greeks and some Indians called Callatiae, whose method of disposing of
their dead was to eat them. Darius asked the Greeks what would induce them
to eat the bodies of their dead fathers, and they replied that they could never
be induced to do so. Then, with the Greeks standing by and listening to what
was said through an interpreter, he asked the Callatiae what would induce
them to burn the bodies of their dead fathers. They reacted with horror at the
very thought.

The story shows an acquaintance with cultural variation, the knowledge
that the custom of one's own group is often directly counter to that of another
group. Yet Herodotus himself (though this point is often neglected) draws no
antinomian conclusions from this story. This is clear from the larger context.
Before this digression Herodotus is discussing Darius' predecessor Cambyses,
who conquered Egypt. While he was in Egypt, Cambyses committed many
heinous crimes not only against his family and his court, but also against
the Egyptian religion since he killed the bull the Egyptians regarded as the
incarnation of their god Apis. This, Herodotus says, was the act of a madman.
He cites Darius' talk with the Greeks and the Callatiae not to show the
irrationality of believing in one's own customs but to show how mad an act
it is to outrage custom. His reason for thinking that Cambyses' act was
crazy is that Cambyses, though not sound of mind before, went mad because
he committed this act. That is to say, he was driven mad by the gods he
had outraged. In other words Herodotus found it plausible to suggest that
the customs of the Egyptians were protected by a divine sanction, and that
Cambyses, though a Persian with different customs, was punished for
outraging them. So *nomos* is not merely human and conventional.

This same theme, the obligatoriness of *nomos* and the divine sanctions
that give force to its precepts, comes out with clarity in the work of Herodotus'
friend, the tragic poet Sophocles. In his *Antigone* the Theban king Creon
makes a decree that the body of Polynices, who brought an army against his
own city, is to be left unburied. Antigone defies this edict and buries her
brother. When she is caught, she tells Creon that his edict has no force:

> In my eyes it was not Zeus who had made this proclamation, nor did
> Justice who dwells with the gods below ordain laws of this kind among
> men. I did not think that your proclamation, being merely mortal, had so
> much strength that it could overrule the unwritten and sure ordinances
> (*nomima*) of the gods. These do not live just now and yesterday but
> forever, and no one knows whence they have come.
>
> (*Antigone* 450–57)

The obligation to bury the members of one's own family is one of those customs, of immemorial antiquity and divine origin, that no human authority can overthrow. Eventually Creon sees how wrong he has been, but by that time it is too late to save the life of his son and his wife. Reality, even for a king, is not infinitely malleable. The gods in the end are guarantors of *nomos*.

In the hands of certain of Euripides' contemporaries, however, *nomos* comes to be regarded as mere convention and is contrasted with *phusis*, nature. The Sophists held that *nomos*, being variable from place to place and a human invention, had no binding validity. If you violate what is customary in your society, it will result in harm to you only if you are caught. By contrast, if you go against your *phusis*, your natural tendency toward pleasure and self-aggrandisement, you are harmed by being deprived of what you want, whether or not anyone is aware of it. *Nomos* is a 'fetter' on nature and something the individual is better off without. We see a reflex of this idea in the argument of Callias in Plato's *Gorgias* and of Thrasymachus in the *Republic* that *nomos* is merely a construct whose purpose is to enable the majority to put a check on strong individuals and prevent them from aggrandising themselves. Such strong individuals should not feel themselves bound by the community's laws. By nature the strong take what they can, unfettered by law, and the weak are simply their slaves. The non-human world, which knows no law, is the model for the successful individual,[15] who will as far as possible ignore *nomos* in the pursuit of self-gratification.

In coming to the defence of Dionysus in the passages cited above, Cadmus and the Chorus mount a defence of *nomos*. Plato's answer to the Sophists' disparagement of *nomos* was to show that the conduct enshrined in it, so far from making those who practise it miserable, is the route to happiness; that justice, temperance, courage and wisdom are the necessary and sufficient conditions for a flourishing life. Euripides, who had not thought of Plato's arguments and could not have incorporated them into his play even if he had, proceeds by other means. In line 331 Cadmus tells Pentheus not to be so clever as to dwell beyond the bounds of established custom and deny the gods, and he cites the punishment of Actaeon. In line 995 the Chorus call down the justice of the gods on Pentheus for being *atheos*, *anomos* and *adikos*: without gods, law or justice. In lines 895-6, quoted above, they go so far as to equate what has always been lawful over the long stretch of time with 'what is grounded in nature'.[16] So much, they seem to be saying to the Sophists, for your exaltation of *phusis* at the expense of *nomos*. *Nomos* is valid *by nature*, and its warrant is divine. In this the sentiments expressed by the Chorus align impressively with those of Herodotus and Sophocles mentioned above.

A third aspect of the power of religion in this play is to be seen, I will argue, in the manner in which Pentheus' death is brought about. From line 780, when he gives the order that the Theban soldiery should arm themselves, Pentheus is determined to use military force against the bacchants. But shortly after line 810 he abandons this plan, deciding instead to go to see the women in person. He is persuaded by Dionysus that the safest way to do this is to disguise himself as a maenad. The change of plan from military action to espionage would seem to require motivation, especially since it means that Pentheus is putting himself at the mercy of someone he has previously regarded as his enemy.

It has often been maintained that Pentheus – who had earlier expressed the belief that the women on the mountain were engaging in illicit sex – has now been seized by the desire to watch them doing so, and that this is why he is lured into the spying that causes his death. Yet neither in the exchange at 810–46 nor in that at 913–76 is there any indication that Pentheus still believes the women are misbehaving sexually: he accepts Dionysus' description of them as *sunkathêmenas*, 'sitting with one another' (810), a participle that in no way suggests intercourse (we might expect *sunkeimenas*), either with men (never mentioned) or with one another. There is nothing to counter the impression this makes that Pentheus has abandoned his earlier suspicion.[17] There is a good reason why Euripides has not written a scene in which Pentheus is destroyed by a perverted desire to watch others copulate: a Pentheus crippled by scopophilia would not only be thematically irrelevant but would lack the representative quality we expect in a tragic protagonist.

If we leave out of account a sexual perversion that is not mentioned or hinted at in the text, what explains Pentheus' change of heart? There are indications that it is the attraction of religion, and not of sex, that motivates Pentheus in the two scenes. When Dionysus suggests dressing as a woman, he at first rejects the idea. But he is much more accepting of other aspects of the plan. When at line 834 he asks 'Will you give me anything else in addition?' he seems to be asking to be given some piece of equipment associated with maenadism. When Dionysus offers to give him a bacchic wand (the thyrsus), he expresses no reluctance to take it up. When he emerges again disguised as a woman, his mind is filled with the details of the rite in which he is about to participate. His new long locks have come loose from his headdress because he has been practising the motions of bacchic ecstasy (930–1). He wants to be instructed in the best way to hold the thyrsus (941–2). That this is not done merely in the interests of a more effective disguise is strongly suggested by lines 945–6 and 949–50, where he imagines that he will have superhuman powers. Pentheus anticipates being a bacchant himself and having the bacchic experience.

We should recall his earlier fascination (465–507) with the mystical bliss that Dionysus promises. In that earlier scene Pentheus asked about the nature of the rites (469–72) and what benefit they conferred to those who practise them (473), but Dionysus had refused to tell him since he was not initiated. Dionysus' refusal, Pentheus had replied, was merely a trick to make him want to hear all the more (475), an admission that his interest has in fact been piqued. Pentheus rejects Dionysiac worship with part of his mind, but it still exercises a strong fascination on him. In the lapidary phrase of J.A. Hartung, Pentheus has a *secretorum spectandorum cupido*, a desire to witness what is secret.[18] But the secrets in question are not those of sex but of a religion that Pentheus rejects but cannot wholly disbelieve in. The power of the bacchic religion, and of religion in general, is to be seen in the dreadful fate that overtakes its opponent and in the bliss it promises to its adherents, a bliss that captivates even the man who is its determined enemy.[19]

Notes

1 Schlegel (1809) led the way.

2 See especially Murray (1913).

3 The historicity of this sojourn is doubted by Scullion (2003) on the grounds that Aristophanes' *Frogs*, written shortly after Euripides' death, does not mention the fact, damning in Scullion's view, that Euripides abandoned Athens for Pella. But there is no reason to think that Aristophanes found Euripides' sojourn damning: he alludes without any apparent criticism to Agathon's similar stay in Macedonia. We can think of Archelaus as wanting to increase Macedon's cultural prestige by starting a sort of MacDowell Colony.

4 See, e.g. Paley (1874) 413–14.

5 Exhibit A might be Socrates of *Clouds*, who in the play is a quack natural scientist and a teacher of dishonest argument to the young. Socrates was neither.

6 See also *Agamemnon* 559–66, in which the Herald describes the hardships, including bedbugs, of being a soldier on campaign.

7 In law a 'colourable' charge is one plausible enough to be entertained in court. In order for a description of, for instance, a tragic poet to be 'comically colourable', it need only build on some recognizable feature of the tragic poet's *oeuvre*. Thus Euripides makes several characters in the course of his plays express doubt about the justice of the gods. The comically colourable charge based on this is that (no matter which character expressed this doubt or in what circumstances) the doubt is to be attributed to Euripides himself. An analogous charge might be that Shakespeare was 'that great proponent of suicide', which would be firmly grounded in Hamlet's 'To be or not to be' speech.

8 The ancient notices about Euripides' life, his career as a tragic poet, and the views about him by contemporary and succeeding generations are collected and translated in Kovacs (1994a). There is a discussion of what they show in Kovacs (1994b) 1–36.

9 Discussion of this evidence in Stevens (1956).

10 The movement to look to the text of the plays themselves as the most reliable source for what view of the world is being presented there has been growing steadily over the decades. Spira (1960) showed that there is no reason to regard the *deus ex machina* endings of Euripides' plays as ironic. Other works in the same vein are Steidle (1968), Lloyd-Jones (1971), Gregory (1979), Heath (1987), Kovacs (1987), Lefkowitz (1987, 1989 and 2002) and Mikalson (1991).

11 The gods' treatment of their mortal enemies parallels mortals' treatment of theirs. A successful mortal in Greek society, as ancient sources often tell us, not only helps his friends but also harms his enemies. The failure to do the latter, in either a god or a mortal, would be, in the eyes of an ancient audience, a damning confession of weakness.

12 For a full list of passages illustrating the ancient and well-accepted view that the gods often destroy innocent persons who are associated with the wicked (which is why sharing a ship voyage with a man guilty of impiety is dangerous), see Nisbet and Rudd (2004) on Horace, *Odes* 3.2.27–9.

13 The Chorus in lines 71–2 say 'I shall hymn Dionysus with the songs that have always been in use'. On this passage see Kovacs (2003a) 114.

14 See Snell (1971) 180–2 (= 43 Critias F 19, *TrGF*). The fragment is translated and discussed in Guthrie (1971) 243–4.

15 Compare the scene in Aristophanes' *Clouds* where Strepsiades is told by his son Pheidippides, who has drunk deep from the new thought, that beating up one's father is justified because it is the behaviour we observe in roosters.

16 A further passage where the idea of *nomos* occurs in highly pointed language is at line 387.

17 The only *prima facie* hint of sexual interest in the two scenes is discussed in Kovacs (2003a) 133–4. There I show that Dodds's translation of lines 957–8 smuggles several words of sexual import into a text from which they are absent.

18 Hartung (1844) 551.

19 My translations are lightly adapted from those I published in my *Euripides 6: Bacchae, Iphigenia at Aulis, Rhesus* (Cambridge, Mass. 2002). I am grateful to Justina Gregory and Jon Mikalson for salutary criticisms of an earlier draft of this piece.

9

Paradoxes and Themes in *Bacchae*[1]

Alex Garvie

Bacchae is a play of paradoxes – the paradox of an oriental god who brings his religion from Asia to Greece, and yet was born to Zeus and Semele in Thebes; the paradox of a new religious cult which Tiresias will claim to be as old as time itself; the paradox of a choral entrance-song whose theme is the cult of an oriental god, yet which takes the form of a traditional Greek hymn; the paradox of Dionysus as a god whose cult proclaims blessedness only for those initiated into his Mysteries, but who is also the god of the ordinary man, and who demands worship from everybody, irrespective of their gender or their age; the paradox of an ecstatic religion which requires of its practitioners moderation, good sense and rational wisdom (*sophia*), at the same time as irrational madness. Perhaps the most striking paradox of all is that the god who throughout the play promises joy will at the end produce only suffering and horror. Binding all the paradoxes together are the play's recurrent themes.

The opening lines suggest that *Bacchae* is loosely connected to a small group of 'return tragedies', which deal with the long-awaited homecoming of a hero from war or other absence abroad. These plays themselves belong to a long poetic tradition which, for Euripides' audience as for ourselves, is represented above all by Homer's *Odyssey*. Often the hero returns in disguise or is otherwise unrecognized, and his recognition forms the climax of the story. So here we look forward to the manifestation of Dionysus. Unusually for such tragedies the protagonist is a god, and no one at home awaits his return. We meet him first as he delivers his monologue in the prologue. Other Euripidean plays begin like this with an introductory monologue from a god, but only here does the god turn out to be the protagonist of the play.

Dionysus explains to us how he has travelled from Asia to introduce his new religion to Thebes. But his aunts deny his divinity and, with all the women, have been driven mad into the mountains as bacchae/bacchants or maenads (the noun derived from the Greek verb 'to be mad'), where they are now sitting peacefully under the pine (or silver fir) trees, while Pentheus, the young king of Thebes, resists the new religion. The tone is unemotional and factual. All the emphasis is on Dionysus' plan to manifest his divinity to

Pentheus and the whole of Thebes before moving on to some other land. There is not a word about punishment for Pentheus, and little to rouse either our sympathy for the god or our disapproval of his plan. Before he departs he explains that he has disguised himself as a human votary of himself. Only at the end of the play will he appear again in his divine form. Despite the unemotional quality of the speech, however, a note of foreboding is not entirely lacking. Many in the audience might recall the fear of the suitors in Book 17 of the *Odyssey* that the unidentified stranger Odysseus could be a god in disguise, one who has come to test their hospitality and to punish the wicked. The motif was common in both myth and literature. For the spectators, therefore, such a *theoxeny* (a god appearing disguised as a human stranger) might seem already to be dangerous.

Already in the prologue Euripides introduces the paradox involved in the ambivalent relationship between rational wisdom and irrational madness in the worship of Dionysus. The god, the first character in the play to use a word with the root *soph-*, applies it disapprovingly to 'a fine excuse' thought up by Cadmus that Dionysus was not the son of Zeus at all. Three lines later he introduces the concept of madness, his instrument of punishment for the unbelieving women. It will be some time before we discover that it is an essential element also in the worship of those who do believe in him.

The onstage action of the play takes place in front of the royal palace. From time to time we are asked also to imagine what is happening in the space behind the central door of the *skene* (the background stage-building). But the most important space of all is offstage on Mount Cithaeron, to which Dionysus introduces us in this prologue, the mountain on which the women are for the moment sitting quietly and peacefully under the pine trees, the mountain to which he departs by an *eisodos* (side passage) at the end of the prologue. As the plot progresses, departures from the civilized city space that the palace represents to the wild untamed space represented by the mountain will become more and more important, until finally we share the horror of what will come back *from* the mountain. And in that development the pine trees will play an increasingly significant role.

The last word of the prologue, 'dance', provides the only preparation for the dramatic change of mood in the chorus's entrance-song, one of the most exciting entrance-songs in the whole of Greek tragedy. While the first line of the prologue marked Dionysus' arrival in the land of Greek Thebes, where he was born, the first word of the song, in the original Greek, is 'Asia', from which he has come. So the irruption of the oriental god into Greece is represented for us by the chorus of his oriental followers, who have travelled with him from Asia, as they irrupt into the theatre, dancing wildly and singing in emotional rhythms, to the accompaniment of drums. In this play of paradoxes their labour brings them 'sweet pleasure in our pain'. More clearly paradoxical is the description, in the Greek, of this new religion as one that has always been practised, and that the form of the song is that of a traditional Greek cult hymn, with praises of the deity and with the telling of the story of his birth. Its keynote is the blessedness of the initiates, and the exciting joy of going to the mountain to dance in ecstasy in a land flowing with milk, wine and honey. Note the mountains as the setting for this worship, and especially the recurring ritual cry, 'to the mountains, the mountains'. Indeed, 'the whole earth will dance'. The pine trees too are mentioned. If this is what Dionysiac worship means, how can anyone be against it? We hardly notice the description of the god as 'bull-horned', or the brief references to the more violent aspect of this cult, the joy of hunting a goat and eating it raw, or the strange description of the maenads' *thyrsoi* (wands) as 'potent' (literally 'hybristic'). And, if we have some faint misgivings about the escapism that it involves (the women on the mountain have abandoned their housework and the civilized society of the city), they are entirely overshadowed by the overall mood of joy. We are certainly not yet encouraged to think about what will come back *from* the mountain at the end of the play. The chorus will play a vital part in this tragedy, as it guides our varying emotional reactions. Joy will be the theme of most of its songs, but there will be a progressive degradation in its, and our, understanding of that joy.

We have noted the dramatic change in mood between prologue and entrance-song. Equally striking is the reversal of mood between entrance-song and the following episode. After the final ritual cry, 'to the mountains, the mountains', the ode has ended with a splendid simile in which the bacchant is compared to a colt skipping along with agile foot beside its grazing mother. This is the cue for the arrival, by the *eisodos* which leads into the city, of the aged, grey-haired, tottering prophet Tiresias, who has come to summon the equally aged Cadmus, the grandfather of Pentheus, from the palace, so that they can go off to the mountain to worship. Clad in Dionysiac fawnskins, carrying Dionysiac wands (*thyrsoi*), and wearing ivy garlands on their heads, they look forward to taking part in the wild dancing on the mountain, claiming that they alone in Thebes have good sense. Cadmus calls Tiresias 'wise', but what is the relationship between rational wisdom and the demands of this emotional religion? Does one not have to be 'mad' to join in Dionysiac dancing? They are joyful because they have forgotten their old age, and feel that they can dance all night and day. Dionysus does not discriminate between young and old worshippers, which means that the irrational is not confined to any one age group. But the two men harp on rather too much about the problems of old age, and there is something a little ridiculous about the spectacle. The mood indeed descends almost into bathos when Cadmus, despite his claim to be rejuvenated, asks pathetically if they cannot drive to the mountain on a carriage. The tragedians usually treat Tiresias with great respect, and those characters who question his wisdom usually find cause to regret it. Here he becomes a figure of gentle fun. But the paradox that he embodies is serious enough; he claims not to practise sophistry (the *soph*-root again) on the gods. The new religion of Dionysus, he says, is as old as time itself, and no rational argument devised by the cleverest intellectuals can ever prevail against it. He will soon himself use such arguments to defend it.

The departure of the two old men for the mountain is delayed by the arrival of King Pentheus, who at first does not notice Tiresias and Cadmus. So far we have seen Dionysus with our own eyes and through the eyes of his followers; now we are to see him through the eyes of his principal antagonist. In his opening speech Pentheus makes clear his reasons for opposing this new religion: it is merely a pretext for luring women into the mountains to indulge in illicit sexual unions. He mocks the effeminate appearance of the supposed votary. Like a typical stage-tyrant he thinks that violence is the solution to all problems, and plans to hunt down the women from the mountain and imprison them. Note the reappearance of the hunting motif and the first invitation to the audience to look ahead to what may come back from the mountain. Pentheus assumes that he will be in control of that. When he does see the old men, he describes the sight as a 'miracle', and laughs at it. Later there will be more serious miracles, and Pentheus will not have the last laugh.

Tiresias and Cadmus do their best to persuade him to change his mind. Tiresias begins with an argument found elsewhere in tragedy, that a clever speech, glibly delivered, like that of Pentheus, may be lacking in sense. He has already claimed to avoid sophistic arguments himself. But he then goes on to spoil it by producing a number of arguments of his own, which Euripides' audience would certainly recognize as belonging to that category, familiar as it was with the rationalizing theories of the sophists, the contemporary teachers and intellectuals. It might be less ready than a modern audience to dismiss Tiresias' explanation of the significance of the word-play on the Greek words for 'hostage' (*homeros*) and 'thigh' (*meros*) and between 'manic' (*maniodes*) and 'mantic' (*mantikos*). Certainly there is nothing false about the first of his arguments, that Dionysus is the god of wine, and that drinking wine gives pleasure, and helps one to sleep and to forget one's worries. The trouble is that Dionysus is much more besides, so that after the excitement of the entrance-song, Tiresias' defence of the new religion is clearly inadequate. When he accuses Pentheus of being mad, he forgets that madness seems to be an essential element in the cult of Dionysus. In response to Pentheus' charge that the women are engaged in illicit sex on the mountain, Tiresias declares that even in bacchic revelry the woman who (in Stuttard's translation) is chaste and moral will not be corrupted. But the two adjectives have also the wider sense of 'self-controlled'. Is it possible to take part in an ecstatic ritual while remaining self-controlled? Cadmus' justification for worshipping the god is still less satisfactory: even if Dionysus is not a god, it will be good for the honour of the family to pretend that he is. He accuses Pentheus of having no good sense (in Stuttard's translation, 'you're not using your head').

It is hardly surprising that by the end of the episode Pentheus remains unconvinced, and orders his men to arrest the 'votary' and bring him back to face execution by stoning.

The choral song which follows deals again with Dionysiac joy, but gone now is all the excitement of the entrance-song. Taking its cue from the arguments of Tiresias, the chorus presents Dionysus in conventional terms as essentially the god of wine and of peaceful convivial parties. The ode is full of the commonplaces of Greek thought. Moderation and wisdom are praised, and their relevance to the ecstatic cult of Dionysus remains problematic. 'Clever is not wise', sings the chorus, but in the Greek a *soph*-word covers both terms, and the audience is left to wonder how it can have a derogatory sense here and at the same time be a term of praise. It is a little disappointing that it is linked at all with moderation and with the opinions of the common man, and that once again madness is used by this chorus as a term of abuse. Again there is something lacking. One stanza, however, stands out from the rest, when the chorus in the face of Pentheus' persecution expresses the wish to be safely far away in Cyprus. This kind of escapist wish is not uncommon in tragedy, but the choice of Cyprus here may be significant; it is the island of Aphrodite, the goddess of sexual love, which for a Greek seemed to be a form of madness. Dionysus is not normally associated with sexual passion, but the similarity between it and ritual 'madness' is obvious. The audience may wonder for a moment whether there was some truth in Pentheus' suspicion of what was happening on the mountain.

At the beginning of the next episode we are suddenly reminded of what the ode omitted. Enter a servant with the 'votary' under arrest. He describes how Pentheus' men 'tracked down' their prey, and here now is the 'animal' which they have caught. The metaphor foreshadows the way in which Dionysus, at this stage of the play the prey, will later turn into the hunter of Pentheus. The prisoner made no attempt to resist arrest; indeed he laughed, an ominous first indication of how the relationship between Pentheus and Dionysus will develop. The servant goes on to report that the women whom Pentheus had imprisoned have miraculously escaped and have gone leaping off to worship the god. 'This man', he says, 'is full of miracles' ('a lot of strange stuff going on' in Stuttard's translation). But Pentheus, who found the sight of

Tiresias and Cadmus so miraculous, is so preoccupied with the sight of the beautiful, effeminate stranger that he fails totally to recognize the significance of the real miracle that has just occurred; he orders him to be untied, because there is no way that he can escape. So begins the first of three confrontations, all of them in rapid single-line dialogue between the god and the man. Pentheus questions the 'votary', and Dionysus accuses Pentheus of folly. It ends with Pentheus apparently in control, as the votary is led off to prison in the palace stables. But already we have a sense that the god is merely playing with him. In the final lines of the episode the 'votary' predicts that the god will take vengeance on Pentheus, the first time in the play that the theme of his punishment has become explicit. Pentheus too departs into the palace.

In the next choral ode, however, it is immediately passed over. Dionysus is again portrayed as the god of wine. The chorus cannot understand why Thebes rejects the joy which he brings, and calls on him not to punish Pentheus, but merely to put a stop to his outrageous behaviour. Unaware of the true identity of the 'votary', the chorus speculates anxiously about where the god may be to hear its prayer. To the audience the answer to the question is obvious: he is locked up in the stables, which we are to imagine as part of the palace, behind the *skene* building. The song is immediately interrupted by the voice offstage of Dionysus, in his own divine person calling to the chorus, while the latter describes an earthquake and stroke of lightning which are destroying the palace, or part of it. The staging of all this is uncertain, but probably most of it is left to the imagination of the audience. What matters is that this, so far the most powerful miracle of the play, takes place inside the palace building, and thus suggests Pentheus' total loss of control over his own home.

So the miraculously liberated 'votary' now emerges through the door to describe how he sat quietly as Pentheus rushed around in a futile attempt to bind a bull, which he mistook for his enemy – a pardonable error, given that Dionysus has already been described in the entrance-song of the chorus as the 'bull-horned god'. The 'votary' ends his speech with the platitude that 'a wise man (*sophos*) should at all times practise equilibrium'. Enter Pentheus, also through the door, totally bewildered by the escape of his prisoner. He ignores his enemy's advice to cool his temper. To his sarcastic 'Oh, very clever (*sophos*)! Very clever! Not where you *should* be clever, though', the 'votary' merely replies 'O, there especially'.

Enter a messenger, a herdsman who has come to report the behaviour of the women on the mountain: 'strange things, like miracles – but more miraculous'. He embarks upon the first of two long, formal messenger-speeches, which although they follow the normal Greek convention of reporting offstage action to an audience, are in this play particularly memorable for their presentation of atmosphere and changes of mood. At first all is peaceful and idyllic; the women lie quietly sleeping, some of them under a pine tree, none of them drunk, nor, as Pentheus had expected, indulging in illicit sex. When they wake up they are a miracle of orderliness. They produce water from a rock, wine from the ground, and honey from their thyrsus wands. The watchers marvel at these miracles. When the herdsmen and shepherds set out to 'hunt' the women, as a pleasant sport, the women have begun their ecstatic dancing, and soon the whole mountain and all the animals join in the worship of the god – a fine example of the pathetic fallacy. But it turns out to be the women who hunt the hunters. They tear the cattle into pieces with their bare hands, and the fragments are hanging from the pines, dripping with blood. For the first time in the play the keynote is violence, but as yet the principal victims are animals, not human beings. The women go on to raid the neighbouring villages, and succeed in wounding men, while the men are unable to wound the women – a further miracle. But this detail is passed over lightly, and the women finally return to the peace of the mountain. So violence and peace are juxtaposed, and it is left to the messenger to draw a wholly inadequate moral: this is a powerful god, who has given us the vine which stops our pain – without wine there is no pleasure for men.

Pentheus, failing totally to appreciate the significance of the miracles that have just been reported and the power of his antagonist, resolves to lead his army against the women on the mountain. What annoys him particularly is the thought of defeat at the hands of a band of women. Dionysus advises him to remain calm (as he himself had done when imprisoned in the stables). So begins the second line-by-line confrontation between the two opponents, the crucial one because it ends with a total reversal of Pentheus' decision. Dionysus offers instead to take him, with no army, to spy on the women sitting on the mountain. The exaggerated eagerness with which he accepts the offer makes sense in the light of his obsession with their supposed sexual activities, which he now looks forward to watching as he sits under the pines. When, however, he learns that he must put on female clothes, he at first recoils, but when Dionysus explains that otherwise he might be detected by the women, he congratulates the 'votary' for having been 'so very clever' (*sophos*). Too eagerly he questions him about what his dress will look like. At several points he tries to backtrack, but all his objections are easily overcome. Having declared that he does not want the bacchants to laugh at him as he goes through the town, he departs into the palace, pretending that he has not yet made his decision, but we know that it is in fact already taken, and that he is already lost. After his departure Dionysus has the last word. It remains for him only to make his enemy mad. Pentheus is heading for a hunter's net.

Dionysus explicitly tells the chorus not only that he is to be punished, by death at the hands of his own mother, but also that he must first become a laughing stock for all the Thebans, as he walks through the city dressed in female clothes. The last line of his speech sums up the paradox of this religion, 'a god of terror and a god of gentle comfort for mankind'. How can we ensure that for us he will not be the former?

The choral song that follows begins with a sense of movement and excitement that we have not heard from the chorus since its entrance-song. It looks forward to its joy, when, like a fawn that has escaped from the hunting-nets, it will be fully free to worship the god. But the sense of excitement does not last. The chorus still identifies itself with the victim of the hunt. Once again it raises the burning question, 'what is wisdom?', but makes no real attempt at answering it. Somehow it seems to be connected only with the pleasure of getting the better of one's enemies. So we return to the platitudes of Greek thought, and the joy at the end of the ode has deteriorated into that of momentary, simple, daily pleasures. Only once does the chorus prepare us for the reversal: it is the impious man whom the gods hunt down, but it is he whom the chorus accuses of being mad.

The third, and most unpleasant, confrontation between Dionysus and Pentheus begins with much emphasis on who sees what. Pentheus, who, in Dionysus' opening words, is 'so hungry to see what should not be seen', is for the audience not himself a pretty sight as he emerges from the palace, now completely under the god's control, totally destroyed from a psychological point of view. He sees things double, and the 'votary' as a bull, recalling his previous encounter in the stable with the bull. Now, says his enemy, 'you're seeing as you should'. He giggles as he fusses about his hair and the fall of his woman's dress, and wonders whether it is better to carry his thyrsus in his right or left hand. He believes the votary when he tells him that he will see the self-control of the maenads on the mountain, but at the same time looks forward to the sight of their uncontrolled sexual activities as he watches them from his hiding place among the pines. So proud is he of himself that he now wants to be taken through the centre of Thebes for everyone to admire. As he finally sets off happily for the mountain, we are invited to look ahead to what will return from the mountain – Pentheus in his mother's arms, a prediction which Pentheus himself completely misunderstands. His last words are: 'Well, I deserve it'. If till now we were unsure whether or not to sympathize with Pentheus, there can no longer be any doubt.

The following choral ode is at least as exciting as the entrance-song. Only in the central stanza is there a brief return to the conventional platitudes of the previous ode, whereby moderation and piety are deemed preferable to madness. But the chorus seems now to have lost interest in defining wisdom.

What matters is only its pleasure in the hunt. The ode begins with the chorus calling on the swift hunting-dogs of Madness to go to the mountain, to incite the women to take vengeance on the man who has gone to the mountain to seek them out. Pentheus, the hunter, is to become the victim of the hunt. In the final stanza, unlike that of the previous ode, the excitement returns, as the chorus calls on the god to manifest himself as a bull or a snake or a lion, and with smiling face to cast a noose round the hunter of the bacchants. Since the manifestation of justice (compare the theme of manifestation in the prologue) is now unequivocally identified with the killing of Pentheus, the violence which was merely hinted at in the entrance-song is now uppermost in our minds.

This is the cue for the appearance of the second messenger, who comes to announce Pentheus' death. Often the tragic messenger brings news that is unwelcome to the recipient, but here the chorus-leader rejoices, a reaction which dismays the messenger: 'It's not right to gloat over another's suffering' (or 'evil things'). So the common man condemns the conception of pleasure inherent in the cult of Dionysus, who is traditionally his god, and the audience is doubtless expected to share in his reaction. In a full-scale formal messenger-speech he describes for us these evil things. Like the earlier messenger he begins by setting an idyllic picture of a peaceful scene on the mountain. Pentheus, ever his own worst enemy, complains that he is unable to see the maenads. If only he could climb a high pine tree he would 'have no difficulty seeing their depravity'. The 'stranger' obliges him by miraculously bending the tree down to the ground to allow him to sit on top of it when it is released. So the tree, till now a symbol of peacefulness, is transformed into the setting for the violence and horror that are about to unfold. Pentheus has failed to realize that, while he can now see the women, they too can see him. At this point the 'votary' disappears, and a voice, that of the god himself, is heard calling on the women to take vengeance on the man who laughed at his rites. In the earlier messenger-speech the whole mountain, in a pathetic fallacy, joined in the worship of the god. Here the whole of nature is silent. The climax comes when, having pelted the tree with branches and other missiles, the women pull it out of the ground, so that Pentheus falls off. The mad Agave's apprehension of her son as an animal to be hunted coincides with *his* return to sanity. At last he understands the error of his ways, but his mother, ignoring all his appeals for pity, together with the other women, tears him limb from limb. She is now on her way back from the mountain, carrying Pentheus' head in triumph on her thyrsus, priding herself on her hunt, in her delusion thinking that it is the head of a lion. This, then, is what Dionysiac joy has become: the joy of a mother who has killed her son. The messenger ends with a moral that is as banal as that which concluded the earlier messenger-speech:

'So what is wisdom? Piety, I think, and godliness. And what is good should be
pursued for ever.' The gulf between the platitude and the horror of what the
messenger has reported is very striking.

In a brief lyric passage the chorus maintains the triumphant tone. And
then Agave enters, carrying, as she says 'from the mountain', her grisly burden,
so that the chorus may see it. In a highly emotional lyric dialogue, in which
the themes of joy and hunting, and the question of what each participant
sees, are interwoven more closely than ever, Agave praises the wise Bacchus
for urging the maenads on against the animal. The derogatory sense 'clever'
may seem more appropriate to the context. There is a telling moment when
even the chorus, till now completely sympathetic to Dionysus and hostile to
Pentheus, expresses revulsion at Agave's invitation to join her in feasting on
the 'lion'. When, therefore, as the metre returns to the language of spoken
Greek, the chorus-leader addresses her as 'poor woman' (omitted in Stuttard's
translation), we should detect not just the conventional language of a tragic
chorus-leader in response to a suffering character but a note of genuine
sympathy.

Cadmus reappears with attendants, carrying the pieces of Pentheus' body
which he has returned to gather together on the mountain. At first his grief
contrasts with Agave's continuing joy in showing him her prize. He declares
that he cannot bear to look at the sight. But soon he begins the process of
enlightening her. At first she tries to evade the truth, feeling perhaps
instinctively that she can remain happy only as long as she is still mad.
Cadmus too wishes that it were possible for her never to return to sanity. Is it
really better not to know some painful truth? Eventually Cadmus does force
her to look more carefully at what she is carrying, and the joy is gone for ever:
'I see such suffering.' And the cause of it all is clear to her: 'Dionysus has
destroyed us all. I now know everything.'

At the end of the play there is no joy for anyone. Even the chorus has
found it too much to bear. Our sympathy lies with Pentheus, an unexpected
side of whose character is now revealed to us; we recognize the Pentheus
who punished those who insulted his old grandfather, but at least he was
good to Cadmus, and Cadmus loved him. The punishment of Cadmus seems
most unfair, as even the chorus-leader acknowledges: 'I pity you your fate.
Your grandson did deserve to die, but you ... I pity you.' He who set off for
the mountain to worship Dionysus, not indeed for the best of motives,
suffers as much as anyone else. We may suppose that this is merely a case of
the innocent suffering along with the guilty, but that is not exactly how
Euripides presents it. The single manuscript breaks off after the chorus-
leader's expression of sympathy, and, when it resumes, Dionysus is on stage,
no longer in disguise, in the middle of a speech, prophesying that Cadmus is

to be transformed into a snake and driven into exile. 'You made your choice', he says. 'Had you been humble' (or 'had you known how to show good sense or moderation') 'you would now be blessed.' Cadmus might, we feel, have replied that he had indeed done his best to behave in the manner that Dionysus now recommends, but that what he has learnt is that moderation and good sense are the last things that are required in the worshipper of this god. Instead, he concedes that 'we did wrong', and complains only that Dionysus has gone too far in his vengeance. 'Gods', he says, 'should not have the passions that men do.' The trouble is that they do.

The paradoxes of the play remain largely unresolved at the end. The use of the same moral terms, but with different connotations, by both defenders and opponents of Dionysiac worship remains a problem. In particular, if in that worship there is a correct relationship to be found between madness on the one hand and wisdom and moderation on the other, it is certainly not exemplified by any of the characters of the play or by the chorus. No one is rewarded for getting it right. We might like to think that we would escape punishment because we do not share the character flaws of Pentheus. To destroy him Dionysus attacked him at his weakest point. Can we be sure that we have no weak points that the god might use to destroy *us* if he chooses to do so? Scholars used to argue about whether in this play Euripides is arguing in favour of Dionysiac religion, or, on the contrary, that the god does not deserve to be worshipped, if he exists at all. Most critics now recognize that to put the question in these terms is mistaken. In terms of the action of the play itself the cult of Dionysus is new to Thebes, but the power of the irrational, which Dionysus represents, does undoubtedly exist, as it has from time immemorial, and there is no point in saying that one is either against or in favour of it. We should not expect a tragedian to present simple morals in response to the great problems of human existence, or to leave no unanswered questions at the end.

Is there any hope at all as the play concludes? The comfort that Cadmus and Agave offer each other is only temporary; for we watch them depart to their separate exile. Richard Seaford, in his 1996 edition of the play, in an interesting interpretation, sees the suffering as a necessary prelude to the foundation of Dionysus' civic and communal cult in Thebes. The royal family had to destroy itself and be driven out before the city could begin to practise it. Pentheus is thus to be seen as a kind of scapegoat whose destruction benefits the whole city. It is true that in the prologue Dionysus announces his intention of manifesting himself to all the people of Thebes, and from time to time we have been reminded that the whole city has been in some way caught up in the worship of the god, most recently very briefly in the line-by-line dialogue between Cadmus and Agave. We might, therefore, expect the effect on the community to play some part at the end of the play. But it has not been a major topic, and at the very end, at least as we have it, nothing at all is said about it, and, from the first line of the messenger onwards, all the emphasis is on the destruction of the house. This may be why the loss of part of the final scene in the single manuscript is so disastrous; for it would have to be there that this optimistic idea was developed. All that we can safely say is that in the play as it stands there is no optimism at all at the end. And, even if Seaford's interpretation of the lacuna is correct, it is surely the horror that predominates. Somehow the despair seems all the darker because of the recurring theme of joy that has preceded it. The play was presented in the theatre of Dionysus, as part of the god's festival. He is the patron god of tragedy as well as of comedy. His concern is with suffering as well as laughter. He may bring joy, but the potential for that joy to turn to tragedy is always present.

Note

1 This essay is a much expanded version of my short paper, 'The paradox of the *Bacchae*', which was published in A. Beale (ed.) (2008), *Euripides Talks*, 15–22, Bristol: Bristol Classical Press. For the most part I have used the translations of David Stuttard, but, in order to emphasize particular points, I have occasionally added or substituted translations of my own.

10

Euripides' *Bacchae* – A Revenge Play

Hanna M. Roisman

Vengeance appears prominently in the extant Greek tragedies. Determination to avenge the murder of Agamemnon drives the plot of the plays involving the House of Atreus (Aeschylus' *Oresteia* and the *Electra*s of Sophocles and Euripides). Vengeance is the central concern of Euripides' *Medea*, figures in his *Hippolytus*, and is an important motif in his *Hecuba*. Strong emotions – anger, a sense of injury and a sense of righteousness – provoke acts of revenge, and these, together with the intrigues involved in accomplishing the action, make for riveting theatre. The accomplishing of revenge also allows the audience to feel the cathartic satisfaction of getting one's own back for an injury.

As Burnett points out, among early Greeks, revenge 'was not a problem but a solution'.[1] It was presented in the revenge plays as a direct means of righting wrongs and obtaining justice (e.g., Aesch, *Eum.* 459–69, 739–43; Soph. *El.* 528–33, 580–3; Eur. *El.* 87–9, 1147–61). In Euripides' *Bacchae*, however, the issue is not human reciprocity. Here a god avenges slights to his divinity, a subject Euripides had dealt with in his *Hippolytus* as early as 428 BCE, more than twenty years before the performance of *Bacchae* (not long after 406 BCE). The similarity between the two plays is evident in the title *Pentheus* (i.e. based on the protagonist's name as is the case of *Hippolytus*), given to *Bacchae* in the Florentine manuscript; Stobaeus, too (fifth century CE), quotes it twice under that name.[2] Pentheus suffers the vengeance of a god whose gifts he refuses to enjoy, and whose divinity he refuses to acknowledge. Similarly in *Hippolytus*, the young hero shows the same contumacy to Aphrodite and suffers a similar punishment.[3] Euripides does not deal with personal gods in either play, but with divinities who are a great factor in the world. Dionysus is not only a god of wine but a higher personification of passion in religion and joy in life, as Aphrodite is a source of joy, continuation of all life, love and happiness. This play teaches, with more focus than *Hippolytus*, that one cannot neglect these sources of joy, enthusiasm and passion. Unlike the earlier play, in which Aphrodite works her pernicious plan through Phaedra, in *Bacchae*, Dionysus (in human form) confronts his disbeliever directly. The absence of a human intermediary strips the play of possible moral dilemmas that complicate human decisions. Therefore the play lacks the moral quandaries tragic characters involved in the workings of revenge usually face, from Orestes' hesitancy in committing matricide to Medea's wavering about the slaughter of her children.

The *principle* of vengeance is usually not endorsed in tragedy. Aeschylus goes to great lengths to justify Orestes' killing of his mother. In the last part of the *Oresteia* (458 BCE) he has Orestes purified by Apollo, who had commanded the murder, and exculpated by Athena, who casts the decisive vote in his trial before the court of the Areopagus. Although in the first part of the fifth century revenge might have been seen as the solution to a wrong done, Athenian attitudes gradually shifted during the protracted Peloponnesian War (431–404 BCE) and the ensuing political strife. Retaliation became an everyday event which threatened civic order.[4] Against this background, matricide is justified in neither Euripides' nor Sophocles' *Electra*. Euripides' *Electra* condemns it outright. At the end of the play, Clytemnestra's deceased brothers are brought onto the scene as *dei ex machina* to declare: 'She got her justice, but you have not worked in justice' (1244) and to confirm Orestes' suspicion that Apollo's oracles were misleading or incorrect. Thus the play's final judgement is that the matricide was a wicked act orchestrated by a headstrong and embittered woman. Sophocles' position is less clear: both Orestes and Electra have qualities of character that might be considered flaws and raise questions about the rightness of their deeds. In *Medea* (431 BCE), the Messenger's hair-raising account of the deaths of Jason's new bride and her father impel the audience to rethink the rightness of revenge. Medea's murder of her children is dramatized in a less graphic and more succinct manner. Yet it is also presented so as to arouse maximum horror. The revenge taken on Hippolytus in *Hippolytus* (428 BCE) is portrayed critically as well. Phaedra, the intermediary of Aphrodite for exacting vengeance from Hippolytus, is portrayed as a passionate and hypocritical woman who does not refrain from calumny to indict the innocent Hippolytus. Artemis' chilling promise to Hippolytus that she will exact a similar vengeance from some ardent follower of Aphrodite reveals the vengeful and merciless ways of gods (*Hipp.* 1416–22).

Unlike these revenge plays, in which the idea of vengeance is either contested or left ambiguous for the spectators to consider, *Bacchae* has the chorus of maenads Dionysus brought from Lydia sing in praise of vengeance without hesitation or equivocation. Their first and second songs prepare the ground (370–432, 519–75). They call upon Holiness, queen of gods, to hear Pentheus' malice, blasphemy and sacrilege against Dionysus, god of dance, music and wine. They call on Thebes to accept Dionysus and they denounce Pentheus as a giant fighting against the gods. Their third song (862–911), with its horrifying disharmony between the refrain, which unabashedly exalts revenge on the impious, and the calm acceptance of what is divine cements their demand for vengeance (877–81, 897–901). The plan that they mastermind in the fourth ode (977–1023) calls for madness to enter into the women on Mount Cithaeron so they will kill Pentheus 'the godless man, lawless man, the man who knows no justice . . . the spawn of Echion' (991–4). Their final chilling song (1153–67) congratulating Dionysus for winning the contest when Agave's hands plunged into her child's blood, 'dripping and glistening and black with his death' (1163–4), surpasses in its brutality even their former insistent calls for revenge.

Divine vengeance does not manifest itself in straightforward murder or death. The process is arduous and tortuous. The victim is assailed or undermined through what he cares most about, or through some latent weakness, or a confluence of both. The madness Athena casts on Ajax in Sophocles' play results in hurting what a Homeric hero cares most about – his honour – when he becomes a laughing stock by killing livestock instead of his enemies. Hippolytus, who belligerently avows his abstinence and virginity, is accused of rape and is unable to prove his innocence. Pentheus' downfall is similar. He dies participating in a cult he had tried to shut down.

In *Hippolytus*, Euripides problematizes the justification for revenge through the characters, especially Hippolytus, an excessively chaste young man who is shown to be more focused on sex than he acknowledges to himself. All the same, we can identify and sympathize with him when a calumnious charge of rape is brought against him, and his promise to keep silent prevents him from fighting the accusation. A similar dramatic principle works in *Bacchae*. Pentheus is a young man (his grandfather is still living and vigorous), passionate about proper behaviour, especially when related to women, while restraining his own libidinous tendencies without acknowledging them. He is the one compelling character in this play with whom the audience can sympathize, if only slightly (see below). Neither completely good nor completely bad, he has enough of the positive in him to arouse our sympathy when he is torn to pieces. As in *Hippolytus*, Euripides connects the quest for revenge with the dichotomy between reason and the irrational,[5] Pentheus standing for reason and Dionysian ecstasy for the irrational. Like Hippolytus, Pentheus is faced with nature's irrational force and tries to solve it by human rational measures.

In this chapter, I will delineate Pentheus' logical solutions to the chaos and turmoil he faces and show the extent to which his actions make sense until Dionysus drives him mad. I will try to show how Euripides' play highlights the horror and harshness of the revenge taken on Pentheus and his family, in a way that forces the audience to reconsider their beliefs in gods, especially in the god whose worship they are participating in as they watch the drama performed in Athens (see below).

I

As a young but responsible ruler, Pentheus does the best he can to preserve the calm in Thebes and the proper conduct of the women who in his eyes have been misled into impropriety. He hurries home from abroad after being informed that the women of Thebes have left their looms and their babies and gone in revelry to Mount Cithaeron, worshipping a Stranger who claims to be Dionysus. As far as Pentheus knows, the baby Dionysus is dead, 'was in fact cremated when the lightning struck and killed his mother' (244–5), because she had the nerve to name Zeus as the father of the unborn baby. He obviously finds the Stranger's story about the baby being sewn into Zeus' thigh unconvincing (242–3); nor is he alone in doubting this story. Teiresias later makes an elaborate attempt to give a corrected version of the story of keeping Dionysus alive (286–97), which only supports Pentheus' doubts. The newly arrived Stranger's claim to divinity therefore looks like blasphemy, the punishment for which ought to be hanging (246–7). So far there is nothing untoward in what Pentheus says or assumes: he acts on the basis of what he knows rather than on a curious tale. We then see him in a series of situations in which his behaviour is easily defensible.

It is natural for him to scold Cadmus for being dressed comically as a bacchant in honour of a stranger whom he considers an impostor. His tirade against Teiresias is understandable, too. How could his revered grandfather do something so silly unless he had been persuaded? He is unaware that Cadmus is attending the revel through political expediency: the possible honour the family might derive from being affiliated with a god, if the Stranger should prove to be one (181–3; cf. 334–6). Pentheus is apparently too young to engage in such shrewd, cynical politicking. Subsequently, angered by Teiresias' speech, he resorts to force, ordering the destruction of Teiresias' augural seat. This certainly is unjustifiable, but again understandable. Oedipus, too, found Teiresias infuriating, and here the seer's homily on the proper use of speech would provoke anyone, but especially a young man sensitive to the respect he thinks is owed him. Teiresias accuses Pentheus of abusing his professional skill: 'For a wise man to speak well when he's got something that's worth saying takes no great effort. Now, *you*, your style is good. You sound *clever*. But the content of your argument lacks thought and substance, and in politics a speaker who has passion without wisdom can be very dangerous' (266–71). Pentheus is cast as a dangerous politician and potential tyrant. No ruler could allow such an accusation to pass, no matter how old and respected the speaker is. We also ought to remember that in Pentheus' eyes Teiresias is a follower of the impostor. Amid the havoc Pentheus is facing in the city, an incitement to revelry from an esteemed seer might be devastating. Pentheus might see force as the only option open to him if he wants to show he is in control. We do not know whether the abodes of the seer were actually destroyed, or not.

Up to now, Pentheus has faced a situation that appeared senseless to him: respected people close to him are following a stranger who claims to be someone Pentheus knows is dead. He has tried to solve the problem by applying force, but to no avail: the townswomen are still on the mountain, and Cadmus and Teiresias have gone to join them in worship. However, he suffers no further personal consequences. He then moves from confronting mortal senselessness to a struggle with divine irrationality. In his direct confrontation with Dionysus, physical force proves again ineffectual, but in addition, his defeat will have personal repercussions. Yet even when facing Dionysus his reactions are rational and not obviously blameworthy.

After being told that Dionysus did not resist capture and that the maenads whom he ordered to be imprisoned got free after 'the keys turned in the locks and the doors swung open, and *no one did it*' (447–8), he resorts to logic and simply doesn't believe the report. After all, keys do not turn by themselves. He is also sure that he can keep Dionysus in his custody. There is indeed no apparent logical reason he should not be able to do this: after all, he is the ruler of the city (506–7). The verbal encounter that follows between Pentheus and the disguised god is both antagonistic and ambiguous and paves the way to Pentheus' doom. While Pentheus' questions are specific and reasonable – who made him a god and what does his new cult have to offer – Dionysus is not only slippery and evasive in his answers, but goads Pentheus into more presumptuous acts: ordering his (Dionysus') imprisonment and threatening to sell or enslave the Lydian maenads (the latter is never realized). Dionysus is specific, however, in his threat of revenge: 'Dionysus will exact his vengeance on you for your arrogance and your ungodliness. In doing wrong by me, you would constrain a god' (516–18). But Pentheus has no logical reason to heed the threat.

Next, Dionysus starts playing with Pentheus' mind: 'I beguiled him. I granted his wish. He thought he was chaining me – he never touched me, though, never came near. It was all in his mind' (616–17), he tells the chorus. He made Pentheus hallucinate: the young king found a bull and bound him, thinking it was Dionysus. Next Dionysus made him think there was a fire in the palace. Pentheus ran frantically about, calling for water, but there was no fire (623–9). A phantom of Dionysus appears in the courtyard, and Pentheus stabs the bright vapour, thinking he is spilling Dionysus' blood (630–1). Finally, Dionysus startles Pentheus by appearing suddenly outside the palace (645–6). All these events destabilize Pentheus, as they would anyone else. When he recovers, a Messenger arrives and reports to him acts of supernatural violence: he and some other shepherds watched three groups of maenads, headed by Autonoe, Agave and Ino, in their sleep, then awake; their play with wild animals; and miraculous springs of water, wine and milk. The shepherds, following the advice of a glibly persuasive townsman, decided to capture Agave for Pentheus, but Agave turned the maenads on them and defeated them. Then the maenads tore the herds to pieces and raided the neighbouring villages. As usual, Pentheus orders out the army. Once again it is hard to condemn him for trying to bring peace and quiet to the mountainside villages. What other measure but force could he have employed against the violent maenads? Now, however, Dionysus deceives Pentheus in a peculiarly horrible way. If up to now some spectators were critical of the young man's easy recourse to physical force, which might have reminded them of a typical tyrant, the following sequence will eventually bring us all to sympathize with the young king.

Dionysus offers to bring the women from the mountains without any use of force. Pentheus is rightly suspicious, thinking this offer is a trick to prevent him from shutting down the cult. Why would the Stranger want to help him? He instead calls again for arms. But Dionysus capitalizes now on Pentheus' latent curiosity about sex, in which Pentheus thinks the women are engaged. Dionysus asks alluringly: 'No, wait! Do you want to see them [the maenads] for yourself – up there on the mountainside?' Pentheus responds: 'Yes! Yes I do! I'd give a lot to see that!' (810–12). But then he vacillates. He agrees (824), then changes his mind (828), while pondering what is on offer. Dionysus perseveres, asking again: 'Have you lost your enthusiasm? Do you not want to see the maenads any more?' (829). Pentheus plays for time, asking questions about the dress he has to wear; finally, clinging to reason, he refuses (836).[6] Dionysus brings up a new point: 'But if you try to fight them, there'll be bloodshed' (837). Pentheus sees the point and agrees to observation as a military strategy: 'You're right. First know your enemy' (839). Dionysus' offer provides him with a reasoned way to mask his inner irrational desire to see the women's activities. Pentheus only gives in to Dionysus when the god frames a logical excuse for him to go to the mountain: reconnaissance. We see the young king lose a struggle with his own irrational impulses, as he had earlier lost the battle with external irrationality. Unreason and revenge are inseparable in this drama. One leads the way to the other. Dionysus wins the argument and acknowledges his deception to the chorus: 'And so he walks into the trap. He *will* go where the bacchae are, and there he'll make amends with his own life' (847–8). He goes on gloating: 'To work now, Dionysus! You're so close. We'll have our vengeance' (849–50). Next, the mortal form of Dionysus asks the god Dionysus to make Pentheus slightly mad so that he may consent to put on female clothing. In order to make the king a laughing stock of Thebes, which is what Dionysus desires, Pentheus must be driven mad. Dionysus' purpose is that when Pentheus dies at his mother's hands, he will know that Dionysus is a god most terrible, but to men most kind (859–61). How Pentheus could learn the second half of the assertion is left unclear.

Accordingly, Pentheus comes out of the palace dressed as a bacchant. He is now completely deranged. He sees two suns and a double Thebes, and thinks Dionysus is a bull. He believes he has the strength to carry Mount Cithaeron and the maenads on his shoulders. This is the ultimate degradation of a rational young man. The horrific revenge follows: Dionysus takes him to the mountain and puts him in the top of a fir tree, then calls to Agave and the maenads to stretch out their hands and catch Pentheus the voyeur as he falls into their grasp. The dramatization of this part of the revenge prevents the audience from being as sanguine about it as they might have been in the earlier sections of the play, where some humour was part of the scenes with Cadmus and with Teiresias, as well as when Pentheus dresses up as a bacchant.

Since violence was not usually shown on stage in the ancient Greek tragedies, the dramatization is effected verbally. The Messenger who witnessed the atrocity reports to Cadmus. He engages first in a brief dialogue with the chorus, who feel only joy that Dionysus has overcome his opponent. However, the Messenger's reprimand, 'I understand your feelings, but it's not right to gloat over another's suffering' (1039–40), prepares the ground for the change in the audience's sympathy that the final scene will produce. The Messenger describes in detail how Agave, thinking her own son is a wild beast, tears him apart with the help of her sisters and other women. Finally she skewers his head on her thyrsus like a trophy to bring it to Thebes. The audience has not seen Agave until now. Her past transgressions were recounted by the Stranger, but not dramatized. Now the tragic irony of a mother carrying her son's head into the theatre, after she has killed him unwittingly, is used to horrify the audience. Violent dismemberment of any human being is gruesome enough, but for a mother to so maul her own son transgresses all bounds of human behaviour. But gods are incapable of mercy. Agave's recognition scene is one of the most painful and harrowing scenes in Greek tragedy. No parent can watch it and not sympathize. The play ends without any remorse from Dionysus or the chorus, no matter how horrible the revenge may be.

There is no question that Pentheus is not portrayed as sympathetically in this play as is Hippolytus in the eponymous drama, even though both young men try to solve irrational situations through rational means. The audience probably saw him as an incipient tyrant. He lacks self-control, is suspicious that Teiresias is profiting from the new rites, assumes the worst on the basis of hearsay, is brutal toward the helpless, and is ignorant enough not to realize that physical force cannot solve mystical problems.[7] And yet, could the spectators have approved of such a horrifying revenge? Beheading is particularly horrendous.

II

Greek tragedy usually presents characters with a moral dilemma that forces them to decide what is right and what is wrong to do. Even when it is their destiny to fail through the decisions they make, the characters still have free choice on how to proceed to their doom. The hopelessness of human choice and the primacy of the situation is brought home in *Bacchae*'s treatment of reason, theoretically the instrument by which the best options should be selected. Sophocles shared this interest in reason. In *Oedipus the King* Sophocles' interest lies in the limited impact of reason on a person's fate. Oedipus tries to find rational means to evade his destiny. He leaves Corinth to avoid committing parricide and marrying his mother; his intellect enables him to defeat the Sphinx; and once the plague descends on Thebes, he acts as a responsible monarch and a logical man. In fact, it is his desire for knowledge and his facility for logical deduction that allow him to recognize his misfortune. Sophocles' play has always been seen as a hymn to the human mind, and thus an *enkomion* to logic, even though the knowledge its hero acquires and the reason he employs do not save him.

Throughout his work, Euripides probes the relation between reason and the irrational, whether in the form of emotion, passion or sexual desire. In *Hippolytus*, rationality and irrationality confront one another in both of the two concentric circles of the plot. In the outer circle, Aphrodite represents the irrational forces and Artemis the forces of reason (even though she is the goddess of wild beasts, too). The characters in the inner circle try to reconcile these forces, but their attempts to solve their 'irrational' dilemmas by rational means all fail.[8] In *Bacchae* two different sets of characters meet the challenge of irrationality with contrasting attitudes and different results.

Cadmus and Teiresias both embrace the new god, each for his own reasons. Teiresias has no logical excuse: he joins the worship because he views Dionysus as equal to natural power, and thus untamed. In his eyes Dionysus is the 'wet principle' of life and the counterpart of Demeter as the 'dry' one

(275–85). His instinct tells him that he faces forces higher than the human mind can perceive and thus he finds it safer to surrender. He serves a god, Apollo, and knows when he is presented with a divinity, acknowledged or not. He is the only human character in the play who is not punished by Dionysus. Cadmus, the family politician, accepts the new god not out of instinct but out of expediency. It might be good for the family to claim kinship with a god. Yet Cadmus is punished, while Teiresias is not. It may be that Cadmus had already earned punishment for disbelieving Semele, but in addition Euripides portrays him as calculating even as he accepts the irrational, and reason cannot win in this play. Pentheus is similarly foiled by his rationality. He sets out to save his city from turmoil through force and logic. But he cannot reason with those who share the ecstasy of Dionysus, and therefore loses to them. Furthermore, Dionysus releases in him his suppressed sexuality, his bottled-up irrationality, which eventually brings him to his doom.

Although the young king does not admit to his sexual desires, they are evident. The first thought that runs through his mind as a reason for the women leaving their homes for the mountains is that they are engaging in sex: 'And one by one they're stealing off to meet men in the forests, to satisfy their carnal lusts. And though they claim they're maenad priestesses, they worship sex more energetically than Bacchus' (222–5). He is certain that Dionysus corrupts the women: 'track him down, this mincing foreigner, who would seduce our women and corrupt them and infect them with his foul disease' (352–4; cf. 237–8, 260–1, 459, 487). His persistent focus on sex is troubling. Even after the first Messenger comes back reporting: 'And I saw the women ... lying there so peaceful ... exhausted, but so chaste, so modest. *It wasn't like you'd said at all*' (my italics, 680–7), Pentheus is unconvinced, and when Dionysus offers him a chance to watch the maenads, he hopes to see them 'like mating birds hugged close in their cock's embrace!' (957–8). Nothing can sway him from thinking of sex when it comes to women. He is both repulsed by sex and at the same time unconsciously desiring it. When he notices Dionysus' handsomeness, his long curls and light complexion, he immediately connects the prettiness with sex: he is sure that these good looks are an asset for Dionysus 'in your pursuit of sex' (459). Unlike his counterpart Hippolytus, who only shuns sex outside marriage but is amenable to sex for procreation, Pentheus seems to shun sex completely.[9] Dionysus is aware of this weakness and takes advantage of it by releasing in him exactly what Pentheus is trying to suppress.

And yet, does Pentheus deserve his fate? Indeed he is a rigid and authoritarian ruler infatuated with power, passionate about law and order, and lacking awareness of his own erotic impulses. The arrival of Dionysus with his followers wreaks havoc on his ordered world. Self-righteous, naive and inexperienced, he serves as the opposite of the confident life-source Dionysus represents. But does all this warrant his death? Pentheus' sole fault is to try to base his decisions on what he sees as logical assumptions (mysterious things do not happen, women are lustful and Dionysus is a fraud). But logic in this play, as in the case of Hippolytus, is not the appropriate answer to illogical problems. Pentheus' death is not due to any single act, but to his attempt to meet irrationality with reason. He did not apply 'like to like', which is a working principle in Euripides: rationality can solve only rational problems, while only irrationality can provide the answer to irrational trouble.[10] While Pentheus tries to annihilate violence with force, which would seem the right response, his refusal to believe in the Stranger prevents him from realizing that the violence he is confronting is based on an irrational natural element which no physical force can overcome. He fails because the only way to respond to Dionysus is to embrace the ecstasy and revelry he represents, which in this play only Teiresias understands. Cadmus is too calculating, and the women of Thebes, including Pentheus' mother and aunts, are deranged by Dionysus and so deprived of reasoned choices. But while Cadmus and his daughters had already encroached on Dionysus' divinity when they refused to believe Semele, the young Pentheus was innocent of this transgression. Dionysus has to goad him into overstepping his human boundaries, so he can become subject to punishment. It is the contrast between Pentheus' helplessness in the face of an irresistible divine force and Dionysus' disregard for human suffering that makes Pentheus' death heart-rending.

Bacchae is starker than other revenge plays due to the immediate, direct and merciless divine engagement in the vengeance. It is clear from the start that humans have no chance to escape the revenge; we can only watch them being marshalled to their doom. Euripides is known for his subversiveness, his innovations, experimentation and challenge to his audiences. It seems natural to ask, then, what he was attempting to tell his spectators. He was known for shunning tradition and undermining popular religion, especially in his later years.[11] Is *Bacchae* then a palinode, as Nietzsche suggested? Did the iconoclastic playwright have a last-minute 'change of mind', a recantation of the 'atheism' of which Aristophanes accused him (*Thesm.* 450–1)? Did he want to say that on a larger scale religion should not be exposed to subtleties of reasoning, that human understanding cannot subvert traditions as old as time? Or was he encouraging the spectators to rethink their belief in and worship of Dionysus, parallel to the way he portrayed Aphrodite and Artemis in *Hippolytus* in 428 BCE? Or, finally, is the play a parody of religious drama?[12] Each of these theses can be supported by some facts but is contradicted by others. We do not even know how much of the play is by Euripides' hand and how much is by his son's (or his nephew's), the younger Euripides. Euripides left Athens in 408 BCE for Macedonia, where he was the guest of King Archelaus. He was 70 years old and there is reason to believe that he was a disappointed man. Judging from the scanty prizes he received in the tragic contests, he could not think of himself as a successful dramatist, and he became the target of the comic poets. In Macedonia he wrote the *Archelaus*, a play about his host's eponymous ancestor, which may have been performed in the newly built theatre in Dion. The *Bacchae*, *Alcmaeon in Corinth* (lost to us) and *Iphigenia at Aulis*, the last probably unfinished, were all found after his death. The younger Euripides eventually brought this trilogy to the Athenian stage at the Great Dionysia (406 BCE). It won the first prize, one of the five prizes Euripides' dramas won in the fifth century BCE. Some think it possible that the *Bacchae* was also staged in Macedonia, but given the many allusions to dramatic characterizations and topics prevalent in tragedies performed in Athens, it is safer to assume that the play was primarily meant for an Athenian audience.

Note

1 Burnett (1998) xvi.
2 For tragedies' titles, see Kaimio (2014).
3 For a helpful comparison between Pentheus and Hippolytus, see Segal (1986), 268–93.
4 Burnett (1998) xvi, 225–6.
5 For rational and irrational in Euripides, see Roisman (1999) esp. 170–2; for the rift between the mythic and the rational see Segal (1982) 220n, 279–80.
6 For cross-dressing in Greek tragedy, see Llewellyn–Jones (2014).
7 Dodds (1974) xliii.
8 Roisman (1999) ch. 7.
9 Roisman (1999) 32–3, 110–12.
10 Roisman (1999) esp. 136–9, 170–7.
11 For Euripides' subversiveness, see Papadodima (2014).
12 See Dodds (1974) xxxix–xl; Thumiger (2014).

The Grandsons of Cadmus

Sophie Mills

'Gods should not have the passions that men do.' This is Cadmus' plaintive comment at the end of *Bacchae* (1348) on the systematic destruction by Dionysus of his family. His grandson Pentheus is not only dead but has been ripped to shreds by his mother Agave. She faces exile, while Cadmus himself and his wife must also leave their home in Thebes and set out on a journey full of unknowns and potential dangers. But in principle, Dionysus has only done what any Greek male might do when faced with disrespect and hostility from an enemy. The principle 'help friends and harm enemies' is most famously expressed by Polemarchus at the beginning of Plato's *Republic* (332a10) as the definition of justice in popular morality, and Dionysus himself alludes to this dictum at the end of the play (1342–3), when he points out to Cadmus that if he had had more sense, he could have had him as an ally. Cadmus himself plainly acknowledges that Dionysus had the right to be angry at his family's disbelief in his divinity (1293–8, 1302, 1346). However, Cadmus' statement at 1348 also assumes that there should be limits on revenge and that there is some sort of reasonable level of anger, which Dionysus has transgressed. What would have been a just punishment? Cadmus does not say, and from Dionysus' perspective, there are no limits: he is a god, the true son of Zeus, and that is enough.

Cadmus' complaint lies at the very centre of *Bacchae* in the portrayal of Dionysus and his human adversary Pentheus. Euripides' earlier play *Hippolytus* handles some similar questions in its portrayal of a young man who considers himself so close to the goddess Artemis that he emulates her hostility to Aphrodite, the goddess of love and sexuality, and is destroyed by Aphrodite for his disrespect. In fact, early in the play, Hippolytus' old servant makes a claim similar to Cadmus' when he expresses his (vain) hope that Aphrodite will not punish her human enemy too severely: 'gods ought to be wiser than men' (Eur. *Hipp.* 120). And yet, though Aphrodite acts very much as Dionysus does, cruelly destroying a young man who crosses her, typically commentators have tended not to express quite as much active revulsion for her actions as for those of Dionysus. Even though the character of Pentheus is also in many ways deeply unsympathetic, 'it is much easier to blacken

Dionysus', as E.R. Dodds, author of one of the most influential of all commentaries on Euripides, states (Dodds 1960: xliii). Why is it that Dionysus' revenge, which conforms to human popular morality and resembles divine revenges in many other tragic and mythological stories, seems so problematic? The answer lies in Euripides' portrayal of Dionysus as an unusually humanized god, and this blurring of divine and human (itself a central characteristic of the Dionysiac religion imagined by Euripides) has some interesting consequences for reading Euripides' *Bacchae*.

Right from the start, Pentheus and Dionysus are adversaries and they appear as visual opposites. Dionysus has long hair, a pale complexion that suggests that he avoids manly pursuits, and the long, flowing clothing of one of his worshippers. The way that Pentheus and others draw attention to these details of his appearance (235–6, 353, 438, 453f) suggests that his form is unconventional for a male and that Pentheus must be his physical opposite, conforming to norms of manly dress and behaviour. The physical opposition between them is aligned with their verbal opposition in a series of long dialogues in which each tries to get the better of the other. But, though opposites in some senses, they are also very similar in the way they view their place in the world. Perhaps this is not entirely surprising, since these two young men are first cousins, sharing Cadmus as their grandfather. Dionysus is the child of Zeus and Semele and is a highly unusual god in having a mortal mother: usually the pairing of a god and a mortal results in a heroic, but human child. So Dionysus, though a god, mixes divine and human in his essential nature. Although Pentheus' parents were both mortals, his father Echion was not of ordinary mortal birth but was one of the Spartoi sprung from the dragon's teeth sown by Cadmus. Thus the god Dionysus has some human elements in his ancestry and the man Pentheus has some supernatural elements in his. The truth of Dionysus' ancestry is obviously central to *Bacchae*, but Pentheus' ancestry is mentioned surprisingly often as well (265, 507, 537–55, 995–6, 1015–16, 1155, 1274). The chorus interpret his birth from 'earth-born' stock as a sign of his opposition to Dionysus, like the giants who fought against divinity (537–55), but his earth-born element may also recall the snake, an avatar of Dionysus: if so, this connection also draws the apparently opposed pair together. Pentheus and Dionysus both come from high-born families and both naturally demand obedience and deference from the world around them. Dionysus is a god in human form; Pentheus is human but aspires to be like a god in some ways. The blurred lines between these two opponents recall the confusion of normal human categories and limits (for example, east and west, male and female, old and young, violence and beauty and, of course, human, divine and animal) that is one of the central motifs of the play and of Euripides' conception of Dionysiac religion (e.g. 15–18, 67, 113–14, 139, 193, 206–9, 526–9, 694).

One of Pentheus' most notable, and unfavourably regarded, characteristics is his emphasis on punishment, confinement and force. Even before he has met the stranger, he has managed to capture and imprison some of Dionysus' worshippers (226–7), and threatens, if he finds the stranger responsible for disrupting his city, to cut off his head (239–41). He considers his 'blasphemy' (*hybris hybrizein*) worthy of hanging (246–7) or even a death by stoning (355–6). Later, he will imprison the stranger, even though the imprisonment of his followers has already proved useless (443–6) and will prove useless in this case as well (644). Though he respects Teiresias' age, he wishes he could imprison him for his part in introducing such harmful rites (258–60) and threatens to turn his prophetic sanctuary upside down as punishment (349; cf. 945–52). Pentheus makes no attempt to find out whether his perception that Dionysus is a false god and his rituals mere excuses for female debauchery is actually true or not: he assumes that he is right and acts accordingly. He has no time for subtleties and his ambitions are large: he plans to hunt down all the women who are in the mountains and imprison them with those he has already put in custody. His behaviour is foolish at best, and only seems more so as the play progresses, and Dionysus reveals more and more miracles – supernatural liberation, an earthquake, and above all the extraordinary events on Mount Cithaeron. Pentheus ought to change his mind and believe, as the audience knows, that Dionysus is divine. But Pentheus does not like being defied or ridiculed.

Dionysus shares many of his cousin's characteristics. He too is absolute in his treatment of the world around him. The female population of Thebes whom Pentheus has imprisoned, or plans to imprison, are in the mountains because Dionysus has sent them there as punishment for the offences of the Theban royal family against him. The language of the prologue in which he explains to the audience what he has done is striking: he has made them 'maddened on the mountain-side, hallucinating and delirious' (32–3; cf. 36, 119), *forced* into being his worshippers (34; cf. 643), because the city must learn who he is, even against its will (39–40). And he is single-minded in his special revenge against Pentheus. Pentheus threatens to hunt the women he has not yet caught: his prey Dionysus (436) will turn Pentheus into the prey of his mother and her fellow devotees at the end of the play (1107–8), and Pentheus' frequent invocation of a literal prison (e.g. 497) is paralleled by the deadly trap (848) that Dionysus lures him into. Pentheus plans to use his army to rid Thebes of the new cult (780–4, 809, 845): at 50–2, Dionysus threatens his own military retaliation if Thebes refuses to accept him. While this unfulfilled threat can be explained by Euripides' fondness for misdirecting his audiences (cf. Eur. *Hipp.* 42), it is also one more means by which the two opponents in the play are given similar tendencies. Pentheus consistently reverts to force when words fail him (e.g. 503) but in a sense the same is true of Dionysus in his imposition of his religion on Thebes (34) and the horrific violence with which he will prove his identity. The death by stoning with which Pentheus threatens the stranger (355–6) will be his at the end of the play as Dionysus' worshippers throw 'branches and boulders' at him to dislodge him from his position high on a fir tree (1096–8), and just as Pentheus threatens to decapitate the stranger (241), Dionysus will preside over his decapitation.

Though ecstatic experience, freed from the boundaries of everyday rationality, is central to Dionysus' cult (and is one of its features that repels Pentheus), the god's prologue speech is coldly rational: he emphasizes that he has disguised himself as a mortal (4–5, 53–4), and makes an explicit connection between his mortal garb and his premeditated punishment for Pentheus (45–55). The god makes no distinctions but wants everyone to give him honour (206–9), but although liberation from the everyday is central to Dionysiac religion, he does not allow anyone the freedom to opt out of worshipping him or deny him. Pentheus' concern that his authority will be undermined by the new religion leads him to attempt to crush all its manifestations.

Pentheus and Dionysus share vocabulary which indicates some interesting common ground between the two apparent opposites. Dionysus is the god who turns everything 'upside down' (602, 741, 753) and Pentheus expresses a desire to upturn Teiresias' prophetic seat at 349. Although Pentheus appears to be the one who binds and Dionysus is a liberator – one of his cult names is *Lyaeus*, 'the loosener' – both Dionysus (39, 492, 656, 948; cf. 181) and Pentheus (489, 655, 780) use the Greek word *dei*, meaning 'it is necessary', which is also connected with the Greek verb 'to bind', and both admit to using force (34, 643). Accusations of *hybris* (translated here variously as 'blasphemy', 'immorality', 'hooligan boasts', 'arrogance', 'insult' and 'beguil[ing]') are notable in the vocabulary of both adversaries or their supporters: Pentheus complains of Dionysus' claim to divinity as *hybris hubrizein* (247) and the religious disturbances as a *hybrisma* (779); Dionysus' worshippers condemn the *hybris* of Pentheus (375, 555); Dionysus complains of Pentheus' *hybrismata* (516) and the *hybris* of Cadmus' family (1347), which Cadmus acknowledges (*hubrin hubristheis*, 1297); and Dionysus expresses some pride (*kathubris' auton*) in tricking and maddening Pentheus (616). The potential for violence in Dionysus' religion becomes increasingly strong throughout the play, but even at 113, the chorus commands reverence around the 'potent' thyrsus (*narthēkas hybristas*; cf. 9, 743).

Neither Pentheus nor Dionysus tolerates ambiguity well. Dionysus sees an insolent young adversary who refuses to give him the respect he deserves and takes considerable pains to entrap him for his disrespect. But scholars more sympathetic to Pentheus' position note that he is a young king who has been given an awesome responsibility to his city in protecting its women and children. He has a right and a duty to speak for his city, and, to his eyes, a foreign cult that takes women away from their homes could be damaging to Thebes. Pentheus sees Dionysus as a fake and his religion as merely an excuse for women to enjoy untrammelled sex and wine (224–5). The chorus, particularly in their early songs, offer a very different story of a genuine, life-changing religious state, full of beauty and miracle. And yet, there is another side to Dionysus which is less benign and which Pentheus' apprehensions – in many ways mistaken though they are – do capture. Wine and sexuality are not the only part of Dionysiac ritual (685–8), but they do play some part, as the first messenger seems to admit (773–4; cf. 279–83), while the chorus implore their god to take them to Cyprus, the island of Aphrodite, 'the land of grace, the land of longing' (403–16). Dionysus is indeed a new (though genuine) god; even Pentheus' claim that the women are involved in false rituals ('pretext of pilgrimage', 218) is in a sense true, given that their worship has been forced upon them rather than been freely undertaken.

Pentheus seeks to limit and confine, while Dionysus transcends distinctions and limits because he is a god, and, in particular, a god who uses his divine power to transcend limitation. Limitation is a quintessentially human characteristic: humans are limited by ignorance, by physical frailty and especially by mortality. Dionysus, however, can be young and old, male and female, Greek and non-Greek, divine and human at the same time. Pentheus does not realize this, thinking in limited, confined ways that will destroy him. Only Teiresias is able at least partially to express a degree of comfort with Dionysus' unhuman illogical multiple statuses (298–309). But he too emphasizes the apparent commonality between humans and gods which mistakenly minimizes the gap between them (319–21; cf. *Hipp.* 8): 'You're gratified when the crowds come out and all the city rings with praise for Pentheus. Well, Dionysus likes being honoured too.' This is true at one level, but, like the disguise that Dionysus deliberately puts on to hide the divinity which gives him power and knowledge vastly exceeding anything human, it also conceals some unbridgeable gaps between them and makes a dangerous equation between god and man. Teiresias' words are designed to make Pentheus accept Dionysus, but they fail and, if anything, he becomes even more vehement against him (343–55).

An analysis of the exchanges between Pentheus and Dionysus shows most clearly the gap in power and knowledge between god and mortal, one of whom thinks he is arguing on equal terms while the other knows that he has completely the upper hand. Until he begins his dialogue with Dionysus, Pentheus' language is forceful, full of first person active verbs in the future or imperatives (228, 232, 239–40, 253, 343–4, 346, 348, 350–1, 352, 355, 451, 460). He is in control as he describes the stranger, defining him in less than flattering terms (453–9), before moving into an interrogation. In a successful interrogation, the interrogator should be clearly in control, asking his subordinate questions and receiving satisfactory answers in return, but repeatedly Pentheus' line of questioning comes to a halt, as Dionysus' responses begin to throw him off balance. For a short time they are matched, but after a series of questions, at 474, in answer to Pentheus' question as to the benefits of Dionysus' rites, Dionysus refuses to say directly and teases him: 'Well worth knowing – but it's not permitted you should know them.' At this point, Pentheus is in control – 'A clever answer, calculated to intrigue' (475) – but his momentum is temporarily checked and at 477 he backtracks to a question he has already raised at 469–70 about how the stranger saw Dionysus. Dionysus' stonewalling response annoys him (479) and at 481 he tries yet another line of questioning, in effect looping back to where he started at 460, with questions about the stranger's origins. After a brief exchange where Pentheus denounces the inferiority of the barbarians who worship the new god, Dionysus parries and Pentheus does not pursue it, so Pentheus again goes back (485) to the 'night and day' question he first raised at 469. When he confidently claims that women are more liable to be corrupted at night (487), Dionysus easily deflects the claim and it is at this point that Pentheus has had enough. This effeminate stranger has proved harder to best than he had conceived, and so he tries to assert himself through threats of punishment. But Dionysus has had enough as well, and turns Pentheus' own words on him (489–90):

Pentheus   You'll pay for your blasphemies *and* your slippery tongue.

Dionysus   And you for your short-sightedness and disrespect to Bacchus.

To this, Pentheus has no good answer and all he can do is exclaim at the stranger's bold speech. In destabilizing his arguments, Dionysus does verbally to Pentheus what he will do to him physically in the earthquake scene, where he watches calmly while Pentheus runs around vainly (616–37), and psychically later in the play (912–70). At this point, the tables now begin to turn as Dionysus takes verbal control of the scene by questioning Pentheus (492), encouraging him in impious threats against the god while repeatedly frustrating his answers or taunting him by suggesting (500–2) that he could see the god if he were not impious. Yet again Pentheus ends the line of questioning (503), relying on his kingly authority by addressing his attendants with another imperative: 'Take him away!' When Dionysus warns him not to proceed (504), Pentheus tries to do what Dionysus did earlier by turning his phraseology against him, mistakenly thinking his own kingly authority much greater than it is:

> **Dionysus**   I'm warning you. Don't touch me. I have the knowledge. You do not.
>
> **Pentheus**   But I have the power.

Dionysus warns him that he does not know what he is doing or saying, or who he is, to which Pentheus' response – his name and parents' name – encapsulates both his human status and his deep ignorance of his enemy. But at this point, he commands his attendants to imprison the stranger and announces his intention to control his worshippers.

The miraculous liberation that Dionysus prophesies for himself (498) happens in the next scene, along with a spectacular earthquake which should be a warning to Pentheus. Dionysus' longest speech since the prologue (615ff) reveals a side of him that resembles Pentheus in its mocking and bullying tone. So here a god is using his divine powers to have revenge on a mortal by manipulating and taking active pleasure in humiliating him (616, 632; cf. 1081) through unconquerable phantoms and illusions (618–20, 624–6, 629–31). Pentheus is made to look stupid and ungainly (620–1) while the stranger watches calmly (622, 636). As Dionysus says: 'He's only a man, / yet he dared fight a god' (635–6). This is Pentheus' offence and Dionysus has the absolute right in the terms of Greek tragedy and Greek myth to punish him: countless stories, including *Ba.* 337–40, tell a similar tale. But a significant number of scholars have expressed repulsion at his revenge, which somehow seems qualitatively more vicious than any other in Greek tragedy. This reaction may partly be explained through Dionysus' unusually humanized characterization: he is not a remote, spectacular deity but a deity who has deliberately disguised himself in human clothing to deceive a mortal into threatening and disrespecting him. Dionysus' behaviour resembles that of his adversary, but his power to inflict hurt does not. Euripides is known for domesticating the big, grand heroes of Greek tragedy, with similarly unsettling effects, and certain elements of his technique with Dionysus, both in characterization and in stagecraft, elicit the same unease. Aphrodite in Euripides' *Hippolytus* offers a useful counter-example. Just like Dionysus, she seeks deadly revenge for human disrespect but, unlike Dionysus, though she has arranged the tragedy right from the start, as she tells us in her prologue speech (*Hipp.* 10–50), she is entirely absent thereafter. While she knows her human characters and how they will enact her disastrous plans, just as Dionysus knows how Pentheus can be entrapped, it is the human characters who unknowingly carry out what she has set up for them by following what they think are their own independent intentions, so that Euripides gives us the illusion that her role in the tragedy is a little less than it actually is. By contrast, Dionysus is on stage for almost the whole of *Bacchae*, deliberately disguised as a human being like Pentheus, and he misdirects and manipulates Pentheus – admittedly culpable for not understanding the significance of the supernatural events he witnesses – into an increasingly inextricable trap.

In 645–59, the reversal of power between king and god is especially clear. Pentheus asks the stranger how he is free from the stables. He gets no answer but just a command (647). When he asks his next question (648) Dionysus answers him with a question, and Pentheus must ask another question, complaining that he does not understand 'riddles' (650). He tries to assert himself again through physical force (653) and is mocked by Dionysus, who points out that no physical force can stop a determined god. This leads to another conversational impasse as Pentheus expresses his frustration: 'Oh, very clever! Very clever! Not where you *should* be clever, though!' (655). But Dionysus turns his words against him: 'Oh, there especially.' The audience knows what he means: irony of this kind will become increasingly prevalent in the play as Pentheus gets less and less capable of understanding what is happening to him and, as we will see, has a particularly horrific effect in Pentheus' last appearance on stage (955–70).

Pentheus' subsequent exchange with the messenger who brings news from Mount Cithaeron is very different from the preceding one with Dionysus. He is back in command, asking questions and receiving clear answers. The messenger is nervous about speaking honestly to him, however, fearing his sharp nature and his king's temper (671): to his underlings, perhaps, Pentheus behaves rather as Dionysus does to him. Pentheus' response is telling as well. He encourages him to speak freely: 'One mustn't take one's anger out on those who're not involved.' Dionysus would hardly disagree. 'But the more I hear about those bacchae, the more flagrant and outrageous their excesses, the more unyielding I shall be to *him*.' This too resembles the sort of treatment that Dionysus gives Pentheus, first luring him into acting so as to arouse his wrath, and then meting out an extreme punishment.

The messenger claims that if Pentheus had seen the sights he had seen he would have supplicated the god whom he now condemns (712–3), but

Pentheus cannot put himself in another position at this stage, and nor can Dionysus. But only one of them will suffer. Thus his response to the messenger's news is his usual appeal to military violence (779–85). He is as determined not to be insulted by women (785–6) as Dionysus is not to be insulted by a human being. Again, Pentheus expresses frustration at being unable to best his adversary, who blocks his every move (800–1): 'This foreigner won't let me go! No matter what I do to him, no matter what he does, he won't keep quiet.'

At this point, Dionysus offers to help him, seizing the initiative once and for all that will lead to Pentheus' destruction. While Pentheus at first retains enough of his judgement to be suspicious of Dionysus' offer to bring the women to him (805, 807) and forcefully tells him to stop talking, Dionysus simply ignores him and asks the fatal question, 'Do you want to see them for yourself?' The chasm between Cadmus' divine and human grandsons gapes open in the contrast of Dionysus' knowledge of Pentheus and Pentheus' ignorance of the god, who plays a complicated verbal game with him, questioning him so that he reveals what he wants, but then makes objections to his replies so that Pentheus must continually be on the defensive. Not only is the god the winner in all their exchanges (811–29), but Pentheus even gratefully and repeatedly praises the wisdom of his malignant advisor (818; cf. 824, 826, 838). At 821 Dionysus drops his bombshell, that Pentheus must wear women's clothing, and Pentheus struggles at length with the idea (819–46). At 824, he accepts Dionysus' advice that this is the only way to see the women unharmed, but by 828, he backtracks. Dionysus teases him: 'Have you lost your enthusiasm? Do you not want to see the maenads any more?' Brought to heel again, Pentheus asks a series of questions which Dionysus patiently answers until 836, when once more he rejects the idea of women's clothing. But this is almost the last point at which he resists: while he thinks that he still retains the option of choosing his way or Dionysus' (843, 845–6), it is clear that he does not.

Pentheus struggles with the temptations offered by Dionysus rather as Phaedra in *Hippolytus* struggles against the shameful desires that Aphrodite has put in her, but whereas Aphrodite is offstage, Dionysus in human form is in front of us in dialogue with his victim. Each time he withdraws, Dionysus comes after him and lures him back in. In *Hippolytus*, though Aphrodite influences events behind the scenes, it is human agency, through the well-meaning Nurse, that ultimately foils Phaedra's attempts to hold off divine power, and although Aphrodite causes Hippolytus' death out of hatred for him, we never see her gloat over his sufferings. Dionysus actively looks forward to Pentheus' incurring laughter among the Thebans (854): Pentheus mocked his rites (1081) and Dionysus will return the injury.

Aphrodite is also directly identified with the impersonal force of sexuality (Eur. *Hipp.* 447–50), so that it is easier to see some symbolism in her revenge as the work of an impartial force of nature. Dionysus also represents some great force, but its specific nature is less clear because he is given so many human characteristics, which make his revenge seem cruel and personally directed rather than an expression of the impersonal forces of the universe in human life. His human disguise represents in visual form the illusion he is offering Pentheus, that they are two equally matched adversaries in a fair fight. Because Pentheus is manipulated into the mistake of believing that he is dealing with an equal, watching the whole experience becomes highly uncomfortable for the audience.

The next scene gives immediate visual expression to the mixture of similarities and differences between Pentheus and Dionysus. Their masks are different, but they now wear the same costume. Dionysus has complete control over a Pentheus who cannot even see normally, though the god describes this as 'seeing as you should' (924, 948; cf. 964). With deadly tenderness, he rearranges Pentheus' hair and Pentheus is quite literally in his hands as he asks his advice on how to be a maenad. Here again, Pentheus asks questions and accepts Dionysus' answers, thanking him for his good advice, as though speaking to an equal (953), but increasingly Dionysus is speaking to someone who has no inkling of what is really happening. Pentheus becomes so bound up in his delusion that he even demands to be carried in triumph right through the middle of Thebes (961). The combination of Pentheus' incomprehension and the multiple plays on words that Euripides gives both characters has a very unsettling effect: since Pentheus does not understand the full import of what he or his adversary are saying, the only ones who do are the audience, so that we become disturbingly complicit in Dionysus' revenge in a way in which we are never complicit in Aphrodite's in *Hippolytus.* The unintentional double meanings in Pentheus' words start as early as 846: the primary meaning of '*toisi soisi peisomai bouleumasin*' is 'I'll take your advice', but the line could also mean 'I will suffer through your advice'. At 934, Pentheus says, 'I've made myself over to you completely', but in another sense of the verb, he is indeed 'dedicated' as an offering to the god. But in the intense set of exchanges between Pentheus and Dionysus (966–70), the double meanings, escaping Pentheus but all too obvious to the audience, abound.

Dionysus . . . Someone else will bring you home.

Pentheus My mother.

Dionysus A most pleasing spectacle.

Pentheus	My destiny.
Dionysus	Raised high.
Pentheus	Too much!
Dionysus	And in your mother's arms.
Pentheus	You want to spoil me.
Dionysus	Yes, I'll spoil you – after my own fashion.
Pentheus	Well, I deserve it.

Earlier, Dionysus gloated over what would happen to Pentheus (850–6). Here, he is even joking with Pentheus, who unwittingly contributes to the joke: he will come home in his mother's arms and – as he deserves – will be spoiled: the Greek word used is cognate with a word that means 'torn into little pieces'. Just after his exchange with Pentheus, Dionysus prophesies that Pentheus' fame will 'fill the sky' (971; cf. 1073, 1083). Such words are made especially unnerving by the god's human disguise and his ever-smiling face (439, 1021). The inhuman mix of playfulness and horror will reach its climax in the ball game that Agave and her companions play with Pentheus' flesh in the woods (1135–6), though a mixture of holiness and violence, beauty and hideousness is strongly emphasized as Dionysiac throughout the play as early as the chorus' *parodos*.

When the messenger announces Pentheus' death, the chorus are jubilant. For the followers of Dionysus, this is simple justice (cf. 991), but he replies: 'I understand your feelings, but it's not right to gloat over another's suffering' (1039–40). As early as the *Odyssey*, Odysseus expresses a similarly sober rejection of rejoicing in an enemy's destruction: 'It is not holy to crow over dead men. The fate of the gods and their own wicked deeds crushed them' (*Od.* 22.412–13). Similarly, Odysseus in Sophocles' *Ajax* rejects Athena's enthusiasm for revenge on an enemy (Soph. *Aj.* 79) because he pities Ajax, seeing that all humans are vulnerable (121–6). Both of these passages express a human wisdom, guided by a sense of the innate limitations of humans which (if they are sensible) must mean that what they are allowed to do is very different from what divinities can do. Pentheus fails to see these limitations in his treatment of Dionysus. And now it is too late, and Dionysus does not need to abide by any limitations.

Certainly he shows no restraint in his treatment of Pentheus. He sets him high upon a fir tree in view of his mother and her fellow bacchants, and his voice calls out twice (1079–81, 1088) to the women to stir them up against Pentheus. The god even gives Agave a superhuman strength to tear her son to pieces (1128). At 507, Pentheus had emphasized his wholly human nature in his naive response to Dionysus:

Dionysus You don't know what you're saying. You don't know what you're doing. You don't know who you are.

Pentheus I am *Pentheus*, the son of Echion by Agave my mother.

Now Pentheus desperately invokes his ancestry again (1119) to use his human, familial relationship with his mother in order to beg her for pity. Pity is an intensely human emotion, stemming from a sense of vulnerability: Aristotle states that we feel pity for the sight of evils that we might expect to come on ourselves or our friends (*Rhet.* 1385b 11–16). Because he is a god, Dionysus does not need to be swayed by pity and has temporarily suspended it in others. Indeed, the whole of this scene is shot through with the negation of humanity or human values. A human is literally ripped to pieces and his flesh used as a plaything (1135–6), and Agave views the son she gave birth to as a beast (1107–8). The women capture their prey without nets or weapons (1175, 1204–10), which some commentators see as a troubling shift from human culture back to an untamed natural state. Agave is proud of her ability to have captured the so-called lion cub and credits Dionysus with her success, calling him her 'companion in the hunt' (1146): he has helped her, not as she believes but in a victory whose 'prize / will be weeping' (1147). Equality between human and divine is an illusion at best and deeply problematic at worst. Dionysus is the god who insists on the erasure of distinction (18, 37, 1131) and turns the world upside down, but erasing the distinctions between animal and human or divine and human in this so-called contest (964, 975) with Pentheus is not the benign erasure that it appears to be at the start of the play.

It is left to his old grandfather Cadmus to search the forest devotedly to put all the pieces of Pentheus' broken body back together again, restoring the best semblance of humanness that he can to him. Already at 1249 (cf. 1297, 1302), Cadmus makes his judgement on what Dionysus has done to his family: 'He had every right to do it, but this – this is too much.' Cadmus also brings Agave back to human reality from her god-sent madness, again through reminding her of her human connections to her son and husband (1274–7). Cadmus' expression of his loss is notable: now he will be vulnerable, with no adult male in the house to protect him from disrespect (*hybrizein*, 1311), as he offers us a slightly different side of Pentheus. Cadmus' Pentheus still focuses on punishment and violence (1311–2, 1320–2; at 945–6, 949–50, violence is on his mind even in his Dionysus-induced delusion), but here his desire to punish is connected with love for his grandfather (1317–8). Like Dionysus, Pentheus likes to punish, but here at least, Euripides shows us the mutual affection between Cadmus and his grandson which impels Pentheus to punish those who hurt him. Dionysus too is both 'a god of terror and a god of gentle comfort for mankind' (861).

The loss of most of Dionysus' speech at the end of the play (between 1329 and 1330) is particularly unfortunate because the god's own account of his revenge might help to contextualize what he does to Cadmus and his family: did he show any remorse or pity to his stricken human foes or was he entirely unmoved by their explicit acknowledgement that they were at fault (as the speculative reconstruction of the speech by Willink (1966: 46–9) has it)? Dionysus' judgement on his actions must remain unknown, but Artemis' speech at the end of *Hippolytus* offers one example of the possibilities for divine contextualization and explanation. Though it was not her plan that caused such misery for Hippolytus, Phaedra and Theseus, her refusal to intervene in Aphrodite's plot against her favourite requires explanation from a human perspective, and she gives it. Indeed, her speech is notable for the way it absolves all the human characters who contributed to the tragedy: Phaedra did wrong but acted nobly in a way (Eur. *Hipp.* 1300–1); Theseus did wrong but he can be forgiven (*Hipp.* 1335–6), since gods do not frustrate other gods' purposes and, when a god decides on something, nothing can be done (*Hipp.* 1328–30; cf. 1433–4). So it is certainly possible for divinities, even when they cause suffering or do not avert it, to give explanations and even some encouragement to the human characters. The two divinities of *Hippolytus* simply frame its beginning and end, but Dionysus (in disguise) announces his plot against Cadmus' family at the beginning, Dionysus (in disguise) works consistently throughout his play to make his plans work, and Dionysus (in his real form) comes to end it.

What remains of Dionysus' speech is a matter-of-fact prophecy that prescribes yet more trials for Cadmus and his wife, who must metamorphose into snakes and go on a long journey far from Thebes (1330–9). Dionysus remains authoritative and firm, asserting his right to prophesy as a true god and god's son (1340–1), before he reminds them that had they 'been humble' (*sōphronein*) they would have had Dionysus as an 'ally' and 'friend for ever'. Cadmus is at last able to confront Dionysus directly, acknowledging that they did wrong, but claiming that the punishment inflicted was too severe. Dionysus will not engage with this – for an insulted god (*hybrizomen*, 1347) there is no such thing as 'too much' vengeance. This is what it means to be a god, rather than a man. Even now, this terrible lesson is one that Cadmus either has not learned or cannot accept: 'gods should not have the passions that men do.' Dionysus' answer seems unsatisfactory – relying on the authority of Zeus, all he can say is that 'this has long been' his father's will. There is no more to be said to him (1351). Agave too must leave her city and her father, and complains about the extraordinary cruelty of Dionysus' revenge on her. It is one of the very striking features of *Bacchae* that her last words repudiate the worship of Dionysus: her family and city might have been forcibly taught to respect the gods, but the religious effect Agave's experience has had on her recalls Dionysus' use of his worship as a punishment for the women of Thebes (23-42) rather than as a genuinely chosen religion. The victory of the god wrapped in human form over his scornful human cousin is total, yet curiously Pyrrhic.

12

Bacchae in the Modern World

Betine van Zyl Smit

The reception of ancient drama includes in its wide embrace productions, translations – some poetic and some scholarly – superficial borrowing and adaptations, sometimes creative and sometimes brutal. Euripides' *Bacchae* provides examples of all of these. It was one of the most quoted and seemingly best-known tragedies in antiquity. It was not only performed in ancient theatres until the fourth century AD, but also provided material for countless vase paintings in Southern Italy. The richness of the dramatic material must partly account for this popularity. The prominent role of Dionysus, the god of the theatre, is clear in the paintings, but the nature of the god, his ecstatic worship, his death and rebirth, also led to him becoming associated with Christ. One of the early Church fathers, Clement of Alexandria, attacked the Dionysian mysteries as they are represented in Euripides' *Bacchae* because they showed the search for salvation through intoxication. In a different mode the Byzantine cento *Christus Patiens* took inspiration for its scene of Mary weeping over the body of her crucified son from the depiction of Agave weeping over the head of Pentheus (1280 ff). About three hundred of its more than two thousand six hundred lines are taken from *Bacchae* and rearranged to fit into the new context.

In spite of its renown in the ancient world, the early reception of *Bacchae* in the modern world was rather muted. Statistics from the Archive of Performances of Greek and Roman Drama show that between 1850 and 1967 there were in total thirty-five productions of Euripides' *Bacchae*, most of them in Anglophone countries and most at educational institutions. However, the tally for the much shorter period of 1968 to early 2015 is one hundred and thirty-seven, a striking increase. Part of the explanation is undoubtedly that records of performance have been kept more accurately in recent times, but that cannot detract from the impression that this tragedy has enjoyed unprecedented interest in theatrical circles in the recent past. Sophie Mills suggests that it was because *Bacchae* was considered so violent that it was seldom performed before the 1960s.[1] In the twentieth century *Bacchae* received extensive and intensive scholarly attention: a number of commentaries and full-length studies were published by distinguished academics such as R.P. Winnington-Ingram, E.R. Dodds, J. Roux, G.S. Kirk, C. Segal and R. Seaford. The play has been read from many different theoretical viewpoints such as deconstructive, structuralist, psychoanalytic and metatheatrical. In tandem with this renewal of attention to performance and study of *Bacchae* has come a number of provocative adaptations of the tragedy. It is unsurprising that this play, with its multiplicity of themes – religion, religious ecstasy, emotion, reason, scepticism, asceticism, role playing and the relationship between gods and humans – should interest creative artists. Pat Easterling has noted that: 'Of the plays in the surviving Greek tragic canon *Bacchae* above all has proved to have special meaning for readers and audiences in the second half of the twentieth century.'[2] The focus of this chapter is on some of the more prominent examples of how the tragedy has been adapted and staged in different countries in the recent past.

The plays reviewed are *Dionysus in 69*, produced in New York by Richard Schechner, well known for his theoretical and practical work in the field of theatre; the Nigerian playwright and poet Wole Soyinka's *The Bacchae of Euripides*, created for the National Theatre in London in 1973; a production of *Bacchae* as part of the first 'Antiquity Project' in Berlin in 1974; and Roy Sargeant's staging of the tragedy at the Dionysus festival in Cape Town in 2002. However, in addition to being transformed into modern plays, *Bacchae* has been adapted to be staged in another modern form which has often been called the closest to ancient tragedy, namely opera. Two examples of opera are described before the rest of the chapter deals with the four plays.

There have been several different operatic versions of *Bacchae* and recently, staged in New York in 2007, even a rock opera, *Rockae*, with music and lyrics by Peter Mills. The Dionysus figure resembled a young metal-rock star, and a variety of musical styles from hard rock to folk was used for the lyrics while part of the dialogue was spoken. One critic was so impressed by this adaptation that he wrote that rock opera might be the best way of conveying the intensity of Greek tragedy to a modern audience.[3] Two more conventionally styled operas which have become part of the repertoire and are both based on Euripides' tragedy engage in different ways with the religious and spiritual themes so prominent in *Bacchae*. The earlier, Karol Szymanowski's *King Roger* dates from 1926 and the second, Hans Werner Henze's opera, *The Bassarids*, had its premiere at the Salzburg festival in 1966 with Gustav Rudolf Sellner as the director. Both these operas clearly reflect influence from Nietzsche's celebrated dialectic between the Dionysian and the Apollonian, which was also a factor in some of the adaptations for drama in the twentieth century.

King Roger, first performed in Warsaw, has a plot invented by Szymanowski, who also co-wrote the libretto with the poet Jaroslaw Iwaszkiewicz. The opera is set in Sicily during the twelfth century. The themes of conflict between the beliefs embodied by Pentheus and Dionysus in *Bacchae* are largely internalized in King Roger, as his own rational approach to life, bolstered by his Arabian adviser, Edrisi, is tested by the seductive message of a newcomer, a Shepherd. His religious message is condemned as blasphemous and King Roger is put under pressure to execute the Indian Shepherd. However, the queen, Roxana, has fallen to the lure of the mysteries of the Indian cult and pleads that the newcomer be given an opportunity to explain his case. The Shepherd does this so successfully that he wins the king over too and is permitted to leave. Thus the incomer leads not only the queen and other Sicilians, but also the king out of the city. While the first act of the opera was set in the cathedral, symbolizing the established faith, the third act takes place in the ruins of a Greek theatre. This location gains deeper significance when the incomer reveals that he is in fact Dionysus. Orgiastic scenes follow in which Roger also participates. He and his adviser, however, stay behind when the Dionysus figure leads the rest of the participants away. Roger's character does not display the arrogance of the ancient Pentheus; he accepts the existence of the new religion, but does not succumb to its lure. He is on the side of reason, as is made clear when the opera ends with Roger greeting the rising sun, Apollo. The queen, Roxana, the Agave character, is Roger's wife rather than his mother. She surrenders to the new god in the guise of a shepherd with all the affinities with Christ that the 'good shepherd' implies. There is a somewhat uneasy amalgamation of Christian and Dionysian in the Shepherd as this aria shows:

My God is as beautiful as I am,
my God is the Good Shepherd,
he roams the stony mountain paths
in search of his lost sheep.
Adorned with a circlet of ivy,
a bunch of grapes in his hand,
he watches over his sheep
in green pastures.
My God sees his smile
reflected in the water's mirror,
in the darkness of the glassy waves!
The rosy dawn is his garment.
His strong, golden feet
take him as if winged
in search of his lost sheep![4]

This combination of imagery from two worlds is perhaps best explained as an indication of the similarities and differences between the beliefs and myths of Christianity and Dionysianism. The theme of the opera is that both should be accommodated. This opera avoids the cruelty and extremes of the ancient tragedy and in the king has a human protagonist who has found a rational way of life which yet permits coexistence with ecstatic religion.

Henze's one-act opera in four 'movements' follows the plot of *Bacchae* more closely. An innovation at the end of the opera is that Dionysus calls on Zeus and Persephone to release his mother Semele from the underworld and she becomes a goddess with the name Thyone. According to Henze[5] it was the poet W.H. Auden's idea to turn Euripides' *Bacchae* into a modern music drama and call it *The Bassarids*, the title of a lost tragedy of Aeschylus. This title also reflects the change from a chorus of female followers of Dionysus, bacchants or bacchae, to bassarids which includes both male and female adherents of the god.

Henze interpreted the themes of his opera as the contrast between the sensual and the intellectual, the repressive and the free, the luxuriant and the austere, and these distinctions are audible. The music for Pentheus (baritone) is dark, dissonant and harsh, while that for Dionysus (tenor) is soft and beguiling with the light timbres of flutes and harps. There are also two types of rhythm: one for Pentheus, associated with marches, with two and four beats in a bar; and the other for Dionysus, whose rhythms are exclusively three in a bar, sicilianas, waltzes and sarabandes.[6] The libretto for *The Bassarids* was written by W.H. Auden and Chester Kallman. Their lines also point up the contrast: Pentheus' lines are jagged and abrupt, while Dionysus' are smooth and fluid. Pentheus is unable to understand the Dionysian elements in his own nature and this makes him an easy victim of Dionysus. Henze saw this work as applying not only to Thebes but to the whole world, and in the whole period between Euripides and the present.[7] The chorus' cries of joy, 'Ayayalaya!', apparently came from the Inuit language and at the end of the opera exotic fertility symbols appeared. At the time of the first presentation Henze was going through a phase of agnosticism and therefore fell out with Auden, whose Christian belief ran counter to his. Auden argued that Euripides had not indicated that Dionysus and the ancient gods were righteous and he therefore wanted to mute the triumphant ending of the opera. But Henze prevailed and in the finale his orchestral music soars three times to heights of transcendent ecstasy. The librettists and Henze fell out over their differences in interpretation. According to Henze[8] Auden expressed his feelings at a press conference by loudly announcing that 'Dionysus ist ein Schwein'. The composer never again collaborated with these librettists.

Henze had regarded the sexual liberation of the 1960s as a suitable context for his interpretation of *Bacchae*. This context undoubtedly also influenced the creation of the radical version of *Bacchae* developed by Richard Schechner in New York in 1968. Revolution was in the air in that year, not only in Paris, but also in the USA where there were widespread protests against the war in Vietnam, and demonstrations and marches by the Civil Rights movement. Greek drama was increasingly being used to identify with causes advocating political and social change in this period. Schechner's production became one of the boldest and most famous of contemporary adaptations. He had established the Performance Group in the SoHo area of New York in a defunct metal-stamping factory. This space was renamed the Performing Garage and their inaugural production was *Dionysus in 69*; although the year was 1968, '69' referred not only to the sexual position, but to a revolutionary proposal for the presidential election of that year, where the slogan would be 'Dionysus for president'. These references already indicate the production's provocative approach to politics and to sexual mores.

Schechner was interested in the ritual origins of performance and what he called 'environmental theatre'. He collaborated with the anthropologist Victor Turner in exploring new ideas. His vision was to integrate the performance space into the world of the play and to break down the traditional opposition between performer and spectator, between interior and exterior, between on- and offstage, between participation and passive observation.[9]

The provocative use of nudity, the blurring of sexual identities, collective movement and dance, and full-on audience participation, which included some spectators removing their clothes and joining the Bacchic chorus 'on stage', all contributed to a sense of theatrical danger and experimental exploration that had never before been experienced in an American production of Greek tragedy.[10]

The Performing Garage was not a conventional theatre. Multi-level wooden platforms lined the sides of a central performance space. The audience sat on the floor or on the platforms at various heights while the actors moved in and around them, blurring the distinction between on- and offstage. Schechner made use of William Arrowsmith's American English translation, but it was merged with dialogue workshopped during rehearsals. This often included allusions to the actors' roles within the play: were they playing characters or performing aspects of their own identity? Performances differed from night to night, both because it depended on audience reaction and because the cast often changed. During its run of more than a year four different actors, including one woman, played Dionysus, and each actor was encouraged to develop their own dialogue. Schechner also made use of familiar songs, handclapping and footstamping to turn the audience into part of the chorus and to engage them in a sense of communal participation in the play. The limits of the theatre space itself were abolished at the end when the actors led a procession that took the audience dancing into the streets.

The use of nudity was part of the performance aesthetics of New York theatre of the time, where it also featured in works like the rock musical *Hair*, Kenneth Tynan's *Oh! Calcutta!* and Terence McNally's *Sweet Eros*. Particularly notable was the opening sequence of *Dionysus in 69* where the birth of Dionysus was presented as an Asmat birth ritual. The male actors lay naked on the floor while the nude female actors straddled them. The actor playing Dionysus was pulled through their legs over the bodies of the men. When the actor emerged from the heaving, swaying and moaning tunnel, he was curled up and wailed like a newborn.

The fact that this play was based on a Greek tragedy was one of the reasons it created considerable controversy. Audiences who had been used to stately and dignified productions were shocked at what many regarded as a lack of respect. When the group took their production on tour in the next year, mainly to American college campuses, it fell foul of the culture wars. It was shut down after one performance at the University of Minnesota, and at the University of Michigan in Ann Arbor ten actors were arrested and charged with indecent exposure. The resulting hullabaloo culminated in a great deal of publicity for *Dionysus in 69*, which became associated with other social issues of the time: the war in Vietnam, the Civil Rights movement, the Women's movement and the Cold War. Schechner felt that when the company resumed their performances in New York, there was a change in the audience and that some came only for titillation. There was great tension in the group and they stopped performing in the nude. Nevertheless, this radical performance was a landmark in its exploration of the meaning of ritual, performance, theatre and community.[11] No wonder that Edith Hall, Fiona Macintosh and Amanda Wrigley called their path-breaking volume on the study of the performance of Greek tragedy in the late twentieth century *Dionysus Since 69*. In that title they captured not only the year, but also the play that heralded a profound change in approach to the performance of Greek drama.

Only a few years later, in 1973, William Arrowsmith's translation was used again, along with Gilbert Murray's, by Wole Soyinka to create his play *The Bacchae of Euripides*. It was first performed at the National Theatre in London, but, although set in ancient Greece, it carries the influence of Nigeria, Yoruba culture, Christian elements and Soyinka's colonial and post-colonial experience. Strong criticism of European colonizers is implied by Dionysos'[12] robust attack on Pentheus' sense of cultural superiority, but the representation of Pentheus as an intolerant, military-style dictator can also be seen as an attack on dictatorships in newly independent African states, including Nigeria. An innovation, an additional chorus of slaves of different races, led by a West African, brings the topic of slavery to the fore and highlights this crime against Africa.

Soyinka was at this time a successful playwright whose work had been produced in London as well as his own country. He was politically committed and after Nigerian independence in 1960 strove to ensure that the new republic would be run in a just and orderly way. This ideal was undermined by the civil war that broke out after the secession of Biafra in 1967. During these years Soyinka was actively involved through his writings, but these led to his arrest and detention for twenty-seven months. After his release he continued his activism and was advised to leave Nigeria for his own safety. He returned to England, where he had lived before, and found that the Eurocentric attitude to Africa had not changed very much. When he wrote *The Bacchae of Euripides* he was able to combine his knowledge of European culture with elements of his own culture and voice criticism of both as well as express his hope that there could be a better future for his own country. It is clear that, although Soyinka was familiar with Schechner's reinterpretation, as indicated by his indirect reference to 'its search for the tragic soul of twentieth-century white bourgeois hippy culture',[13] his aim was to rewrite Euripides' tragedy in a different way with reference to his African roots.

Soyinka's approach is thus one of syncretism. He retained the broad outline of the Greek tragedy, but added characters and plot elements of his own, made changes in the depiction of the characters and also altered the ending. Soyinka's depicts Dionysos as a life force and a liberator. At the start of the play there is an annual ritual where a scapegoat, an old slave, is flogged to death to purify the land. This time Tiresias has offered himself as victim to be sacrificed. Dionysos announces himself just in time to save Tiresias, but this scene of ritual cleansing is important in that it is taken up again at the conclusion of the play where a different victim is substituted.

Soyinka's Dionysos is not androgynous, but clearly masculine, like the Yoruba god Ogun with whom Soyinka had indicated his Dionysos had many affinities. This assimilation of some of the characteristics of Ogun, whom Soyinka describes as having a 'Dionysian-Apollonian-Promethean essence',[14] with his Dionysos, explains some of the differences in his portrayal of the god. The play starts, like *Bacchae*, with Dionysos introducing himself. However his monologue is much shorter. These are his opening words:

> Thebes taints me with bastardy. I am turned into an alien, some foreign
> outgrowth of her habitual tyranny. My followers daily pay forfeit for
> their faith. Thebes blasphemes against me, makes me a scapegoat of a
> god.
> It is time to state my patrimony – even here in Thebes.
> I am the gentle, jealous joy. Vengeful and kind. An essence that will not
> exclude, nor be excluded. If you are Man or Woman, I am Dionysos.
> Accept.[15]

It is noteworthy that Dionysos emphasizes his status as outsider and that his
divinity has been denied, but also that he mentions the habitual tyranny of
Thebes. It is possible to see a parallel between his exclusion from Thebes and
Soyinka's from his native country. The entry of Pentheus considerably later
immediately shows up the clear contrast with the god as well as Tiresias
and the Chorus Leader, who have already appeared. The stage directions
describe Pentheus as 'straight, militaristic in bearing and speech' and his first
words are:

> I shall have order! Let the city know at once
> Pentheus is here to give back order and sanity.
> To think those reports which came to us abroad are true!
> Not padded or strained. Disgustingly true in detail.
> If anything reality beggars the report. It's *disgusting*!
> I leave the country, I'm away only a moment
> Campaigning to secure our national frontiers. And what happens?
> Behind me – chaos! The city is in uproar. Let everyone
> Know I've returned to re-impose order. Order!
> And tell it to the women especially, those
> Promiscuous bearers of this new disease.[16]

Pentheus is the only character whose words are in verse. This emphasizes the
gulf between him and the other characters, and contributes to his seeming
harsh and unnatural.

There are two silent tableaux inserted as plays within the play. These
scenes portray two weddings: the first ends in wild revelry after the
consumption of much wine and replaces Aphrodite with Dionysos, while the
groom throws off his conventional suit and reveals that he is wearing a
fawnskin underneath. In the second scene a traditional Christ-figure wearing
a crown combining Christian and Dionysiac elements, thorns and ivy, is
present while the stories of Martha and Mary are enacted and also the miracle
of the changing of water into wine at Cana. After Pentheus has seen these

scenes, he wants to drink and to go to the mountain with Dionysus. He insists on wearing armour, but Dionysus manages to dress him in female clothes without Pentheus realizing it. When they have left for the mountain, the slave chorus and the Bacchae join to reject Pentheus' regime and mime the hunt and capture of Pentheus. A messenger appears and, as in Euripides' tragedy, Agave returns and is gradually confronted with what she has done. Tiresias explains that the old ritual was cruel without the power of cleansing and renewal, but Pentheus' death will bring about renewal in Thebes. This is Soyinka's way of creating what he regarded as a more fitting ending. Soyinka gave his play a subtitle: *A Communion Rite*. That comes out most clearly in the final scene because the head of Pentheus produces spouts of wine which is drunk by all the characters. This constitutes the communion rite and symbolizes a measure of healing and restoration, unlike the destruction at the end of the Greek tragedy. However, it is hard to accept that Agave, who has to come to terms with the horror she has perpetrated, would 'tilt her head backwards to let a jet [of wine from Pentheus' head] flush full in her face and flush her mouth' (stage directions).[17]

Soyinka's rewriting of Euripides' *Bacchae* seems to have attempted to combine too many elements from disparate worlds so that it becomes rather long-winded and, instead of providing a cathartic ending as is intended, provides a different kind of gruesomeness. There have been more positive interpretations of this play, however. Wiveca Sotto, who has made a detailed study of the play, concludes:

> Agave, Tiresias and the Slave Leader all function as interpreters of the Dionysian message and as mediators, both between god and man and between the different groups of the Theban community. In this context it is interesting to note that in the cast list Soyinka emphasizes that the Slave Leader should be black and the Slaves and Bacchantes of mixed origins. The *Bacchae* is a play intimately linked with 'a particular moment in a people's history' – the Nigerian Civil War – but it is also, and perhaps above all, a play in which Soyinka expresses ideas of universal concern, and like Euripides' *Bacchae*, Soyinka's play is imbued with 'a hovering eternal presence'. To the same extent as Pentheus represents the military leaders of Nigeria *and* is a prototype of the dictator, the Slaves are seen as a particular group of people in a particular situation *and* as any oppressed people or social class struggling for justice and freedom.[18]

Sotto interprets Agave's reconciliation, expressed in the act of drinking the wine spurting from her murdered son's head, as her realization that she has offered Dionysos something which will benefit the entire community.

Soyinka's changed ending completes his introduction of the scapegoat motif earlier in the play. As Kadmos is moved to say that he does not understand why the god had to bring about Pentheus' killing by his mother, Tiresias offers his explanation:

> Understanding of these things is far beyond us,
> Perhaps . . . perhaps our life-sustaining earth
> Demands . . . a little more . . . sometimes, a more
> Than token offering for her own needful renewal.[19]

The one aspect of the play that does seem worthy of celebration is the removal of the dictator, and from that perspective the cruelty could be seen as the sacrifice and suffering demanded by civil war.

Another painstaking and methodical remaking of Euripides' *Bacchae* was the fruit of the first *Antikenprojekt* of Peter Stein with the Schaubühne in Berlin in the 1970s. The aim of this project was to research the origins of theatre, specifically Greek theatre, and to put their findings into practice.[20] The Schaubühne was an actors' collective and left-wing alternative to the established theatre. They chose *Bacchae* because the role of Dionysus, god of theatre, went to the heart of the project. The group's research was underpinned by a wide-ranging theoretical base. The early 1970s saw many changes in research in the humanities. Structuralism and anthropological approaches dominated and interdisciplinarity became commonplace. The work of Foucault and Lévi-Strauss revolutionized research in Classics too. Vernal and Vidal-Naquet opened Greek studies to religion, myth, ritual, anthropology and visual images and published influential works, especially on Greek tragedy. Walter Burkert's *Homo Necans* (1972), which combined human ethology, biology, and sociology with the insights of the Cambridge Ritualists, put violence and sacrifice as well as myth and ritual at the centre of his interpretation of Greek religion and tragedy, while René Girard's theories in *La Violence et le Sacré* (1972) dealt with the relationship between aggression and the way in which society overcomes it by choosing a scapegoat and collectively killing it. This collective act then works to reintegrate the community. Girard used *Bacchae* as a key text. The Schaubühne group spent more than a year on studying the background of the play. They studied the academic literature mentioned above and incorporated these ideas into their approach to performance. They travelled to Greece and applied their findings by trying out different ways of presentation.

The actual performance was presented over two evenings. The first, for which Stein was responsible, was named *Exercises for Actors*. It was an attempt to go back to the possibilities of expression pre-dating dramatic representation as well as establishing the link between ritual and performance. This event took place not in the theatre but in a long rectangular room heaped with earth where the audience was seated on planks laid on the floor. The *Exercises* were made up of six parts: first *Anfangen* (start) showed experiments of bodily movements, breathing, grunts etc. and interaction by means of voice and glance. Rituals connected to the very beginning of theatre were attempted. Next in *Jagd* (hunting) one actor, clad in an animal skin, was chased by the group, playing dogs, until he was exhausted and they surrounded him. In *Opfer* (sacrifice) choral action followed: an object was created from animal bones and wool to restore the victim. After an interval filled by scenes similar to those of satyr-play, *Initiation* showed a few men and women being separated from the group. They were stripped, tortured and buried, but later reintegrated into the group. The audience were then taken to another room where an actor was suspended high on a wall and encased in plaster while reciting the famous lines (443–61) from Aeschylus' *Prometheus* in which Prometheus describes how helpless human beings were before the introduction of knowledge and civilization. This passage symbolizes the Greek enlightenment and emancipation from mythical prehistory, ritual and physical action to speech. This first evening displayed a debate about whether physical action or speech was more important for theatre play. In the vein of the performative turn the emphasis is clearly on the performance as an emergent event, since modern logocentrism, i.e. theatre without corporeality and movement, is pure text and implies rational but lifeless rigor. Therefore Prometheus finally disappears into the rock.

The first evening provided a prelude to Klaus Michael Grüber's legendary staging of *Bacchae* on the second evening. Hunting, sacrifice and initiation and the indirect debate on the predominance of the tools of theatre were also key themes of the production of this tragedy where Euripides himself raises metatheatrical themes.

The dichotomy of the contradictions between Pentheus, representative of rational order, and Dionysus, who embodies the principle of ecstasy and loss of self, was shown as revolving around modern human existence and the danger of destruction embedded in Western civilization. The key of the production was in the performative and visual: glaring neon lighting revealed a white space that seemed sterile. The backdrop opened into three rooms into which the audience could see. In the room on the left stood a huge road-sweeping machine, while on the right there were two live horses behind a glass wall. Accompanied by the bewitching string melody of the famous apotheosis from Stravinsky's ballet *Apollo*, the god was wheeled in on a hospital bed. A light focused on the god's stretcher showed him quite nude, with white makeup, his hair in disorder and his expression wild. In his hand he held a woman's high-heeled shoe, as a fetish. He formally uttered the first words as he stutteringly articulated 'Ich bin'. The Apollonian *principium individuationis* commenced. Slowly the spoken voice freed itself from the body and semiotic diction as speech act separated itself from the world of symbols. The chorus of bacchantes now entered, the neon lighting was dimmed and the wild-haired women in peasant dress tore up the floorboards. From underneath these they brought up fruit, clumps of wool and other natural elements. They also unearthed Cadmus and Tiresias, both covered in slime. Finally the cleansing machine came on with a great din and tidied up. Pentheus' first words were two diary entries of Wittgenstein (31 May 1915 and 8 July 1916) regarding name, death and eternity.

The visual tableaux, signs and actions remained enigmatic. Any attempt at making sense was undermined. Voices and speech became ragged, seemed fragmented and disjointed. Opposites, like the Dionysian and Apollonian, met, only to fall apart again immediately. Meaning became lost behind the visual mystification. Thus there was no fusion of horizons, no precipitate identification of past and present. The ruling aesthetic was one of disorder, of rupture and fracture, of dispersion and withdrawal. The contrast with contemporary productions, especially those of Schechner, became very explicit. Schechner wanted to make clear the revolutionary potential of the Dionysian. But here there was a strange remoteness.

Erika Fischer-Lichte[21] saw this performance as a *sparagmos* of texts. The text had to be sacrificed, to be dismembered, in order that a performance could take place in the theatre. Image, action and performance took precedence over the text in this example of director's theatre. Grüber in this way pointed to aspects that Euripides himself already addressed, but which were only later discussed in research on Greek drama. Euripides in this late drama created a metatheathrical tragedy, a play within a play, which works out the nature of tragedy, under the sign of the god of tragedy, as fragmentation. Here ritual and myth, especially the terrible dismemberment of Pentheus, who denies the divinity, served him as elements in his composition.

In contrast to these adaptations of *Bacchae*, there was a very successful performance of the tragedy in Cape Town in November 2002 that aimed at reproducing many of the authentic features of an ancient Greek enactment. It took place as part of a 'Dionysus festival' that included lectures on Greek drama, the god Dionysus, wine and wine-tasting. The play was directed by Roy Sargeant, who had been a professor of drama and theatre studies and was an experienced radio and theatre director. Sargeant acknowledged that staging *Bacchae* was the fulfilment of a long-held desire instilled by his first reading of Mary Renault's novel *The Mask of Apollo*. Renault's novels based on ancient Greek history and mythology were scrupulously researched.

The Mask of Apollo recounts the adventurous life of an Athenian actor, Nikeratos, who is a younger contemporary of Plato and travels all over the Greek world to participate in dramatic festivals. It was Renault's description of Nikeratos performing in *Bacchae* in the theatre at Syracuse which first drew Sargeant's interest and was to influence many aspects of his direction of the play.

The tragedy was played in a small open-air stone theatre on the back slopes of Table Mountain in the Kirstenbosch National Botanical Garden. The perfect acoustics and the beauty of the natural setting added to the excitement of the performance. In addition to evening performances there were two in the early morning, as in ancient Greece. The director maintained that he wanted to stay as true as possible to the original Greek style of performance. In contrast to most modern directors, and inevitably adaptors, Sargeant had no wish to stress any relevance to the modern world.[22] He thought the play stood for itself and that the sparseness of the production would highlight the richness of the text. In this way Sargeant aimed, like Mary Renault, 'to tell the truth about the past'. The audience could draw their own conclusions about the themes of the drama: East and West, order and freedom, male and female, life and death. The parallels between Pentheus and some modern politicians, who are smart but not wise and want to be in total control, came out clearly; as did the violence that follows when repressed emotions break out and the high price paid for freedom. These are timeless themes of universal application. Perhaps seeing them encapsulated in the formality of the ancient drama did enhance their authority.

The English translation chosen for the production was that by David Epstein because Sargeant judged that it captured the poetry of the original in language that actors can speak. The only modification of the text was ironing out some gross Americanisms. As part of the striving for authenticity, the cast was three male actors, and a half chorus of six young men. Masks were worn and the parts were divided among the actors so that the first actor, Matthew Wild, played Dionysus and Tiresias, the second actor, Tauriq Jenkins, played Pentheus and Agave, while the third actor, Ralph Lawson, played Cadmus, the first soldier and a herdsman. The chorus played a central part. They remained on stage from the *parodos*. Their foreignness was suggested not only by their costumes, masks and musical instruments, but also by the fact that they were males representing women. The six young men moved as one, in Sargeant's words, 'like a shoal of fish or a flock of starlings, connected, yet disconnected'. They were dressed identically and wore identical half masks. Passages of heightened emotion were sung, while weightier pronouncements were spoken. The music was all performed on stage by their castanets, drums and tambourines. The final words of the play,

In vain man's expectations;
God brings the unthought to be,
As here we see

were not taken from the Epstein translation used for this staging of *Bacchae*. These lines form a tailpiece which also occurs at the end of four other Euripidean tragedies and were probably added in performance, but Sargeant adopted them from the *Mask of Apollo*, where Nikeratos uses them repeatedly at points of crisis in the narrative.[23] Sargeant's use of this tag was an explicit homage to Mary Renault and the world of Greek actors she created in her novel.

Roy Sargeant was well aware of the various modern adaptations of *Bacchae*, but he wanted to remind theatregoers of the force, beauty and impact of the original tragedy. Eight years after democracy had arrived in South Africa, there was no need to make use of adapted versions of Greek drama to bring ideas about justice and freedom to the public, as had been done in many previous local rewritings of ancient plays, most famously in Fugard, Kani and Ntshona's version of *Antigone* in *The Island*.

The divergences in interpretation of Euripides' *Bacchae* evident in the various operatic and dramatic adaptations discussed in this chapter are well captured in the extremes of Auden's judgement of Dionysus as a swine and the Performance Group's campaign for Dionysus as president. These few examples of how *Bacchae* has been explored and presented in the modern world indicate that it is once again, as in the ancient world, one of the Greek tragedies which engages the attention not only of audiences, but also of playwrights and directors who are most involved in the nature and craft of the theatre itself.

Notes

1 Mills (2006) 105.
2 Easterling (1997a) xii.
3 Foley (2012) 110–16.
4 Quoted in Cowan (2010) 324–5.
5 Henze (1998) 206.
6 Henze (1998) 260.
7 Flashar (1991) 217.
8 Henze (1998) 215.
9 My description of this production is heavily indebted to Meineck's chapter (forthcoming).
10 Meineck (forthcoming).

11 There is not space in this overview to do justice to the complexity of Schechner's conception and re-enactment of Euripides' *Bacchae*. Zeitlin (2004) has a lucid and critical discussion with further references.
12 This is the transliteration Soyinka uses. It will be used here to refer to his character in Soyinka's play.
13 Soyinka (1992) 7.
14 Soyinka (1992) 157.
15 Soyinka (1973) 233.
16 Soyinka (1973) 256.
17 Soyinka (1973) 307.
18 Sotto (1985) 176.
19 Soyinka (1973) 306.
20 Information about this project is based on Bierl (forthcoming) and Fischer-Lichte (2004).
21 Fischer-Lichte (2004) 340–2.
22 This information is taken from a lecture, 'My *Bacchae*', that Roy Sargeant gave to the Western Cape Branch of the Classical Association of South Africa on 15 March 2003, as well as on the programme notes of the production.
23 Renault (1966) 22, 45, 187.

Euripides' *Bacchae*

Translated by David Stuttard

Dramatis Personae

The action takes place outside the royal place of Pentheus, king of Thebes. Close to the palace is a shrine to Semele (Dionysus' mother) with an eternally burning flame.

Although there are no stage directions given in the original text, certain conventions are presupposed: the *skene* (stage building) represents the palace, with entrances and exits being made through its central door; the two *eisodoi* (passageways) on either side of the *skene* generally represent roads to different parts of the city or countryside – in *Bacchae* one represents the road to Teiresias' home, the other to Mount Cithaeron.

In the first production three special effects may have been employed. One was the *mechane* (crane), a pivoted device which allowed gods and other heavenly characters to 'fly' over the heads of those performing in the *orkhestra* ('dancing floor'). The second may have provided for the flame burning in Semele's shrine suddenly to flare up in one scene. The third may have involved a means of suggesting an earthquake, which included the partial destruction of the palace. However, given that one of the play's themes is the blurring of the real and the imagined, the audience may have been expected simply to envisage the flame and earthquake, perhaps aided by onstage choral movement.

Bacchae was probably written around 407 BC for performance at the court of King Archelaus I of Macedon. It was produced posthumously (by Euripides the Younger), possibly at the Athenian Dionysia in 405 BC as the third part of a trilogy which also included *Iphigeneia at Aulis* and *Alcmaeon in Corinth*. The trilogy was awarded first prize.

Within the translation, choral passages or passages which use verse forms other than iambic trimeter are usually identified both by a change of layout and through the use of lowercase lettering throughout, including of proper names.

Dionysus Thebes. First city in all Greece. I have come back. I, Dionysus, back to Thebes, the son of Zeus by Semele.

Semele . . . Semele, my mother was a mortal, and the lightning fire that gave me birth tore through her womb, and so it was by her death she delivered me . . .

I've changed my form, shape-shifted, god become flesh to pay his honours at a cenotaph, a mother's tomb, a blackened crater smouldering for ever with the living fire of Zeus, the living hatred of his wife against my mother.

Cadmus, though – old Cadmus – he's earned my respect – my mother's father. He's made this a memorial, a place of sanctity, a shrine for a dead daughter. And I – I've shaded it with dappled ivy, green and dripping leafy with black berries like the vine.

My journey, then, the path I took to get here: first Lydia, all golden, glittering, and Phrygia, the sun-baked plains of Persia, the fortress-towns of Bactria, and Media, so cold, so grim, Arabia, Arabia, rich, fertile, blessed, and Asia, her cities sparkling like jewels beside the dancing sea, so many cities, high towers gleaming in the sun, streets teeming, Greeks and foreigners all mingling as one. I danced my dances there; I taught my mysteries, that men might know me as a god, and so I came to Thebes, first city in the whole of Greece. And so in all of Greece it was in Thebes – here – that the women's screaming moans of pleasure first were heard. In Thebes I first draped deerskin on their naked shoulders, put my weapon in their hands, my thyrsus, missile matted green with ivy shoots . . .

My mother's sisters, her own sisters!, said that Dionysus – I – am not the son of Zeus, that Semele gave her virginity to some mere man and then pretended Zeus had bedded her, blamed him, a fine excuse (they said) thought up by Cadmus. So they smirked behind their hands and smeared the rumour round the streets that this is why Zeus killed her, because she'd lied that she had slept with him. My mother's sisters . . .!

So I've driven them like cattle from their houses, maddened on the mountainside, hallucinating and delirious. I've dressed them in the clothing of my cult, my mother's sisters, Cadmus' daughters, and with them all the women from all Thebes all herded crazed and frenzied from their homes. And now they're lolling in each others' arms, all indiscriminate, in mottled shadow of cool shady pine or on the sun-drenched rocks.

The city must learn once and for all, against its will if it must be, that it is yet to be initiated in my rites, my Bacchic rites, the rites of Dionysus; while I – I must redeem my mother's memory. I must reveal myself to all men as a god, son of the heavenly Father, son of Zeus.

Now, Cadmus is no longer king. He's given up the throne and handed power to Pentheus, his grandson and my enemy.

Pentheus . . . Pentheus has challenged my divinity, banned all and any offering to me, forbidden any mention of my name in prayer. And that is why I'll show him and all Thebes I am a god. And once I've done it, I'll move on. But if Thebes mobilizes troops to try to take my women from the mountains forcibly, well, I'll join battle. I'll unleash on them the savage anger of my maenads, crazed and maddened, and I myself, their master, at their head.

But now, my girls, my Lydians, my sleek young hunting pack, my fellow-travellers, so faithful to me on my journey here, and so companionable too, awake, asleep –

> beat the rhythms of the east
> my rhyming rhythms
> rhea's rhythms
> beat the rhythms loud
> for pentheus to hear
> for thebes to hear
> loud
> loud
> and louder still
>
> and i'll go to cithaeron
> and to the mountain glens
> to where my women are
> my bacchae are
> and there with them
> i'll beat the rhythm loud
> and loud
> and louder still
> and dance
> and dance
> and dance

Chorus   strange places
                always to the west
            strange faces
                always to the west
            and asia behind us
            and the holy mountain tmolus

            but the journey's good
                when it's with dionysus
            sweet pleasure in our pain
                when it's for dionysus
            and the thunder's low
                and it is dionysus
            dionysus
            dionysus
                always on our lips

            who's in the streets
            who's in the alleyways
            who's in their homes
                in the cool slanting shade
            leave the streets
            leave the alleys
            and leave your cool houses

            and silence
                no sound now
            just silence
                and sanctity
            silence
                and
            praise
                to the god dionysus
            praise to him
                now and forever

            blessèd is he
                the initiate
                god-kissed
            walking the path
                of the mysteries of god

soul joined with god's soul
and high in the mountains
worshipping
    bacchus
    the lord dionysus
    in ritual
    purity
worshipping
    cybele
    mother god
    earth god
beating the thyrsus
embraced in the ivy
    for bacchus

go bacchae
now bacchae

link arms with bacchus
    the thunder god
    son of god
lead him in triumph
    from tmolus
    from phrygia
bringing him home
    through the broad streets
    of greece

    wings flashed
    fire exploded
semele
    so heavy with
    her child
    her dionysus
    burning and convulsing
    in the pain of her miscarriage
    premature delivery
    her baby not quite formed yet
    consumed in the explosion
    of the lightning fire
    of zeus

zeus
   snatched
   his child
   his dionysus
   wrapped him in his own flesh
   in his thigh
   until his own time came
   his god flesh
   stitched
   with golden needles
   god-child
   hidden from his wife
   and when his time came
zeus
   gave birth to him and
destiny
   delivered him
   the bull-horned god and
writhing serpents
   wrapped him close
   the snakes his maenads gather now
   to wrap close in their hair

wrap your hair close
in the ivy
   thebes

   semele's city
   when she was young

scarlet blood berries
stain dark leaves
   of bryony

burgeon and blossom now
wrap yourselves close
   in soft fir down
   and oak leaves

cool naked shoulders
dappled with deerskins
   white wool

all innocent
fringing the pelt

the thyrsus is potent
revere it

the whole earth will dance
and the dancer is bacchus
leading his pack
to the mountains
the mountains
where women and
young girls throng
    homes all abandoned
    dazed and delirious

all's
    dionysus

cult caves
cult caverns
    deep
    in crete
gave birth
to zeus

and corybantes
deep
in caverns
stretched
skin
taut
on
hollow
drums

and so the dance began
the dance of madness
    bacchic frenzy
    phrygian flutes
    wild harmony
the mother god
the earth god

rhea
pounding the drum
   to the screams of the bacchae
passing the drum
   to the satyrs
     wild goat men
     leaping the years
     in a wild tarantella
     dancing and dizzy
     for bacchus

it is good to be on the hillside with the hunting pack
it is good to let yourself fall naked
   only the deerskin to clothe you

and you're blooded with the goats' blood you've been hunting
and its flesh is quivering and warm
and you taste it
and you tear it

and he comes
where his mountains
straddle phrygia
and lydia
and bacchus
great cult leader
smiles in triumph

and the earth flows with milk
and the earth flows with wine
and the earth flows with honey and nectar

the bacchus leaps high
and smoke billows
   like frankincense
   trailed from his pine torch

he dances
he dances

there's none won't dance with him now
wild with his bacchic cries

head
   thrown back
hair
   blowing free in the breeze

his dancers scream loud
and he answers in thunder
   go bacchae
   now bacchae

embrace dionysus
and dance in the wind
like the gold dust of tmolus
drumming the rhythm
ecstatic
exalting god
gasping
   in ecstasy
gasping
the lotus flute throbbing
   in ecstasy
joining its voice
to the voice of the dancers

go to the mountains
the mountains

and
like a colt
straining its limbs
its swift hooves
in the meadows
galloping close
to its mother
exultant

like a colt
all exultant
the dancer leaps high

Teiresias Where's the doorman, eh? Where is he? Ask Cadmus to come down, the son of Agenor, who set out west from Sidon once to ring Thebes round with towers. Well, go on! Tell him Teiresias is asking for him. He knows why I'm here. I may be old – and he's older than I am – but we've arranged to meet to make our thyrsuses and put on deerskins and wrap our heads in sprigs of ivy.

Cadmus Teiresias, my dear friend! I heard you from inside! I recognized your voice. Wise words from a wise man, eh? I've come prepared. I've got the gear, god's sacred tackle. You see, we must do all we can to increase his prestige. He *is* my grandson, after all: Dionysus, god made manifest to men. So, where have we to go to do the dancing – all that stamping and tossing our white hair?! Lead on, Teiresias! The old leading the old! Yes, you know what you're doing. I hope I don't get tired what with constantly banging my thyrsus night and day! It's good to forget how old you are when you get to our age.

Teiresias My sentiments exactly. Yes. My sap is rising, and I'm going to try some dancing.

Cadmus Do you think we should drive to the mountain?

Teiresias No, no. That wouldn't be the same at all. Not sufficient veneration if we drive.

Cadmus You're an old man – *I*'m an old man! You don't expect me to support you all the way?

Teiresias The god will guide us there with ease.

Cadmus And will we be the only men there doing the dance for Bacchus?

Teiresias Oh yes – none of the others understands. Just us.

Cadmus It's going to be a long journey. Take my hand.

Teiresias There. My hand! A united front!

Cadmus I am a man, and I respect the gods.

Teiresias And with the gods, the best thing's total honesty. No clever argument can overturn traditional morality built over many years, no matter what new theory some smart thinker might invent. Oh, I can hear them now saying how it's inappropriate for me at my age to be going out dancing with ivy in my hair. But the god doesn't discriminate on grounds of age ('young people mustn't dance; old people mustn't dance') – no, he wants everyone to pay him honour equally. Total honour. No exceptions.

Cadmus   Teiresias, I must act the seer now – you're blind. It's Pentheus.
He's on his way and in a hurry. Yes, my appointee, my successor, King
Pentheus! He's looking agitated. What's he got to say?

Pentheus   I've been receiving reports, in my absence, of an
unprecedented danger facing Thebes. Our women have been leaving
our homes on pretext of pilgrimage, and flocking to the mountains and
the forests, to dance in worship of a new god, Dionysus – whoever
Dionysus is.

And they have wine with them. A lot of wine. And one by one they're
stealing off to meet men in the forests, to satisfy their carnal lusts. And
though they claim they're maenad priestesses, they worship sex more
energetically than Bacchus.

I've had reports that there's a foreigner involved, some charismatic leader
who can magic miracles, with scented hair and golden curls, and dark
seductive eyes, a magnet to our girls all day, all night, enticing them with
promises of an initiation that will bring them ecstasy. If once I get him here,
I'll put an end to him. I'll stop him pounding his thyrsus, and tossing back
his hair. I'll sever his pretty head from his pretty body.

He claims to be a god. He claims he's Dionysus. He claims Zeus sewed him
in his thigh, when Dionysus was in fact cremated when the lightning struck
that killed his mother. This blasphemy, this total blasphemy, has earned his
death by hanging, whoever he might be – and him a foreigner.

Behold, another miracle! Teiresias, the prophet, draped in deerskin, and my
own grandfather too, acting the bacchant with his thyrsus! How ridiculous.
Sir, I can hardly bring myself to look at you, so venerable, and yet so stupid.
You are my *grandfather*! Get rid of it and get rid of that ivy too!

Teiresias, you made him do this. And why? Because you hoped that if you
introduced some new religion you'd have more excuse to watch for omens
and earn more baksheesh for reading runes. Only your age has spared
you, or I'd have had you thrown in chains with all the other bacchae, for
promoting immorality. And women . . . wine and women do not mix.
These new rites are abhorrent, an abomination!

Chorus   Sneering at gods – irreverence – and at Cadmus too, Thebes'
founder and your grandfather! No respect at all for any of your
family.

Teiresias   For a wise man to speak well when he's got something that's
worth saying takes no great effort. Now *you*, your style is good. You sound

clever. But the content of your argument lacks thought and substance, and in politics a speaker who has passion without wisdom can be very dangerous.

This new god you mock – I can't even begin to tell you how significant he'll be. But listen. Let me give you some advice.

For mankind, there are two first principles: earth – Demeter, whatever term you want to use – earth provides food. Now, Dionysus provides drink – wine. And when you drink enough of it, wine washes all your cares away and lets you sleep, and so forget the worries of the day. Wine is the only cure for worry. And so a god is poured in offering to gods, and so through him flow blessings for mankind.

And then you mock him for being sewn in Zeus' thigh. I'll tell you what's behind that. When Zeus snatched the baby from the lightning fire and took him to Olympus as a god, Hera, Zeus' wife, was desperate to throw the child from heaven. But Zeus resisted her, and in a godlike way. He took some of the ether which surrounds the earth, and moulded it to look like Dionysus, and gave this to his wife, a sort of love-tie, to show his good intentions. Over the years, men got confused and said he'd been sewn up in Zeus' *thigh*, since thigh and love-tie sound so similar.

And Dionysus is a mystic, too. The bacchic trance and ecstasy are very mystic states, and when the god possesses you, you can foretell the future.

He's warlike too. You've seen an army, well drilled, well equipped, turn tail in terror before a shot's been fired? Well, that mad panic comes from Dionysus.

And you will see him on the crags of Delphi, leaping the twin peaks, his torches blazing as he beats his thyrsus, thundering the earth, and Greece will worship him.

Listen to me, Pentheus. Don't be so certain that your power has any power to govern men, or that because you have some thoughts you have some understanding, when what you think is wrong. Receive the god in Thebes. Make offerings to him. Take part in his rituals, and put his garland on your head.

It's not for Dionysus to make women chaste. You only need to look at human nature. Even at the height of bacchic passion, a moral woman will not be corrupted.

Look. You're gratified when the crowds come out and all the city rings with praise for Pentheus. Well, Dionysus likes being honoured too. So, though

you ridicule him, Cadmus is going dancing in his ivy crown, and so am I.
We may be old, but we must dance his dance. And I won't challenge god for
all your arguments. It's you that's mad and cruelly so, and you're rejecting
the one cure that might just bring you sanity.

Chorus   Teiresias, your words do credit to the prophet's god Apollo, and
you are wise to honour Dionysus. He is a powerful god.

Cadmus   My boy – Teiresias has given you good advice. Live as we do.
Don't turn your back on traditional values. You're up in the air. You're not
using your head. Look – even if you're right and he's not a god, you still can
say he's one. Massage the truth – it's in a good cause. This way, everyone will
think that Semele's the mother of a god, and we – you, me, the family – will
get the glory.

You saw how Actaeon died up there in the wilds, on the mountainside,
torn apart and mauled by the self-same hunting dogs he'd bred in his own
kennels, because of all those boasts of his of being a better hunter than the
goddess Artemis. Don't let the same thing happen to you. Come on! Come
here! Drape a bit of ivy round your head, and join with us in honouring
the 'god'.

Pentheus   Don't touch me! Go to your bacchic rituals if you must, but
don't taint me with your stupidity.

It was Teiresias who schooled you in this nonsense. I'll punish him.
(*to some of his attendants*) Go, someone! Quickly! Now! Go to his lair,
go where he watches for his prodigies! Smash it to pieces! Tear it apart!
Turn the whole place upside down! And throw his sacred hangings for
the winds to snatch and tear to ribbons! And so I'll get him where it hurts
the most.

(*to the remainder of his attendants*) The rest of you, go, comb the city, comb
the whole of Thebes, and track him down, this mincing foreigner, who
would seduce our women and corrupt them and infect them with his foul
disease. And if you find him, bring him here in chains, that he might die by
public stoning here, and see the celebration of his cult's last rites in his own
suffering and death.

Teiresias   You utter fool! You don't know what you've said. You were
irrational before, but this is madness!

Cadmus, we'll go, and, for all his bestiality, we'll pray for Pentheus, and for
Thebes too, that we should suffer nothing unexpected at the hands of god.

Come on. We'll try to support each other. It would be embarrassing for two
old men like us to fall over. Still, go we must, and pay our dues to Dionysus
son of Zeus. I pray that Pentheus does not bring pain on your house,
Cadmus. That's not a prophecy – merely an observation based on what
I've seen. Yes. He's a fool, and he talks like one.

Chorus   sanctity
        sanctity
           goddess of the
           golden skies
           who skim the earth
           on golden wings
        look upon
           pentheus
           all he has done

        his malice
           blasphemy
        his sacrilege
           against
        the thunder god
           the son of semele
           god garlanded at banquet
        god
           of all the gods
           most bless'd
        lord of the dance
           who unites all mankind
        god of the flute
           of laughter
           soothing all our cares

        and when the sacrifice is over
        and the feast begins
        and squares are swathed in dappled ivy
           purple berries glistening like dew
        the wine is passed from hand to hand
           each drinker wreathed in ivy
        and with the wine comes sleep

rough unchecked tongues
rough uncurbed ignorance
   dies in disaster

a gentle rhythm
   mind in harmony
   unruffled
keeps the house secure

and though gods may inhabit
   the high stratosphere
they still can see
   the smallest act of man
clever
   is not wise
nor thoughts
   no man should entertain

man's life is short

too high an aim
and even what's within your grasp
   escapes you

this way lies
   madness
   blasphemy
and
   there is no escape

i wish i were in cyprus now
the land
   of love
   of aphrodite
land
   of lust and longing
   sweet seduction
   in soft eyes
in paphos
   where the foreign river
   river
   with a hundred streams

brings her crops to fruitfulness
no need for any rain

or in the fertile valleys
tumbling
    from mount olympus
tumbling
    where muses dance
    in fair pieria

take me there
    bacchus
take me
    my thunder god
    bacchus
    my ecstasy
    my inspiration

take me to
the land of grace
the land of longing
    where all undisturbed
    your bacchae
    join with you
    in sweet communion

dionysus
    son of zeus
    god of feasting
    peace
    content
    young men growing
    to strength and manhood
gives
    to rich and poor alike
his well-being
    that will wash away
    all tears

embrace life
    in the sunlight
    in the dark of night

live well
and he will love you
live meanly
   strut
   and boast
   superiority
and he will loathe you
   all your life

the common way
   that's best for all
is best for me

Soldier   Here we are, Pentheus. This is him. We tracked him down like you told us to, no wild goose chase for us. No, but this beast of yours was nice and tame for *us*. *He* didn't try to run away. No! He held his hands out quite the thing – no worries – not so much as a tremble, looking at us all the time with those big eyes of his, and smiling, staying right where he was, and telling us to tie him up and bring him in. He made things nice and easy. I felt a bit embarrassed, so I said to him, I said: 'I'm just following Pentheus' orders, mate. I'm not *enjoying* this.'

Just one more thing. Those women you took into custody, those bacchae you put under lock and key in jail – well, they've got out. They've gone back to their dancing and their rituals, and they're calling up the thunder god, the Bacchus. Their manacles just came off by themselves; the keys turned in the locks and the doors swung open; and *no one did it*.

Since he got here, there's been a lot of strange stuff going on. But what to *do* about him – well, that's up to you, sir.

Pentheus   You can stop holding him. He's in *my* custody now, and he's not quick enough to get away from *me*.

Well, stranger, you're quite pretty. At least, *women* would probably think so, which is why you've come to Thebes. Nice long curls – you're not a soldier then? Look how they frame your face – enchanting! And your complexion – that must take a lot of care. You must have to stay inside a lot, keep out of the sun, your good looks your chief asset in your pursuit of sex.

So. First question. Where are you from?

Dionysus   Well, that's an *easy* question. Have you heard of a mountain called Tmolus? Its slopes are carpeted in wild flowers.

Pentheus   I've heard of it, yes. The city of Sardis is built at its foot.

Dionysus   That's where I'm from, then – Lydia.

Pentheus   So why are you introducing this cult of yours to Greece?

Dionysus   Dionysus *brought* us here – the son of Zeus.

Pentheus   Oh? So in Lydia you have a Zeus who's fathering new gods?

Dionysus   No. Zeus joined in love with Semele. She was from *Thebes*.

Pentheus   Did you get your calling in a dream, or did you see him face to face?

Dionysus   Oh – face to face! He initiated me in his mysteries.

Pentheus   And what mysteries would those be, then?

Dionysus   It is forbidden to reveal them to the uninitiated.

Pentheus   And the benefits of this new religion are?

Dionysus   Well worth knowing – but it's not permitted you should know them.

Pentheus   A clever answer, calculated to intrigue.

Dionysus   God's mysteries disdain all artifice and all impiety.

Pentheus   This god – you say you saw him. What was he like?

Dionysus   Whatever he wanted to be. It was nothing to do with me.

Pentheus   You counter well, but it's all empty words.

Dionysus   There's no use being profound if you can't be understood.

Pentheus   Is this your first port of call with your new religion?

Dionysus   No. I've introduced the mysteries throughout all Asia.

Pentheus   Foreigners are so much less sophisticated than we Greeks.

Dionysus   Except in this. They do have different customs, though.

Pentheus   And are your rituals performed by night or day?

Dionysus   Night mostly. Darkness lends a great solemnity.

Pentheus   And is for women the best time for debauchery.

Dionysus I think you'll find that you can be debauched by daylight, too!

Pentheus You'll pay for your blasphemies and your slippery tongue.

Dionysus And you for your short-sightedness and disrespect to Bacchus.

Pentheus The priest's got a temper in him. He's quite manly when it comes to words.

Dionysus So what would you do to me? Torture me? How?

Pentheus First I'm going to cut off your lovely long curls.

Dionysus My hair is sacred. It belongs to Dionysus.

Pentheus And then – give me your thyrsus.

Dionysus Take it yourself. It belongs to Dionysus.

Pentheus I'm going to have you locked up.

Dionysus The god himself will set me free. I only have to ask him.

Pentheus Without your women you've no power. Your god won't come for you.

Dionysus But he's here now. He sees how I'm being treated.

Pentheus Where is he then? He's not at all obvious to me.

Dionysus He's here. Where I am. Your own ungodliness is blinding you.

Pentheus Take him away! He's no respect for me or Thebes.

Dionysus I'm warning you. Don't touch me. I have the knowledge. You do not.

Pentheus But I have the power.

Dionysus You don't know what you're saying. You don't know what you're doing. You don't know who you are.

Pentheus I am Pentheus, the son of Echion by Agave my mother.

Dionysus Pain, Pentheus, pain – a man of sorrow and your name means pain.

Pentheus Take him away. Lock him in the stables, in the darkness. Dance your dances there! As for those women, who've been part of this debauchery – I'll either auction them as slaves or keep them for myself to work for me. They'll put their hands to good use then – no more drums and tambourines for them!

Dionysus   Let's go then. Nothing will be that will not be. But know this – though you deny him, Dionysus will exact his vengeance on you for your arrogance and your ungodliness. In doing wrong by me, you would constrain a god.

Chorus   pure water
    dirke
virgin daughter
    of the river god
you bathed the bacchus
in ripples of rock-pools
cool
    from the searing fire

when zeus
    the father
stole him to salvation
stitching him close
    in his thigh

and he thundered

    come twice-born come
    safe to your father's womb
    my revelation
    my bacchus
    for thebes

pure water
    dirke
why do you shun me
no room on your banks
    for the garlands of bacchus
why do you scorn me
why do you shrink from me

soon you'll flow
    fertile and cool
through broad vineyards
rich with the grape
    of the god of the thunder

lush with the rich grace
  of bacchus

a new revelation
a mud man
king pentheus
  born of the dragon's blood
  fathered by echion
  mud man
  and monstrous
not born of woman
  but bloated
  and bloody
  and brawling with gods

soon he will bind me in ropes
  me
  the bacchic girl
now that my master's
  in bondage
  in chains

look on us now
  dionysus
  you
  son of zeus
look on your servants
  oppressed
  and enslaved
and come to us now
  with the blaze
  of your thyrsus
and grind all his
  hooligan boasts
  in the dust

dionysus
dionysus

are you on nysa now
  urging your hunting pack

high to the haunts
of the wild mountain beasts
or high on parnassus
the crags of corycia
or deep in the deep
forest folds
of olympus
where orpheus
magicked
the trees
with his music
magicked
the wild forest beasts
with his music

and bacchus honours you
fertile pieria
and he will come
with his bacchae
and dancing
and fording
the fast swirling eddies
of axios
leaping
the mad whirling dance
with his maenads
leaping
the lydia's
lazy clear waters
winding through fields
grazed by sleek arab stallions
bacchus
the blessèd
bestower of riches

Dionysus   hear my voice!
hear my voice!
go bacchae!
now bacchae!

Chorus listen
        the thunder
        the bacchus
        is calling me

Dionysus hear my voice
        semele's son
        son of zeus

Chorus master
        come now
        come to us
        to your hunting pack
        thunder god
        come
        dionysus

Dionysus and shiver
        the world
        to its roots
        in the earthquake

Chorus the palace must fall
        and the whole house
        of pentheus

        dionysus
        is here

        worship him
        we are worshipping

        look
        look
        the marble façade
        is exploding
        roaring
        the ricocheting
        voice of the thunder god

Dionysus fireballs and
              lightning and
              holocaust
              holocaust
              firestorm
              engulfing
              the whole house
              of pentheus

Chorus look
              the fire's
              lapping
              round
              semele's shrine now
            fire
              born
              of fire
              of the fire's conflagration
            lightning explosion
              of zeus
              that engulfed her
            throw yourselves
              down
              on the earth
              down

            the master
              is turning
              the whole house
              to liquid
            burning
            and churning
              the house
              to destroy it

            bacchus
            the master
            the true son of zeus

Dionysus Ladies! Little Lydians! Was it all so frightening for you? Did you
have to cower away for your protection? It seems you heard Bacchus rattling the
house. Come on! Up now! You're safe now. No need for any more trembling.

Chorus   We were alone and you came for us, a mystic light of revelation blazing out for us.

Dionysus   Were you so worried when they took me away, when they locked me up in the darkness?

Chorus   Of course I was. Who would protect me if you were not there for me? Pentheus is an evil man. How did you manage to escape?

Dionysus   I set myself free. It was not difficult.

Chorus   But you were handcuffed and chained.

Dionysus   No. I beguiled him.
I granted his wish.
He thought he was chaining me –
he never touched me, though,
never came near.
It was all in his mind.

It was a bull that he led to his stables,
not me.

And he hobbled its hooves
blind with fury and panting
and pouring with sweat
as he bit his lips bloody.
I saw it all

(I was sitting near, watching).

And then Bacchus came
and he shivered the palace
and fed the flame blazing
on his mother's tomb.

When Pentheus saw it
he thought the whole palace
was burning.

And he dashed about madly
and ordered his house-slaves
to fetch water – 'Water!' –
and so all the house
was in turmoil, confusion.

But there was no fire.

And he stopped in his tracks then –
he thought I'd escaped him –
and drew out his blade
and stormed into the palace.

And then it was, Bacchus,
the lord of the thunder –
this is my guess, now;
this how I saw it –
created a phantom
outside in the courtyard.

And *he* blundered out
and kept stabbing at thin air,
thinking that it was *me*
he was attacking.

But Bacchus had one last disgrace
left for Pentheus.
He tore down his palace
to rubble and ashes.
And now all's collapsed.
My imprisonment's ended
and all he has left is his humiliation,
exhausted and drained
by his duel with a phantom.
He's only a man,
yet he dared fight a god.
I've walked out unharmed.
Here I am. I've come back to you.
And as for Pentheus,
he doesn't worry me.

I can hear his hobnailed boots now! I think he's coming back outside. What can he have to say after all this, I wonder? Me, I'll be calm and cool, for all his bluster. A wise man should at all times practise equilibrium.

Pentheus This is outrageous! He's escaped – the foreigner – and I only just got him under lock and key! Look! There he is! What's this? What's going on? How can you show your face here of all places – outside my own house?

Dionysus Stay where you are. Be calm. Relax.

Pentheus How did you escape?

Dionysus I told you that he'd set me free. Were you not listening?

Pentheus That who'd set you free? You always speak in riddles.

Dionysus 'He who plants the fecund vine for mankind to enjoy.'

Pentheus A spiritual liberator? Very *comme il faut.*

Dionysus But this is Dionysus' greatest gift, and you'd insult it?

Pentheus (*to guards*) Lock all the city gates!

Dionysus You can't lock up a god! Gods can pass *through* gates!

Pentheus Oh, very clever! Very clever! Not where you should be clever, though!

Dionysus Oh, there especially. But there's someone coming for you now – down from the mountains – listen to their news. And don't worry about me. I won't go away.

Herdsman Pentheus! King! I've just come from Cithaeron – right from the peaks where the snow never melts.

Pentheus Why such urgency? What's your news?

Herdsman I've seen the women on the mountainside – pale flesh glimpsed just – running – possessed – glimpsed just and gone – and I came to tell you and the city, sir, all that they're doing, the strange, strange things, like miracles – but more miraculous. But I need to know, sir – should I tell you what's going on there, or should I keep quiet? You see, I know you've got a temper, sir – well, you're a king; you have a lot to think about – and I must admit I'm nervous.

Pentheus Tell me. Whatever your news, I won't punish you for it. One mustn't take one's anger out on those who're not involved. But the more I hear about those bacchae, the more flagrant and outrageous their excesses, the more unyielding I shall be to him when I pass sentence on him for corrupting them with his black arts.

Herdsman It was at sunrise. We were herding our cattle, driving them high to the uplands to pasture, and the heat of the sun just beginning to be felt.

And I saw the women, in three hunting packs, and each with its own leader: Autonoë; Agave, your own mother; and Ino. And they were sleeping – all of them – asleep – lying there so peaceful, so untroubled, soft on beds of deep fir fronds or downy drifts of oak leaves, pillowing their heads, each where she'd fallen, spent, exhausted, but so chaste, so modest.

It wasn't like you'd said at all. They weren't drunk or drugged. No hypnotizing flutes. No furtive scouring through the woods for sex.

It was your mother heard the cattle first. And she stood up – the bacchae still were sleeping all around her – and she began to keen a throbbing high-pitched scream to rally them, to wake them.

The women rubbed their eyes, and then, together, all began to stand, close-ordered, well-drilled, disciplined – not what we'd thought to see at all – young girls, old women standing side by side.

And they unpinned their hair and let it fall loose to their necks and shoulders, tied their deerskin dresses, knotted the cords firm and bound the dappled hides . . . with coils of serpents, writhing, flickering their tongues.

And any who had lately given birth, their breasts still full and swollen, cradled wild fawns in their arms and wolf-cubs too and suckled them.

One struck her thyrsus on a rock and water splashed out cool and glistening. Another struck the earth – god answered, and a new spring bubbled up – but not of water: wine. And others scored their nails across the cracking earth and milk gushed, arcing high in fountains, and they drank it deep. And from the ivy shoots wound round each thyrsus, honey oozed in sticky rivulets.

If you'd been there, if you had seen it, you'd have given praise to Dionysus, though you now disparage him.

We held a meeting – herdsmen, shepherds – and compared what we had seen. And each report outdid the last, so much that we could not explain, so much and all so strange.

There was one man there – he spends a lot of time in town, so he's a clever talker – and he spoke up and said: 'This mountain and these moors, this pasture-land is ours – it's where we live. Come on! Let's hunt Agave, trap her, take her to her son, King Pentheus, and earn his gratitude.'

We thought this good advice, so crawled off to conceal ourselves in ambush in the undergrowth.

And then it started. It was as if they'd all been waiting for the moment. The women started up a rhythmic beating with their thyrsuses, and all the crowd began to chant the name of Bacchus, Iacchos, the son of Zeus, the thunder god.

And all the mountain, all the creatures were possessed by Dionysus, and nothing moved that did not move in harmony with god.

And as she danced, Agave came near where I was. I leapt out from my hiding place and tried to catch her. But she shouted loud: 'My hunting pack! My hunting hounds! These men are hunting us! Follow me now with your thyrsuses raised! Follow me in the attack!'

We turned and ran and so escaped the carnage and the mutilation, and the women fell with their bare hands on our defenceless herds.

One seized a heifer in both hands – a lovely creature, a good milker – it was bellowing with fear – and as we watched, she tore the beast in two, while others in their frenzy ripped and clawed our cattle in a writhing mass of limbs, a bloody welter, ragged carcasses and hooves, and ribbons of raw bleeding flesh flapped down from dripping pines.

And massive bulls, till now so noble, and their spirits huge and surging through their horns, collapsed and fell, dragged down by all those hands, by all those girls. And in the blinking of an eye, a royal eye even, they had stripped the creatures bare of any flesh.

Then – like a wheeling flock of birds – they turned and raced across the wheat-fields by the banks of the Asopus, and they surged into the villages, Hysía and Eríthra, pouring through the lanes that climb the slopes of Mount Cithaeron, looting, plundering. They ransacked everything.

They snatched young children from their homes, and anything they carried on their backs stayed firm – no need to strap it on. No matter what it was – metal, bronze or iron – it didn't fall.

And in their hair they carried firelight, and they did not burn.

The village men were outraged at this unprovoked attack, and grabbed their weapons. And then what I saw . . . what I saw then, king – it was so strange, so strange, so inexplicable. Their weapons would not pierce the women's skin, while they – they launched a volley of their thyrsuses. The men began to fall, some badly wounded, others turning, running, wild with panic, and the women at their heels. A god was with them.

And then they turned and went back up the mountain to the springs the god had made, and washed their hands of blood.

And snakes were coiling themselves gently round them, licking their cheeks clean and purifying them all of all their killing.

Receive the god into the city, king, whoever he might be. He has an awesome power. I've heard it said his wine can liberate a man from any care. And wine adds so much pleasure to so many things, king – even sex!

Chorus   I hesitate to speak so freely to a king. But it must be spoken. Dionysus is a god.

Pentheus   No. This immorality, this new fanaticism's spreading like a fire through all of Greece, contaminating it. It must be stopped.

(*to guards*) Go to the Electran Gate. Pass on this order to the garrison – we're marching on the bacchae.

It's gone too far. We've put up with enough. I won't allow us to be treated in this way by women!

Dionysus   Won't you listen, Pentheus? You've treated me shamefully, but still I must warn you: don't take arms against a god. No. No – it's best if you do nothing. The mountain's the god's now, and Dionysus won't allow his bacchae to be moved.

Pentheus   For a criminal, you preach a lot of sermons! You'd best be careful – do you want me to imprison you again?

Dionysus   If I were you, I'd worship him, make sacrifices, check my temper. Yes. I wouldn't try resisting him when you're a man and he's a god.

Pentheus   Oh yes, I'll sacrifice. Their blood will be my sacrifice, the only sacrifice all this deserves, and all the gullies of Cithaeron will be *choked* with blood.

Dionysus   No. They'll easily defeat you. They'll put your men to rout. Imagine the humiliation: well-armed soldiers running from a bunch of women and their thyrsuses!

Pentheus   This foreigner won't let me go! No matter what I do to him, no matter what he does, he won't keep quiet.

Dionysus   Of course, there is another solution.

Pentheus   What? To take orders from you, from a criminal?

Dionysus   I'll bring the women here. No need to send in troops.

Pentheus   You're trying to trick me.

Dionysus   No. I'm trying to save you.

Pentheus   It's a conspiracy to stop me shutting down their cult.

Dionysus   It is, yes, but my co-conspirator's a god.

Pentheus   I've heard enough. (*to his attendants*) Bring me my weapons. Now!

Dionysus   No, wait! Do you want to see them for yourself – up there on the mountainside?

Pentheus   Yes! Yes I do! I'd give a lot to see that!

Dionysus   Why such desire?

Pentheus   No – not desire – distress! I'd be distressed to see them all so drunk.

Dionysus   But even so, you want to see them?

Pentheus   Yes. I'll observe them – quietly – from behind a tree.

Dionysus   But they'll track you down, no matter if you try to hide.

Pentheus   Then I'll go openly. Yes. Yes. That's good advice.

Dionysus   So I'm to lead you? You do want to go?

Pentheus   Yes – now! We're wasting time.

Dionysus   Before we go, you must put on a dress.

Pentheus   What? And pretend to be a woman?

Dionysus   They'll kill you if they think you're a man.

Pentheus   Well said. Yes. Yes – you've always been so very clever.

Dionysus   The idea came from Dionysus.

Pentheus   How best to do it then?

Dionysus   Come inside the house. I'll dress you.

Pentheus   What? Like a woman? I'd be so embarrassed.

Dionysus   Have you lost your enthusiasm? Do you not want to see the maenads any more?

Pentheus   What sort of dress did you say I should wear?

Dionysus   I'll give you nice long curls.

Pentheus　And then?

Dionysus　A long dress to your ankles, and a ribbon for your hair.

Pentheus　What else?

Dionysus　A dappled deerskin and a thyrsus.

Pentheus　I couldn't dress up as a woman.

Dionysus　But if you try to fight them, there'll be bloodshed.

Pentheus　You're right. First know your enemy.

Dionysus　Yes, better that. You don't want to invite more problems than you need.

Pentheus　How to get out of Thebes without being seen?

Dionysus　By empty streets. I'll be your guide.

Pentheus　The great thing is the bacchae don't think I'm ridiculous. I'm going inside now to consider what must best be done.

Dionysus　Yes. Go. I've done everything I need to do.

Pentheus　Perhaps I'll go inside. Yes. And it may be that I take the army. Or it may be I'll take your advice.

Dionysus　And so he walks into the trap. He will go where the bacchae are, and there he'll make amends with his own life.

To work now, Dionysus! You're so close. We'll have our vengeance.

And – for Pentheus – first ecstasy, skewed thinking, febrile madness. Yes, if he'd been sane, he'd never have admitted to such passion for being dressed in women's clothes; possessed, he'll relish it. And all his threats, and all his blustering – I need to hear the mocking laughter, see him ridiculed by Thebes, led through the streets, a woman.

So now to dress him in his robes for death, his robes he'll meet his mother in. And so she'll slaughter him. And he'll know Dionysus as the son of Zeus, a god born truly of a god, a god of terror and a god of gentle comfort for mankind.

Chorus　night
　　　　dances
　　　night
　　　　dancing

will i
pound my feet hard
on the earth
   in the
night
   dance
and
throw back
   my head
   in the
cool
   mountain air

   like
a fawn
leaping high
   in the
lush
meadow grasslands

   ecstatic
   alive

and the hunt's
   far behind now
the beaters
the terror
the hunting nets
   cleared

and
the shouts
   of the men
   to their dogs
all growing distant

they're calling them back
and their quarry's escaped

and its muscles
   are rippling

it's racing
   the breeze now
and bounding
   with joy
in the fens
   by the river

and on
to the wild woods
the deep
   untamed forests
and dark
   dappled shadows
ablaze
   with new life

what is wisdom
   and
what better
   gift
   is given us
   by god
than power
to overcome
   our enemies
to bring
   our hands
   down
   heavy
   on their heads
   and
what is good
should be pursued
   for ever

the justice
   of the gods
   grinds
   slow
   inexorable
   unfailing

to make
   the cold
   the cruel
   the crookèd
straight
   the irreligious and
   the blasphemous
   the crazed
   the megalomaniac

time
stretches

stealth
conceals
   the hunter
tracking down
   the heretic

knowledge
has its bounds

faith
is more simple
(and yet more profound)—
pure
understanding
arching
to eternity
born
at the birth of time

so
what is wisdom
   and
what better
   gift
   is given us
   by god
than power

to overcome
    our enemies
to bring
    our hands
    down
    heavy
    on their heads
    and
what is good
should be pursued
    for ever

blessèd is he
    who outraces the storm wind
    and anchors his boat
    safe in shelter
blessèd is he
    who survives

there is an inequality to power and wealth
and countless men have countless hopes
and some will wither, some will flower to richness

but
the richest man's
the man who's blest
with what he needs
to let him live
from day to day
in peace
and happiness

Dionysus   Pentheus! Come out now! So hungry to see what should not be seen, so eager where you should be cautious! Come out and show me how you look as a woman, a maenad, a nymph of Dionysus, as a voyeur spying on your mother and her company!

You could be one of Cadmus' daughters!

Pentheus   I think I see two suns, two Thebes! And you – you – you're a bull and you're my guide and you've got horns. Or have you never really been a man at all? Look! You've become a bull.

Dionysus The god is here. He was angry with you before, but he's on your side now, and so you're seeing as you should.

Pentheus How do I look? Don't I have just the identical poise to Ino and my mother, Agave?

Dionysus When I look at you, it's like I'm seeing them. Keep still! This hair's come loose, and I'd taken such care with those ribbons.

Pentheus When I was inside, I was tossing my hair like the dancers do. It must have worked loose then.

Dionysus We'll sort it out. Head up! I can see I'm going to have to be your dresser.

Pentheus My make-up boy! Yes! I've made myself over to you completely.

Dionysus And look at your bodice! It's all saggy. And your dress is rucking badly at the ankles.

Pentheus Oh, yes! Yes! Badly on the right side, yes. It's hanging nicely on the left, though.

Dionysus When you see how gentle the bacchae are – such unexpected gentleness – you'll know how good a friend I am.

Pentheus Which hand should I use to hold my thyrsus to blend in better with the bacchae?

Dionysus Your right hand. And now bring up your right arm at the same time as your right leg. I'm glad you're so different to the way you used to be.

Pentheus Do you think I could carry all Cithaeron on my shoulders – all the women, too?

Dionysus If you wanted. You know, you used to have such delusions, but you're all right now.

Pentheus Should we take winches? Or maybe I can get my shoulders underneath and lift the mountain up with my bare hands.

Dionysus What, and destroy the grottoes of the nymphs, and the cave where Pan plays on his pipes – such haunting melodies?

Pentheus Yes. Yes, you're right. No need for any force to get the better of those women. I'll hide in the pine-trees.

Dionysus You'll find a perfect hiding place to spy on women when they've been inspired by Dionysus.

Pentheus   Imagine! I expect they're in the bushes now like mating birds hugged close in their cock's embrace!

Dionysus   Indeed. I understand now why you've taken on the rôle of watchman! Perhaps you'll catch them . . . if they don't catch you.

Pentheus   Take me there now – through the centre of Thebes, along the main roads! I am the only man in all of Thebes who'd have the courage to dare do this.

Dionysus   You are the only man. The only man. The weight of Thebes is on your shoulders, and the trials that lie ahead are all for you. This way. Come on. I'll make sure that you get there safely. Someone else will bring you home.

Pentheus   My mother.

Dionysus   A most pleasing spectacle.

Pentheus   My destiny.

Dionysus   Raised high.

Pentheus   Too much!

Dionysus   And in your mother's arms.

Pentheus   You want to spoil me.

Dionysus   Yes, I'll spoil you – after my own fashion.

Pentheus   Well, I deserve it.

Dionysus   You terrible man!

You. Terrible. Man. And terrible the horrors that will meet you. And all the world will know your name. Your fame will fill the sky.

Stretch out your arms, Agave! Cadmus' daughters, stretch out your arms! I'm leading a young soldier to his last great battle, and with Bacchus, with the thunder god, I shall defeat him. And what shall be, shall be revealed.

Chorus   vengeance
               vengeance

          go
               vengeance
          now

vengeance
goading
   your hunting dogs
race
   to the hills
race
   to thebes bacchic
   hunting pack
goading them
lashing them
maddened with rage
   at the gibbering man
   dressed as gibbering woman
   the gibbering spy
   as he leers at their rites

and his mother will see him first
   leering and ogling
   high on a crag
   or a sheer rocky outcrop
she'll call to the bacchae

who's come to the mountain
to pry on the bacchae
to pry on us
   racing the breeze
   on the mountain
who is he
what is he
what savage beast spawned him
not born of a woman
a lioness for mother
a libyan gorgon

let
justice come that we might see her
justice with her sword held high
   against
   the godless man
   the lawless man
   the man who knows no justice

the mud man
the mad man
the spawn of echion
let
justice with her sword held high
come now to slice his throat

bacchus
bacchus

death
    to the man
    who would seek
    to destroy you
his mind cruel and rotten
his heart cold with hate
    to destroy any worship
    of you or your mother
the man
    crazed with cunning
    who'd seek to match force
    with a force that's unmatchable

death
    is the only due

gods
    must be honoured
and all men must die
    to accept that brings peace
and though we might
    push back the bounds
    of our knowledge
the world is more complex
    and life's more profound
for man's life should be
    a great journey to purity
    banishing blasphemy
    honouring god

    let
justice come that we might see her

justice with her sword held high
   against
   the godless man
   the lawless man
   the man who knows no justice
   the mud man
   the mad man
   the spawn of echion
let
justice with her sword held high
come now to slice his throat

come bacchus
now bacchus

come as a bull
or a hydra
   its snake heads
   all writhing
a fire-breathing lion

come bacchus
come
   with a smile on your sweet lips
to cast the grim noose
   round the neck of the hunter
the grim noose of death
   round the neck of the hunter

and bacchae
   are swarming
   to fall
   on their prey

Messenger   Until today all Greece admired the dynasty of Thebes and Cadmus and the dragon's teeth. I am a mere slave, but still I mourn its passing.

Chorus   What's happened? Have you some news of the bacchae?

Messenger   Pentheus is dead.

Chorus   divine revelation
                     revealed in your majesty
             bromius
                     god of the thunder

Messenger   What are you saying? How can you speak like that? How can you gloat at the news of his suffering?

Chorus   it's
                     the cult cry of bacchus
                     the song of the foreigner
                     sweet liberation
                     an end to our fear

Messenger   Do you think Thebes so weak . . .?

Chorus   thebes
                     has no power now
             it's all
                     dionysus

Messenger   I understand your feelings, but it's not right to gloat over another's suffering.

Chorus   the man was evil
                     his actions were evil
                             but tell us
                     please
                             how did he die?

Messenger   We made our way up out of Thebes. Soon there were no more houses, no more villages. And we crossed the Asopus, and struck out deep into the foothills of Cithaeron – Pentheus and I (I went as his servant), and the foreigner who acted as our guide.

And so we went on, picking our way carefully in silence, no one speaking, till we came to a valley with tall grasses, where we could hide and watch without being seen. Ahead, a gorge. On both sides, sheer cliffs. Water streaming down the rock face. And dark pines. And women, maenads, sitting so contented, so absorbed, so concentrating on their work.

Some were repairing thyrsuses, binding the tips round with swathes of ivy; others, innocent, like colts set free to race the breeze, were singing hymns to Dionysus, each one picking up the melody in turn.

For Pentheus, though, this was not enough, and he whispered to the stranger: 'From where we are, I can't see any of the other maenads. I can't see the debauchery; I can't see the perversions. But there's a tall pine high on the ravine, and from the top of that I'd have no difficulty seeing their depravity.'

And then I saw the stranger work a miracle. He took the pine-tree's topmost bough and bent it like a bow down down down until its tip was brushing the black earth. He took the tree-top in both hands and dragged it down – no man could do that – and on a branch he seated Pentheus. And slowly slowly he released the tree, and it began to bend back straight and tall, and all the time so careful not to topple Pentheus, till it rose up so high, so straight, so towering in the towering sky. And on the highest branch of all clung Pentheus.

But now he could be seen more easily than he could see, and in a moment he would be exposed.

I looked around. The foreigner was nowhere to be seen. And then a voice – I think it was the voice of Dionysus – shivered through the air:

'Look, bacchae! Now, bacchae! Here is the man who's been mocking my mysteries, mocking me too. Take your vengeance!'

And as he spoke, a blade of firelight shot between the earth and sky and all the air fell silent.

Time stopped. Nothing. Silence. Not even the rustle of wind in the leaves. No birds. No animals. The women standing motionless, confused, their faces blank, expressionless.

And then it came again. And when they heard it, they all recognized the voice of Bacchus, and they understood its meaning.

And they poured out like doves, all the swarm of the bacchae, and splashed through the gorge, crossed the torrent of boulders, and God's breath was in them.

And there was Pentheus clinging to the branches of the pine-tree.

And some scaled the cliffs which towered over the gorge and launched volley on volley of branches and boulders, and others threw thyrsuses hurling them high, but he was too far for them. For all their efforts he was out of reach.

And so he sat there, trembling and trapped, and there was no escape.

And now they were stripping an oak of its branches and driving them deep in the base of the pine-tree and trying to uproot it, but it would not move.

And then she spoke, Agave, Pentheus' mother:

'Now, bacchae, now – hold the tree trunk round firmly. The beast's in the branches. We must catch it now before it exposes the god's sacred mysteries!'

And they stretched out their hands, all the mass of the bacchae, and tore the pine out of the earth.

He was so high. He had so far to fall. And his scream seemed to go on for ever.

And then the ritual of slaughter. The first rites were his mother's rites. And as she closed in for the kill, he tore the ribbon from his hair so she would know him, so she'd spare him, and he screamed as he clawed at her cheeks in his terror:

'Mother! Mother! It's me, mother! Pentheus! Me! Me! Your son! Pity me, mother! I know I've done wrong, but don't kill your own son!'

But foam was pouring from Agave's mouth. Her eyes were rolling wildly, and her reasoning was all gone. The god was riding her, and she was deaf to all his screaming.

And she drove her foot hard down on Pentheus' ribcage and grasped his left elbow ... and wrenched off his arm. She never would have had the strength, but god was in her and he gave her power.

And then Ino was with her crouched, huddling over him, tearing his flesh, and Autonoë too, and the whole mob of bacchae, a bestial mass writhing, savage and feral and shredding him raw. And the noise was so deafening: Pentheus shrieking till all screams were silent, and the baying of the bacchae in triumph.

I saw one drag an arm into the undergrowth. One held a foot, and the shoe was still on it. And all the others thrashed and clawed in frenzy, stripping his ribs clean, and tossing lumps of flesh as if it were some gruesome game of catch and everything was spattered with his blood.

So his remains are scattered over jagged rocks or high in branches swaying in the silence of the forest. To recover all of them would be impossible.

But his mother has his head. She skewered it on her thyrsus like a trophy from a lion-hunt, and then she turned away. Her sisters are still there in the dance of Dionysus but Agave's coming back to Thebes.

And she's laughing and she's bragging and she's boasting of her bloody prize and calling out to Bacchus, her companion in the hunt, to Bacchus, wreathed in victory, although for her the only victory is tears.

I'll not stay. I've no wish to see more suffering, and she'll be with you soon.

So what is wisdom? Piety, I think, and godliness. And what is good should be pursued for ever.

Chorus   dancers
      soar high
      in the dances
       of bacchus
    roaring
      the cry
      of the death
      of king pentheus
    spawn
      of the dragon
    he dressed
      as a woman
    and clutched
      at the thyrsus
      his death rod
      his death god
    and followed
      the bull
      to destruction

    and you
      theban bacchae
    have won
      a great victory

    but your prize
      will be weeping
      and sore lamentation
    a fine contest this
      to plunge hands
      in your own
      child's blood

dripping
and glistening
and black
with his death

but look
    look
agave
    king pentheus' mother
her eyes
    staring
    wild
in the wild
    dance of bacchus
her soul
    staring
    wild
in the wild
    dance of ecstasy

welcome her now
to her city

Agave   lydian bacchae

Chorus   no
              what do you want of us

Agave   i've brought home
             a gift
                 from the mountain
             a vine shoot
                 a tendril
                 sliced
                 dripping
             the spoils
                 of the hunt

Chorus   i see you
              i welcome you

              you've joined
                  his dance now

Agave i snared it myself
   and i needed no nets
   for the lion cub

   look
   look at it

Chorus where?
    on the mountain?

Agave cithaeron

Chorus cithaeron?

Agave i killed it

Chorus who shot it

Agave i shot it
   the prize
    is mine
   and all
    my hunting pack
   call me
    the blessèd one
    blessèd agave

Chorus who else was there

Agave cadmus

Chorus what? cadmus?

Agave his daughters
    were with me
   they joined
    in the death
   but i killed it
   i killed it

   the hunt
    has been good today
   now
    for the feast

come
   and join me

Chorus   what? no

Agave   but the bull calf
      is young
   and its cheeks
      soft and downy
   and look
      how its hairs
      curling over its brow

Chorus   yes its hair
         is a beast's hair

Agave   the hunter
      was bacchus
   he unleashed
      his maenads
   to bring down
      the beast

Chorus   he's the lord of the hunt

Agave   and so i shall be famous

Chorus   yes famous

Agave   in thebes

Chorus   and your son?
      what of pentheus?

Agave   pentheus too
   and my fame
   is his fame

      i've brought home
         the lion cub

Chorus   a hard prize

Agave   and hard won

Chorus   and so you'll give thanks

Agave   for my ecstasy
                  yes
             for this great revelation
             laid bare
                  in the hunt

Chorus   So. Now. The revelation. Show us, show all of Thebes your trophy.

Agave   Thebans! Thebes! What a beautiful city! Everyone, come here and gaze on the beast! We hunted it! We killed it! The daughters of Cadmus! And no need for spears or for hunting nets! Only our white hands, our soft hands, our women's hands! So after this, who'll listen to a huntsman boasting how he's built up such a stock of hunting gear and all the best equipment when he doesn't need it! We killed this beast with our bare hands! We ripped this beast apart with our bare hands!

Where's my father? I want my father. And Pentheus! Where's Pentheus? Where's my son? He must get a ladder and climb up and nail up the lion head there – there above the door as a trophy of my hunt!

Cadmus   Bring him home, now. Bring home poor Pentheus, this poor sad bundle that was Pentheus. I tried so hard to find his body – it was scattered all across Cithaeron: in the gullies, in the woods. It was so hard to find.

I'd only just got home. Teiresias was with me. We'd been out at our bacchic festival. And they told me what had happened, my daughters' cruel atrocities. So I went back up the mountain for my grandson. The bacchae killed him.

They were still there – Autonoë – she had a son once, Actaeon (he died), and Aristaeus was his father – they were all there. And I saw Ino too. And they were running maddened through the woods in their sad ecstasy.

And someone told me that Agave'd come back here, and she was still possessed. And it was true. And it was true. It breaks my heart to see her.

Agave   Father! You've so much to be proud about! You've got the best daughters in all the world! All your daughters, but me specially. I gave up domesticity for bigger things, for hunting wild beasts with my own bare hands.

I'm cradling it – look! Look! Look! It's my prize! I'm going to nail it up there – there – above your door.

You hold it, father! Aren't you proud of me? Aren't you proud how I hunted the beast? Invite all our family and friends to a banquet. They'll see what I've done and they'll think you're so lucky!

Cadmus   The grief is never-ending, and I can't bear to look. Cruel hands! Cruel slaughter! O, what a sacrifice is this to offer to the gods? And you'd invite all Thebes – and me – to banquet? And all the horror. All the horror. You're suffering the most, but I'm suffering … I'm suffering … The god has crushed us. He had every right to do it, but this – this is too much. Dionysus was my daughter's son, and now he's crushed us.

Agave   Old men can be so disagreeable. Always frowning. Always discontent. I wish that Pentheus could be as good a hunter as his mother, and he'd go out with his hunting pack, with all the youth of Thebes, to hunt wild beasts. Not Pentheus! He's only good for fighting with the gods! Father, you must speak to him. Get him here, someone. I want to see him. I want him to see how happy I am.

Cadmus   If you ever find out what you've done, the pain will be too much. But if you stay like this – if you stay like this for ever – you may not be at peace, but in your mind you'll never suffer.

Agave   There's nothing ugly here – nothing distressing.

Cadmus   Lift up your eyes and look at the sky.

Agave   What should I be looking at?

Cadmus   Does it seem the same to you, or is it different?

Agave   It's brighter than it was. And more transparent.

Cadmus   And you feel more calm?

Agave   Calm? I don't understand. But somehow … somehow clearer. Something's changing in my head.

Cadmus   So can you listen to me now? Can you answer me clearly?

Agave   What were we saying just now, father?

Cadmus   Whose family did you marry into?

Agave   You gave me to Echion, one of the dragon's brood.

Cadmus   And who was the son you had by Echion?

Agave   Pentheus.

Cadmus   And whose head are you cradling?

Agave   A lion's. The hunting pack killed it.

Cadmus   Look at it carefully.

Agave   (*screams*) What!? In my own hands?

Cadmus   Keep looking. Understand more clearly.

Agave   I see such suffering.

Cadmus   Do you still think it's a lion's head?

Agave   No. It's Pentheus.

Cadmus   Before you even knew, I mourned him.

Agave   Who killed him? How did he come into my hands?

Cadmus   The truth is hard. Now's not the time.

Agave   No. Tell me. My heart's filled with foreboding.

Cadmus   You killed him. You and your sisters.

Agave   Where? Here at home? Or where?

Cadmus   Up there, where Actaeon once was killed by his pack of hunting dogs.

Agave   Why was my son on Cithaeron?

Cadmus   He went there to sneer at the god and at you, at the bacchae.

Agave   What? We were on Cithaeron?

Cadmus   You were all possessed. The whole of Thebes was gripped by bacchic madness.

Agave   Dionysus has destroyed us all. I now know everything.

Cadmus   Yes. In your arrogance you denied he was a god.

Agave   Where's Pentheus' body?

Cadmus   I looked for it. I brought it home.

Agave   Is it laid out properly?

. . . .
. . . .

Agave Why Pentheus? Why did he have to suffer for my madness?

Cadmus You both refused to honour Dionysus, and so he passed this sentence on us all – on you and Pentheus and me. So he wiped out a dynasty.

I had no sons of my own, and now my grandson's dead, and his death was so cruel, so barbaric. He was our hope.

You gave my house new strength, my Pentheus, my grandson. And all of Thebes respected you. When you were near, no man would dare to disrespect your grandfather. You took swift action then!

And now I, Cadmus, Cadmus who was once so strong, who founded Thebes, who sowed the dragon's teeth and reaped their shining harvest, I, Cadmus shall become a shabby refugee.

I loved you, Pentheus. And now in death I love you still. You'll never stroke my cheek again. You'll never fling your arms around me, say, 'Grandfather! Who's wronged you now? Who's injured you? What's worrying you? Who's been upsetting you? Tell me, and I'll see he pays!'

But now it's over, and I'm just a poor old man. You're gone, and with you all your mother's hopes, and all her future. We won't recover now.

And if a man should ever question the authority of heaven, let him remember Pentheus and how he died and recognize the true power of the gods.

Chorus I pity you your fate. Your grandson did deserve to die, but you . . . I pity you.

Agave All ruined. All reversed.

```
 .   .   .   .   .   .   .   .
 .   .   .   .   .   .   .   .
 .   .   .   .   .   .   .   .
 .   .   .   .   .   .   .   .
```

Dionysus Cadmus, you will shape-shift and become a snake; your wife too, Harmonia, whom Ares gave you though you were a mortal, shall become a beast like you, a snake.

This is the word of Zeus.

And together you will lead a swarm of foreigners to Greece, riding in an ox-cart with a cruel barbaric horde. And so you'll sack so many cities, countless cities. But in the end they'll plunder Delphi and Apollo's sacred shrine, and so their homecoming will be a plague, a pestilence.

But Ares will deliver you and your wife safe. And so you'll live for ever with the gods.

I am Dionysus, son of Zeus, god born of gods, not man.

You made your choice. Had you been humble, you would now be blessed and you would walk with me, with Dionysus, son of Zeus, your ally and your friend for ever.

Cadmus   Dionysus, we did wrong! Forgive us!

Dionysus   No. You learned too late. And when you should have known me, you rejected me.

Cadmus   I know now. But to punish us like this – it's more than we deserve.

Dionysus   I am a god and you insulted me.

Cadmus   Gods should not have the passions that men do.

Dionysus   This has long been the will of Zeus my father.

Agave   It is our fate, then? Exile?

Dionysus   It is your fate. Now, go!

Cadmus   Agave, we're consumed by all our suffering, you and your sisters, you and I. I am an old man and I must become a refugee. And more – it is the gods' will I must lead a foreign army against Greece. My wife and I must become serpents. I must lead an army against all that's sacred in the land of Greece. And there will be no end to all my suffering. The gods won't even let me rest in death.

Agave   I'll never see you again, father!

Cadmus   Your arms can't save me now.

Agave   Where will I go, a refugee, a beggar?

Cadmus   I don't know. I don't know. I won't be there for you.

Agave   This was my city and my home. Now all there is is sorrow. My tears are for you, father.

Cadmus   And mine for you and your sisters.

Agave   Dionysus has unleashed a terrible revenge on all our family.

Cadmus   Yes. For all he suffered at our hands, dishonoured by the whole of Thebes.

Agave   Goodbye, father.

Cadmus   Goodbye. There's no good left now.

Agave   so now i shall go
and i'll look for
     my sisters
that they too
might share in
     my grief
and
     my exile

so come with me
be with me

i want to go
     where i won't see
     cithaeron
and the plague
and the shame
     of cithaeron
     won't see me

     and i can forget
     the god's thyrsus

     it must pass
     to others now
     to other bacchae

Chorus   gods
shape-shift

and
they walk among us
though we may not know
that they are gods

and
when we think

we can control
our future
nothing is
as we had thought
and that is god
and that is god
and that is god

Bibliography

Adkins, A.W.H., *Merit and Responsibility: A Study in Greek Values*, Oxford, 1960.

Artaud, A., *The Theatre and Its Double*, trans. Mary Caroline Richards, New York, 1958.

Balot, R.K., 'The Virtue Politics of Democratic Athens', in S. Salkever (ed.) *The Cambridge Companion to Ancient Greek Political Thought*, Cambridge, 2009.

Bierl, A., 'Maenadism as Self-referential Chorality in Euripides' *Bacchae*', in R. Gagné and M.G. Hopman (eds) *Choral Mediations in Greek Tragedy*, Cambridge, 2013.

Bierl, A., 'Germany, Austria and Switzerland', in B. van Zyl Smit (ed.) *A Handbook to the Reception of Greek Drama*, Malden, MA, forthcoming.

Braund, D., 'Dionysiac tragedy in Plutarch, *Crassus*', *Classical Quarterly* 43, 1993.

Brooke, N., *Horrid Laughter in Jacobean Tragedy*, New York, 1979.

Brooke, R., 'Drama', in C. Hassell (ed.) *The Prose of Rupert Brooke*, London, 1956.

Burnett, A.P., 'Pentheus and Dionysus: Host and Guest', *Classical Philology* 65, 1970.

Burnett, A.P., *Catastrophe Survived: Euripides' Plays of Mixed Reversal*, Oxford, 1971.

Burnett, A.P., *Revenge in Attic and Later Tragedy*, Berkeley, Los Angeles, and London, 1998.

Butler, S., *Aeschyli tragoediae quae supersunt, deperditarum fabularum fragmenta, et scholia Graeca*, 8 vols, Cambridge, 1809–16.

Carey, C., 'Comedy and the Civic Chorus', in E. Bakola, L. Prauscello and M. Telò (eds) *Greek Comedy and the Discourse of Genres*, Cambridge, 2013.

Carrara, P., *Il testo di Euripide nell' antichità*, Florence, 2009.

Cartledge, P., '"Deep plays": Theatre as Process in Greek Civic Life', in P.E. Easterling (ed.) *The Cambridge Companion to Greek Tragedy*, Cambridge, 1997.

Collard, C. and Cropp, M., *Euripides: Selected Fragmentary Plays*, vol. I, Cambridge, MA, 2008.

Collard, C., Cropp, M. and Gibert, J., *Euripides: Selected Fragmentary Plays*, vol. II, Oxford, 2004.

Cowan, R., 'Sing Evohe! Three Twentieth-century Operatic Versions of Euripides' *Bacchae*', in P. Brown and S. Ograjenšek (eds) *Ancient Drama in Music for the Modern Stage*, Oxford, 2010.

Csapo, E. and Slater, W.J., *The Context of Ancient Drama*, Ann Arbor, 1995.

Cusset, C., *Ménandre ou la comédie tragique*, Paris, 2003.

Diggle, J., *Euripidis Fabulae*, 3 vols, Oxford, 1981–94.

Dittenberger, G., *Sylloge Inscriptionum Graecarum*⁴, Hildesheim, 1960.

Dodds, E.R., *Euripides'* Bacchae, *Edited with Introduction and Commentary*, Oxford, 1960.

Dodds, E.R., *Euripides'* Bacchae, *Edited with Introduction and Commentary*, reprint, Oxford, 1974.

Droysen, J.G., *Kleine Schriften zur alten Geschichte*, vol. ii, Leipzig, 1894.

Easterling, P.E., 'The End of an Era? Tragedy in the Early Fourth Century', in A.H. Sommerstein, S. Halliwell, J. Henderson and B. Zimmermann (eds) *Tragedy, Comedy and the Polis*, Bari, 1993.

Easterling, P.E., 'Foreword', in R.P. Winnington-Ingram, *Euripides and Dionysus: An Interpretation of the Bacchae*, second edition, London, 1997a.

Easterling, P.E., 'Form and Performance', in P.E. Easterling (ed.) *The Cambridge Companion to Greek Tragedy*, Cambridge, 1997b.

Easterling, P.E., 'From Repertoire to Canon', in P.E. Easterling (ed.) *The Cambridge Companion to Greek Tragedy*, Cambridge, 1997c.

Eitrem, S., Amundsen, L. and Winnington-Ingram, R.P. (eds), 'Fragments of Unknown Greek Tragic Texts with Musical Notation (P. Oslo inv. no. 1413)', *Symbolae Osloenses* 31, 1955.

Eliot, T.S., *Elizabethan Essays*, London, 1934.

Else, G.F., *Aristotle's Poetics: The Argument*, Leiden, 1957.

Esslin, M., *The Theatre of the Absurd*, revised edition, London, 2001.

Fischer-Lichte, E., 'Thinking About the Origins of Theatre in the 1970s', in E. Hall, F. Macintosh and A. Wrigley (eds) *Dionysus Since 69*, Oxford, 2004.

Fisher, N.R.E., *Hybris: A Study in the Values of Honour and Shame in Ancient Greece*, Warminster, 1992.

Flashar, H., *Inszenierung der Antike: das griechische Drama auf der Bühne der Neuzeit 1585–1990*, Munich, 1991.

Foley, H.P., 'The Masque of Dionysos', *Transactions of the American Philological Association* 110, 1980.

Foley, H.P., 'Marriage and Sacrifice in Euripides' *Iphigenia in Aulis*', *Arethusa* 15, 1982.

Foley H.P., *Ritual Irony*, Ithaca, NY, 1985.

Foley, H.P., *Reimagining Greek Tragedy on the American Stage*, Berkeley, 2012.

Fowler, R.L. *Early Greek Mythography*, Oxford, 2000.

Frazer, J.G., *Apollodorus: The Library*, 2 vols, London and Cambridge, MA, 1961–63.

Garvie, A., 'The Paradox of the *Bacchae*', in A. Beale (ed.) *Euripides Talks*, 15–22, Bristol, 2008.

Goldhill, S., *Reading Greek Tragedy*, Cambridge, 1986.

Goldhill, S., 'The Great Dionysia and Civic Ideology', *Journal of Hellenic Studies* 107, 1987.

Green, J.R., *Theatre in Ancient Greek Society*, London, 1994.

Gregory, J., 'Euripides' *Alcestis*', *Hermes* 107, 1979.

Gregory, J., *Euripides and the Instruction of the Athenians*, Ann Arbor, 1991.

Griffith, M. and Most, G., *Euripides V: Bacchae, Iphigenia in Aulis, The Cyclops, Rhesus* (including the translation by D. Grene and R. Lattimore), Chicago, 2013.

Gurd, S.A., *Iphigenias at Aulis: Textual Multiplicity, Radical Philology*, Ithaca and London, 2005.

Guthrie, W.K.C., *The Sophists*, Cambridge, 1971.

Gutzwiller, K.J., 'The Tragic Mask of Comedy: Metatheatricality in Menander', *Classical Antiquity* 19, 2000.

Hall, E., *Inventing the Barbarian*, Oxford, 1989.

Hall, E., 'The Sociology of Athenian Tragedy', in P.E. Easterling (ed.) *The Cambridge Companion to Greek Tragedy*, Cambridge, 1997.

Hall, E., 'The Singing Actors of Antiquity', in P.E. Easterling and E. Hall, *Greek and Roman Actors*, Cambridge, 2002.

Hall, E., 'Iphigenia and Her Mother at Aulis: A Study in the Revival of a Euripidean Classic', in S. Wilmer and J. Dillon (eds) *Rebel Women: Staging Ancient Greek Drama Today*, London, 2005.

Hall, E., *The Theatrical Cast of Athens*, Oxford, 2006.

Hall, E., *Greek Tragedy: Suffering under the Sun*, Oxford, 2010.

Hall, E., *Adventures with Iphigenia in Tauris: A Cultural History of Euripides' Black Sea Tragedy*, New York, 2013.

Hall, E. and Macintosh, F., *Greek Tragedy and the British Theatre*, Oxford, 2005.

Hall, E. and Wyles, R. (eds), *New Directions in Ancient Pantomime*, Oxford, 2008.

Halleran, M., *Stagecraft in Euripides*, London, 1985.

Hammer, C., *Rhetores Graeci, ex recognitione Leonardi Spengel. Vol. 1, Pars II*. Leipzig, 1894.

Hanink, J., *Lycurgan Athens and the Making of Classical Tragedy*, Cambridge, 2014.

Hansen, M.H., *Polis: An Introduction to the Ancient Greek City-State*, Oxford, 2006.

Hartung, J.A., *Euripides restitutus*, volumen alterum, Hamburg, 1844.

Haug, D.T.T., *Relative Chronology in Early Greek Epic Poetry*, Cambridge, 2012.

Heath, M., *The Poetics of Greek Tragedy*, London, 1987.

Henderson, J., 'Comic Scenes in Greek Tragedy', in H.M. Roisman (ed.) *Encyclopedia of Greek Tragedy*, vol. I, Hoboken, NJ, 2014.

Henze, H.W., *Bohemian Fifths, An Autobiography*, trans. S. Spencer, London, 1998.

Hunter, R.L., *The New Comedy of Greece and Rome*, Cambridge, 1985.

Hurst, A., 'Ménandre et la Tragédie', in E.W. Handley and A. Hurst (eds) *Relire Ménandre*, Geneva, 1990.

Huys, M., *The Tale of the Hero who was Exposed at Birth in Euripidean Tragedy: A Study of Motifs*, Leuven, 1995.

Isaac, D., 'Review of *Dionysus in 69*', *Educational Theatre Journal* 22.4, 1970.

Jodrell, R.P., *Illustrations of Euripides on the Ion and the Bacchae*, London, 1781.

Jouan, F. and van Looy, H., *Euripide: Les Fragments*, vols I–IV, Paris, 1998–2003.

Kaimio, M., 'Titles of Tragedies', in H.M. Roisman (ed.) *Encyclopedia of Greek Tragedy*, vol. III, Hoboken, NJ, 2014.

Kalke, C.M., 'The Making of a Thyrsus: The Transformation of Pentheus in Euripides' *Bacchae*', *American Journal of Philology* 106, 1985.

Kamerbeek, J.C., 'On the Conception of ΘΕΟΜΑΧΟΣ in Relation with Greek Tragedy', *Mnemosyne* 1 (4th series), 1948.

Kampourelli, V., *Space in Greek Tragedy*, London, 2015.

Kannicht, R., 'Zu Aeschylus fr.23 und trag. adesp. fr.144 N²', *Hermes* 85, 1957.

Kannicht, R., *Tragicorum Graecorum Fragmenta (TrGF)*, vol. V 1–2: *Euripides*, Göttingen, 2004.

Karamanou, I., 'Euripides' *Alcmeon in Corinth* and Menander's *Periceiromene*: Similarities in Theme and Structure', *Actas del XI Congreso Español de Estudios Clásicos*, Madrid, 2005.

Karamanou, I., 'Euripides' "Family Reunion" Plays and their Socio-political Resonances', in A. Markantonatos and B. Zimmermann (eds) *Crisis on Stage: Tragedy and Comedy in Late Fifth-Century Athens*, Berlin and New York, 2012.

Katsouris, A.G., *Tragic Patterns in Menander*, Athens, 1976.

Kepple, L.R., 'The Broken Victim: Euripides *Bacchae* 969–970', *Harvard Studies in Classical Philology* 80, 1976.

Kirk, G.S., *The Bacchae by Euripides: A Translation with Commentary*, Englewood Cliffs, 1970.

Kovacs, D., *The Heroic Muse*, Baltimore, 1987.

Kovacs, D., *Euripidea*, Leiden, 1994a.

Kovacs, D., *Euripides 1: Cyclops, Alcestis, Medea*, Cambridge, MA, 1994b.

Kovacs, D., *Euripidea Tertia*, Leiden, 2003a.

Kovacs, D., 'Toward a Reconstruction of *Iphigenia Aulidenis*', *Journal of Hellenic Studies* 123, 2003b.

Lefkowitz, M.R., 'Was Euripides an Atheist?', *Studi Italiani di Filologia Classica* 5, 1987.

Lefkowitz, M.R., ' "Impiety" and "Atheism" in Euripides' Dramas', *Classical Quarterly* 39, 1989.

Lefkowitz, M.R., 'Apollo in the *Orestes*', *Studi Italiani di Filologia Classica* 20, 2002.

Llewellyn-Jones, L., 'Men in Female Roles', in H.M. Roisman (ed.) *Encyclopedia of Greek Tragedy*, vol. II, Hoboken, NJ, 2014.

Lloyd-Jones, H., *The Justice of Zeus*, Berkeley and Los Angeles, 1971.

Lucas, D.W., *Aristotle: Poetics*, Oxford, 1972².

Luschnig, C.A.E., *Tragic Aporia: A Study of Euripides' Iphigenia at Aulis*, Berwick, 1988.

March, J.R., 'Euripides' *Bakchai*: A Reconsideration in the Light of Vase-Paintings', *Bulletin of the Institute of Classical Studies* 36, 1989.

Markantonatos, A., 'Leadership in Action: Wise Policy and Firm Resolve in Euripides' *Iphigenia at Aulis*', in A. Markantonatos and B. Zimmermann (eds) *Crisis on Stage: Tragedy and Comedy in Late Fifth-Century Athens*, Berlin and New York, 2012.

McGinty, P., 'Dionysos's Revenge and the Validation of the Hellenic World-view', *Harvard Theological Review* 71, 1978.

Meineck, P., 'Greek Drama in North America', in B. van Zyl Smit (ed.) *A Handbook to the Reception of Greek Drama*, Malden, MA, forthcoming.

Mendelson, E., *Later Auden*, London, 1990.

Michelakis, P., *Achilles in Greek Tragedy*, Cambridge, 2002.

Michelakis, P., *Euripides: Iphigenia at Aulis*, London, 2006.

Michelini, A.N., 'The Expansion of Myth in Late Euripides: *Iphigeneia at Aulis*', in M. Cropp, K. Lee and D. Sansone (eds) *Euripides and Tragic Theatre in the Late Fifth Century*, Urbana, 1999/2000.

Mikalson, J.D., *Honor Thy Gods: Popular Religion in Greek Tragedy*, Chapel Hill, 1991.

Mills, S., *Euripides: Bacchae*, London, 2006.

Moloney, E., '*Philippus in acie tutior quam in theatro fuit*... (Curtius 9,6,25): The Macedonian Kings and Greek Theatre', in E. Csapo, H. Rupprecht Goette, J.R. Green and P. Wilson (eds) *Greek Theatre in the Fourth Century BC*, Berlin and Boston, 2014.

Murray, G., *Euripides and his Age*, London, 1913.

Nagle, D.B., *The Household as the Foundation of Aristotle's Polis*, Cambridge, 2006.

Nisbet, R.G.M. and Rudd, N., *A Commentary on Horace, Odes, Book III*, Oxford, 2004.

North, H., *Sophrosyne: Self-knowledge and Self-restraint in Greek Literature*, with an introduction by Edith Hall, London, 1966.

Ober, J., *Mass and Elite in Democratic Athens: Rhetoric, Ideology and the Power of the People*, Princeton, 1989.

Page, D.L., *Actors' Interpolations in Greek Tragedy*, Oxford, 1934.

Page, D.L., *Poetae Melici Graeci*, Oxford, 1962.

Paley, F.A., *Euripides with an English Commentary*, vol. 2, London, 1874.

Papadodima, E., 'Euripides and Subversiveness', in H.M. Roisman (ed.) *Encyclopedia of Greek Tragedy*, vol. I, Hoboken, NJ, 2014.

Patterson, C.B., *The Family in Greek History*, Cambridge, MA and London, 1998.

Pearson, A.C. (ed.), *The Fragments of Sophocles*, vol. 1, Cambridge, 1917.

Podlecki, A.J., 'Individual and Group in Euripides' *Bacchae*', *Acta Classica* 43, 1974.

Pomeroy, S.B., *Families in Classical and Hellenistic Greece: Representations and Realities*, Oxford, 1997.

Reinhardt, K., 'Die Sinneskreise bei Euripides', *Eranos* 26, 279–317, 1957, reproduced in English translation in J. Mossman (ed.) *Oxford Readings in Euripides*, 16–46, Oxford, 2002.

Renault, M., *The Mask of Apollo*, London, 1966.

Revermann, M., 'Euripides, Tragedy and Macedon: Some Conditions of Reception', in M. Cropp, K. Lee and D. Sansone (eds) *Euripides and Tragic Theatre in the Late Fifth Century*, Urbana, 1999/2000.

Reynolds, L.D. and Wilson, N.G., *Scribes and Scholars: A Guide to the Transmission of Greek and Latin Literature*, Oxford, 2013[4].

Roisman, H.M., *Nothing Is As It Seems: The Tragedy of the Implicit in Euripides' Hippolytus*, Lanham, MD, 1999.

Roselli, E.K., *Theater of the People: Spectators and Society in Ancient Athens*, Austin, 2011.

Rosenbloom, D., 'Scripting Revolution: Democracy and its Discontents in late Fifth-Century Drama', in A. Markantonatos and B. Zimmermann (eds) *Crisis on Stage: Tragedy and Comedy in Late Fifth-Century Athens*, Berlin and New York, 2012a.

Rosenbloom, D., 'The Panhellenism of Athenian Tragedy', in D. Carter (ed.) *Why Athens? A Reappraisal of Tragic Politics*, Oxford, 2012b.

Roux, J., *Euripide Les Bacchantes*, Paris, 1970.

Schlegel, A.W. von., *Über dramatische Kunst und Litteratur: Vorlesungen*, Heidelberg, 1809.

Scott, W.C., 'Two Suns Over Thebes. Imagery and Stage Effects in the *Bacchae*', *Transactions of the American Philological Association* 105, 1975.

Scullion, S., 'Euripides and Macedon, or The Silence of the *Frogs*', *Classical Quarterly* 53, 2003.

Seaford, R., *Reciprocity and Ritual: Homer and Tragedy in the Developing City-State*, Oxford, 1994.

Seaford, R., *Euripides' Bacchae with an Introduction, Translation and Commentary*, Warminster, 1996.

Seaford, R., 'Dionysus, Money, and Drama', *Arion* 11.2, 2003.

Seaford, R., 'Mystic Light in Aeschylus' *Bassarai*', *Classical Quarterly* 55, 2005.

Seaford, R., *Cosmology and the Polis*, Cambridge, 2012.

Segal, C., 'Etymologies and Double Meanings in Euripides' *Bacchae*', *Glotta* 60, 1982.

Segal, C., *Interpreting Greek Tragedy*, Ithaca and London, 1986.

Segal, C., *Dionysiac Poetics and Euripides'* Bacchae, Princeton, 1997^2.

Seidensticker, B., *Palintonos Harmonia: Studien zu komischen Elementen in der griechische Tragödie*, Göttingen, 1982.

Silk, M.S., *Aristophanes and the Definition of Comedy*, Oxford, 2000.

Snell, B., *Tragicorum Graecorum Fragmenta*, vol. 1, Göttingen, 1971.

Sommerstein, A.H., 'Aeschylus' *Semele* and its Companion Plays', in G. Bastianini and A. Casanova (eds) *I papiri di Eschilo e di Sofocle*, Florence, 2013.

Sotto, W., *The Rounded Rite: A Study of Wole Soyinka's play* The Bacchae of Euripides, Lund, 1985.

Soyinka, W., *The Bacchae of Euripides* in *Collected Plays* 1, Oxford, 1973.

Soyinka, W., *Myth, Literature and the African World*, reprint, Cambridge, 1992.

Spira, A., *Untersuchungen zum Deus ex machina bei Euripides*, Kallmünz, 1960.

Steidle, W., *Studien zum antiken Drama*, Munich, 1968.

Stevens, P.T., 'Euripides and the Athenians', *Journal of Hellenic Studies* 76, 1956.

Stockert, W., *Euripides: Iphigenie in Aulis*, 2 vols, Vienna, 1992.

Sutherland, D., *The Bacchae of Euripides*, Lincoln, NE, 1968.

Swift, L., 'Conflicting Identities in the Euripidean Chorus', in R. Gagné and M.G. Hopman (eds) *Choral Mediations in Greek Tragedy*, Cambridge, 2013.

Taplin, O., *Greek Tragedy in Action*, London, 1978.

Teevan, C., *Alcmaeon in Corinth: After a Fragment of Euripides: First Performed as 'Cock of the North'*, with an introduction by Edith Hall, London, 2004.

Thumiger, C., 'Euripides: *Bacchae*', in H.M. Roisman (ed.) *Encyclopedia of Greek Tragedy*, vol. I, Hoboken, NJ, 2014.

van Looy, H., *Zes verloren Tragedies van Euripides*, Brussels, 1964.

Webster, T.B.L., *The Tragedies of Euripides*, London, 1967.

West, M.L., *Introduction to Greek Metre*, Oxford, 1987.

West, M.L., *Studies in Aeschylus*, Stuttgart, 1990.

Wilkins, J., *Euripides: Heraclidae*, Oxford, 1993.

Willink, C.W., 'Some Problems of Text and Interpretation in the Bacchae', *Classical Quarterly* 16, 1966.

Wilson, P., *The Athenian Institution of the Khoregia: The Chorus, the City and the Stage*, Cambridge, 2000.

Winnington-Ingram, R.P., *Euripides and Dionysus: An Interpretation of the Bacchae*, Cambridge, 1948.

Winnington-Ingram, R.P., *Euripides and Dionysus: An Interpretation of the Bacchae*, second edition with foreword and bibliography by P.E. Easterling, London, 1997.

Zagagi, N., *The Comedy of Menander*, London, 1994.

Zarrilli, P.B., *Theatre Histories: An Introduction*, London, 2010.

Zeitlin, F.I., 'Dionysus in 69', in E. Hall, F. Macintosh and A. Wrigley (eds) *Dionysus Since 69*, Oxford, 2004.

Zielinski, T., 'De *Alcmeonis Corinthii* Fabula Euripidea', *Mnemosyne* 50, 1922.

Zuntz, G., *An Inquiry into the Transmission of the Plays of Euripides*, Cambridge, 1965.

Index